ADIRONDACK WILDERNESS

A Story of Man and Nature

JANE EBLEN KELLER

SYRACUSE UNIVERSITY PRESS · 1980

Library of Congress Cataloging in Publication Data

Keller, Jane Eblen.
Adirondack Wilderness.

(A York State book)
Bibliography: p. 233
Includes index.
1. Adirondack Mountains.   I. Title.
F127.A2K43   974.7'53   79-28188
ISBN 0-8156-0147-6
ISBN 0-8156-0150-6 pbk.

Manufactured in the United States of America

Lake Colden reflecting Avalanche Pass in the Adirondack High Peaks. *Collection of the New York State Museum*

For George

Jane Eblen Keller, a native of Knoxville, Tennessee, is a free-lance writer and historical researcher who during the last ten years has worked for Harvard University, the City of Boston, and the New York State Museum in Albany.

CONTENTS

Preface   ix

Acknowledgments   xiii

Introduction   xv

The First Adirondack Wilderness (Creation–1830)   1

    1. Maps and Man in New York State   3

    2. The Final Frontier   8

    3. How a Hat Won the West   18

    4. Dreams of Glory and Times of Trouble   24

    5. Land for Sale   34

    6. The Rock   43

    7. The Forest   56

The Wilderness in Transition (1830–85)   77

    8. Timber!   79

    9. There's Ore in Them Thar Hills   99

    10. How the Adirondacks Got a Name   111

    11. New World Cathedrals   117

    12. A Pound of Flesh   130

    13. Roughing It   143

    14. A Public Pleasure Ground   161

The Contemporary Wilderness (1885–Present)   171

    15. Wilderness Economics   173

16. The Mellowing   180
17. Love Unto Death   189
18. For Beauty's Sake   201
The New Problem of Man and Nature   211
19. Saving For or From?   213
20. Taking Charge   225
Bibliography   233
Index   235

PREFACE

N o ONE," wrote William Chapman White in 1954 of the Adirondack Mountain region of northern New York State, "knows all of it." Counting foothills, the Adirondacks take up about one-third of the state and occupy an area as big as Connecticut plus most of Vermont. Hundreds of mountains and many more hills roll across the region, some craggy, rock-pocked peaks, some gentle, undulating mounds.

Two thousand lakes and ponds shine like diamonds throughout the mountains. Lake Champlain and Lake George, the biggest lakes, form the eastern boundary of the region. It would take most of this book to name the others: Long Lake, Lake Placid, Tupper Lake, Upper, Middle, and Lower Saranac lakes, Blue Mountain, Schroon, Raquette.

Six thousand miles of rivers run down mountains and through valleys. Five of these rivers are major water suppliers to New York and much of the East. The Hudson, the Mohawk, the St. Regis, the Ausable (whose water feeds Lake Champlain and eventually the St. Lawrence River), and the Black River all originate and gather strength in the Adirondacks. Some flow north and others south since the water divide of the state is near the top of the highest Adirondack peak, Mt. Marcy.

Covering the mountains and lining the edges of the rivers and lakes is forest, miles and miles of the "Green Mosiac" or "leaf-shadowed mystery" as the Adirondack forest has been called. More than 70 percent of the entire region is blanketed in trees, thirty native species. In the forest wildlife thrives: 50 species of mammals, 200 species of birds, and 66 species of fish. Eagles, loons, pine martens, and other rare creatures live alongside the more common white-tailed deer, beavers, rabbits, mice, and squirrels.

Perhaps the only way to grasp the immensity and variety of the whole Adirondack region is to fly over it. Yet to get such an impression is to forego an intimacy with one of the lakes, the satisfaction of climbing one of the forty-six peaks over four thousand feet, or even the tame pleasure of driving to the top of Whiteface Mountain.

But intimate and cursory knowledge of the Adirondacks both reveal one paramount fact: this is wilderness or the closest thing to it in New York, and the largest remaining protected chunk of it in the United States.

More than six million acres of the Adirondack wilderness now comprise a state park, the biggest park—federal or state—in the nation. It is bigger than Yosemite, Yellowstone, Grand Teton, and the Great Smoky Mountain parks put together. About half the Adirondack Park is Forest Preserve land, owned by the state and strictly protected. The remainder of the land is privately owned and scattered throughout the park: islands of industry, tourist attractions, towns, lumber company resources, and other private holdings and acreage in a sea of "forever wild" land, as the Forest Preserve is called.

The mixture of private and public land in the Adirondack Park is one of several unique aspects of the region. The flora, the fauna, the people, the rock, the way New Yorkers have perceived the merits and demerits of their wilderness up north all contribute additionally to a special flavor about the place.

"Of this region," wrote one of the Adirondacks' most devoted explorers, Verplanck Colvin, in 1879, "for a hundred years or more, civilized man has held the most diverse opinions." The sheer variety of topography would have assured that. The different attitudes toward nature that men and women brought with them as they gazed at or exploited or preserved the Adirondacks also made diverse opinions inevitable.

As a result, today the essential character of the Adirondacks remains both as distinct as the profile of Mt. Marcy and as elusive as a mountain trail buried under a winter's snowfall. There is a continuity in that the whole region looks like wilderness, but there is variety in that sophisticated cultural events take place in some of the towns. There is a long history of hardship for natives along with an indomitable spirit of hope for a better, prosperous future. Rich men and poor men have loved the Adirondacks, as have loggers and conservationists, hunters and fishermen, painters, writers, and sculptors as well as illiterate hermits and criminals in search of sanctuary. While the year-round population, now about one hundred and twenty-five thousand people, has long been noted for conservative politics and deep suspicion of outsiders, they at least once welcomed and befriended a self-confessed Marxist, the artist Rockwell Kent who lived for many years on a farm in Keene Valley. Many Adirondack hotels in the late nineteenth century were outspokenly anti-Semitic. Yet one of the most famous Adirondack personalities was the radical libertarian John Brown, who set up a farm in North Elba for fugitive slaves and later led an abortive attempt to end slavery in the South. For a time, the Adirondacks were thought to be a rich man's private paradise of elegant "camps" and exclusive resorts. Yet the mountains were also known as a haven for tuberculars from every background, and the famous Trudeau Sanatorium in Saranac Lake was the first private nonprofit clinic in the nation catering to those who could not afford expensive treatment elsewhere.

A land of contrasts, paradoxes, and inconsistencies, affected for better and for worse by the hand of man, loved, despised, exploited, cared for, argued over, and eulogized, the Adirondacks and the men and women who have made their history are like America as a whole. Certainly few places in all the United States have elicited the changing feelings and behavior toward nature quite so dramatically or prototypically as have the Adirondacks in the last 150 years or so. The way man perceived nature in the Adirondacks and behaved toward it was remarkably similar to the way Americans all over the country were perceiving and behaving toward nature in general. In fact, the twists and turns that characterized New Yorkers' attitudes about their North Country wilderness in many ways anticipated country-wide trends.

For example, it is astonishing how many leaders of the conservation movement learned to love nature as a result of childhood or adult experiences in the Adirondacks. Many of these men and women who boosted Americans' appreciation of natural wilderness first honed their skills by boosting New Yorkers' appreciation of the Adirondacks. The battle to preserve portions of the Adirondacks foretold many later struggles to preserve forests, canyons, plains, and deserts in the South, West and Midwest.

A study of the Adirondacks, then, is a study not just of trees, rocks, and animals, but also of contrast, conflict, and change in man's attitudes toward nature. Exhibits in the New York State Museum in Albany, New York, deal with these subtle relationships, emphasizing neither man nor nature exclusively, as a historical or scientific museum might, but focusing on the way man and nature confronted each other most directly, with the most telling consequences.

This book attempts to extend the same theme by describing in more detail the ways man and nature played into each others' hands, waged war against each other, or cooperated like willing partners throughout Adirondack history. The book also tries to explore why man behaved as he did, but does not propose to pass judgment on the way man has manipulated nature. In the Adirondacks, as in the rest of New York State, the dual tenancy lies at the heart of human history and will continue to have profound effects upon natural history.

ACKNOWLEDGMENTS

TWO OF MANY, many books on man and nature were especially important in helping me shape the outline of this book: Arthur A. Ekirch, Jr.'s *Man and Nature in America* (Columbia University Press, 1963), and Roderick Nash's *Wilderness and the American Mind* (Yale University Press, 1967). To both I owe an enormous debt, although my interpretation of their work, as well as the work of Adirondack scholars and writers, must be judged on its own merit.

This book is less a new history of the Adirondacks than a synthesis of others' work. I have tried to use their material to take a new look at how man and nature affected each other in the Adirondacks. Further, I have tried to see how general trends in the American way of seeing nature over the years helped answer some of the why's in Adirondack history. Since other men and women, in their research about the Adirondacks, paved the way for me, I am deeply indebted to dozens of people. A selected bibliography appears at the end of this book, but two sources stand out and deserve mention. William Chapman White's *Adirondack Country* (Knopf, 1954) has a character and scope unparalleled in Adirondack literature. And Norman J. VanValkenburgh's unpublished manuscript tracing the history of "forever wild" saved me many hours because he gathered carefully so much otherwise scattered and difficult material.

Many people worked hard to help me find material and formulate the ideas presented here. Especially insightful about the current economic problems in the Adirondacks were Roger and Anne Tubby of Saranac Lake. Mr. Tubby is Governor Hugh Carey's Advisor on the Adirondack Economy and Special Host for the 1980 Olympics in Lake Placid. Richard Beamish, formerly with the Adirondack Park Agency, was

xiv ACKNOWLEDGMENTS

generous with his time and information as was Robert Flacke, Chairman
of the APA. Assemblyman Glenn Harris, who represents much of the
Adirondack region in the New York Legislature; William K. Verner, formerly curator at the Adirondack Museum in Blue Mountain Lake; Gary
Randorf of the Adirondack Council; Luke Patnode at the Olympic Games
Organizing Committee; and many others, too many to name here, all
shared their enthusiastic devotion to the Adirondacks, a devotion that
unites otherwise differing individuals.

Special thanks, too, go to Paula Metzler, who pointed me toward
valuable source material, Judy Jesse, on the staff of the New York State
Museum, who led me patiently through the geology of the Adirondacks,
and to the entire staff of the Museum. Noel Fritzinger, then Assistant
Commissioner in the State Education Department, and G. Carroll
Lindsay, Director of Museum Services, asked me to do this book; Dale
Fanning, Assistant to the Director, with unfailing courtesy took care of
many of the details and loose ends; and Robert Maurer, Deputy Commissioner for Cultural Education, helped overcome some peculiar hurdles. I
thank them all.

Many of the photographs in this book came from the personal
scrapbook of W. F. Kollecker, long a resident and photographer of Saranac
Lake and environs. I am very grateful to the Saranac Lake Free Library for
allowing these to be published for the first time.

Finally, my husband, George Keller, gave me the kind of help that
made all the difference. This book is his, too.

Selkirk, New York   Jane Eblen Keller
Fall 1978

INTRODUCTION

NOW AND THEN someone will scoop up a dozen fuzzy ideas, a handful of new facts, original insights, and dated opinions, shake them up like dice in a cup, and present the world with a reappraisal of itself.

In 1836, to only limited acclaim at the time, a soft-spoken American poet, essayist, and former minister, Ralph Waldo Emerson, gave the world a slender volume called *Nature*. In it he treated an age-old problem: is it man or nature that has ultimate authority on earth? He took two dominant views of the problem and divided the responsibility between the two. In a pleasant phrase, Emerson said his work was an exploration of the "occult relation between man and the vegetable."

Emerson's work had two long-term consequences. First, he provided generations of scientists and thinkers with an intellectual basis for much of modern ecological theory by emphasizing the "wonderful congruity which subsists between man and nature." Secondly, his approach to the man/nature dilemma reconciled the uncertainty many Americans have always felt toward nature and their role in it.

The bridge Emerson and his followers built was between two basic and opposing views about the relationship between man and nature. One view held that man was a part of nature. In Europe, many persons, including the Romantic poets who were Emerson's close contemporaries, were reviving a more or less pagan, pretechnological attitude that extolled the virtues or at least the supremacy of all-powerful, all-beautiful nature, of which man was only a fragment. Shelley, Wordsworth, Byron, and others developed themes expressed by one of the most important early Romantic poets, William Blake, who wrote that man was "only a slave of each moment . . . wrapped in mortality," while nature was immortal, grand, free, and omnipotent.

In America, toward the middle of the 1800s, a group of painters awed by the gorgeous expanses of the land, were expressing a similar feeling. Monumental scenery painted in oils characterized the influential, New York-based Hudson River School of artists, for example. Many followers of this school painted scenes of the Adirondack Mountains, where a beneficent nature seemed to reign magnificently. "Twilight in the Adirondacks" by artist Sanford R. Gifford is just one of many examples. The painting concentrates not on people but on nature. Gifford made his "figures . . . small, nature large," as Adirondack historian William Verner summarized.

American writers, too, were beginning to express the idea that nature was the truly benign and authoritative power on earth. Emerson's friend, Henry David Thoreau, was one such figure, immersing himself in the natural surroundings of the Merrimac River and Walden Pond in Massachusetts.

In short, a number of people believed that nature, by some automatic hegemony, rules us all—for better, as some Romantics thought, or for worse, as some fatalists imagined. Yet this idea that man belongs, like an oak tree or beaver, to the whole fabric of nature was, of course, an age-old assumption. It often characterized the thought and behavior of primitive men and cultures without sophisticated technological tools or means of manipulating nature. Without these, man tended to see himself as little more than a child, alternately abused and caressed, of "Mother Nature."

The opposite view, usually developed along with increased technological achievement, was that man was the ultimate creation, destined to assume a place of authority over all nature. Nature being cruel, capricious, and unjust, as many had reason to think because earthquakes, disease, drought, and floods seemed constantly to buffet man about, man had to assert control over it.

Emerson understood both views. He, with Lord Byron and others, was awed by natural beauty and uplifted by the sight of a flower or a field, a mountain or a sunset. In the woods it was easy for him to submit his senses to nature and to feel a part of it. But he also understood the benefits of certain of man's assertions of authority over the dark side of nature, such as disease. (Tuberculosis, for example, wiped out most of Thoreau's family, finally killed Thoreau himself, and continued to kill one out of every seven Americans well into the nineteenth century.)

Whether to fight or worship nature has led many persons throughout history to gather evidence in favor of one or the other tactic. Emerson, however, urged his readers (and later his audiences when he lectured all over the country) to do both. He thought of the world as a whole, with man and nature occupying equal stations, each affecting the other with equal force, sharing equal responsibility, equal shame. He emphasized the harmony of the universe. He advised neither abject submission to nature nor total assertion of human control; he wanted balance. He realized that man had to cultivate the fields, manipulate rivers and rocks, fend off disease and seek shelter. He respected farmers. As the political historian Arthur Ekirch put it, Emerson thought farmers "kept the world in repair." Yet he worried that man "masters [the earth] by penny-wisdom," without sufficient awareness of the effects of his mastery. "To speak truly," he lamented, "few adult persons can see nature. . . . At least they have a very superficial seeing."

To cultivate one's eye as well as one's field could be rewarding beyond measure. "The whole of nature is a metaphor of the human mind," Emerson thought. If only man could learn to read the natural world, he would learn just how much he could do to it, and how much he should refrain from doing. He would learn discipline and restraint. He would experience intense joy, too. "I am thrilled with delight by the choral harmony of the whole," Emerson reported, "the waving of the boughs . . . is like that of a higher thought or a better emotion coming over me."

Emerson also believed that "nature was the part of creation closest to God" and served as an avenue to religious insight. This idea had profound effects upon man's attitude toward the Adirondack Mountains in the late nineteenth century.

In retrospect, Emerson's approach and the steady acceptance of his ideas among many Americans seem almost inevitable. Modern ecological research derives in part from his ideas, and modern historians, scientists, and philosophers now accept man *and* nature as the "basic fundamental fact of history," Ekirch wrote.

Furthermore, Emerson's questioning of nature, which led him to accept both man and nature as fundamental partners, reflected a widespread, especially American attitude. So many people, including the legendary pioneers, seem never to have been entirely comfortable with either of the two possible extreme solutions to the question of ultimate authority on earth.

From the beginning of written American history, when explorers and fur trappers and weary settlers encountered an apparently endless wilderness, people saw the raw land of the new world as both magnificent and terrible. A man's best hopes and worst fears could be realized in the forests and on the plains and along mountain slopes. Nature turned a divided face, half beast, half beauty.

Even after the pioneering era, when the necessarily direct confrontation between man and nature had passed, the tension remained. The ubiquitous presence of the hand of man represented both the fulfillment of many hopes and at the same time the prospect of calamity when resources were seen to be diminishing.

In the State of New York, man and nature have come to terms with each other in different ways. In New York City, for example, man has asserted a great deal of control over the environment. Rivers 300 miles away from Manhattan have been tapped, redirected, channeled, and even rebuilt to provide water for the millions of people living there. With true Ciceronian mastery—"We are the absolute masters of what the earth produces," wrote Cicero, the Roman statesman and orator in the first century A.D.—man first subdued then created a second nature to better suit his needs. Even the great city parks—Central Park, Prospect Park, and the Bronx Park—were the creation of men who razed the natural formations and built new ones.

In Upstate New York, by contrast, man and nature were more directly adaptive. The subjugation of the wilderness, agricultural supremacy, the marvelous transportation network of canals, then railroads, then highways, were evidence of man's shaping of the environment; but they were also results of man's desire to use nature for the utmost productivity. In Manhattan the emphasis was on man. Upstate the emphasis was on man working close to nature.

In the Adirondack Mountains the matter of who was in charge did not have such a neat resolution. For centuries it was not the subjugation of wilderness that produced ambivalent feelings on the part of man; it was the apparent implacability of the wilderness. Nature has tended to prevail throughout Adirondack history, and not just nature as it can be analyzed, reshaped, and integrated by man, but wilderness—the state of nature most challenging to man.

Every phase of Adirondack history is concerned with different states of wilderness. This book divides Adirondack history into three phases: the First Wilderness, Creation–1830, an era when man made little or no difference whatever to the natural wilderness; Wilderness in Transition, 1830–85, a period encompassing man's attempts to assert his power over the mountains for exploitative purposes; and the Contemporary Wilderness, 1885–Present, during which time man came to appreciate wilderness for its own sake and did something to preserve it in the Adirondacks.

While the wilderness in transition and contemporary wilderness would seem to represent a Ciceronian view as opposed to a Romantic one (and indeed the two attitudes did prevail, one after the other, historically), the two phases are not really so inimical as a first glance might indicate. Their opposition has been neutralized to a large degree by the application of Emersonian concepts of harmony. It is, in fact, possible to say that in the Adirondacks a marriage of human and natural history, of romantic idealization and raw exploitation, of the typical American irresolution toward nature, has taken place.

Today there are still those who believe, as many loggers, miners, farmers, and businessmen did in the nineteenth century, that nature even in the Adirondacks is there for man's use. A nineteenth-century admirer of the region, Reverend John Todd, spoke for many people when he wrote that "these forests shall be cut down, and along the lakes and valleys there shall be a virtuous, industrious Christian population."

Others disagree. "Civilization," wrote newspaperman S. H. Hammond, also a nineteenth-century admirer of the Adirondacks, "has no business among these mountains . . . I would consecrate these old forests."

What has, for the most part, allowed a kind of marriage to take place between these opinions is the fact that man in the twentieth century realized that the best way to exploit the Adirondack wilderness was to retain it. Today wilderness and civilization exist side by side in the Adirondack Mountains, though certainly not without tension. But since a tenuous balance between the two does seem to be working moderately well, it may be said that man and nature in the Adirondacks have cooperated in such a way as to give substance to Emerson's ideas.

THE FIRST
ADIRONDACK WILDERNESS
(Creation–1830)

Maps and Man in New York State

THE SHAPE OF NEW YORK STATE is neither geometrical and man-made like the nearly square Wyoming; nor is it like Hawaii, its boundaries determined entirely by nature. Instead, half of the borders of New York are natural; half are man-made. Lakes Erie and Ontario, the St. Lawrence and Delaware rivers, and ocean-edged Long Island mark the outer ends of about 50 percent of the state.

The remaining borders are something else again. Unlike the convolutions of shorelines, the other 50 percent of New York's boundary lines are ruler-straight, as man-made as steel. From the southern tip of Lake Champlain all the way down to New York harbor; from the crotch of the Delaware River at Port Jervis, east to Dobbs Ferry on the Hudson; from Hogansburg on the south shore of the St. Lawrence River, to Rouses Point on the banks of Lake Champlain; and running most of the length of the Pennsylvania line between the New York towns of Deposit and Clymer, these borders cut across rivers and mountains and slice through valleys, ignoring nearby natural delineations. Such hard-edged demarcations seem almost to flaunt the mathematical precision of man over the asymmetrical meanderings of nature.

Nature as man found it and history as man created it are twin forces in the story of New York. Within the nearly fifty thousand square miles of land that by 1800 came to compose the state of New York, settlers found examples of most of the natural formations known to man: mountains, waterfalls, valleys, gorges, lakes, oceans, conifer and deciduous forests, fertile fields, and bare mountain tops.

Although the state has never been the biggest in the nation—it was third in size in 1800, and twenty-seventh in 1977—nor does it have the highest mountains, the longest rivers, the deepest harbors, the richest ores, or the tallest trees, what enchants and impresses is its variety. "It is not a land of staggering wonders but one of varied loveliness," wrote noted historian and loyal New Yorker Dixon Ryan Fox. As if to complement its varied geography, New Yorkers have long been noted for their versatility and enterprise. New York's human achievements are the truly staggering wonders of the state.

Within twenty-five years of 1800, barely time enough for one generation to mature, New York had burst out of a kind of slump characterized by the wreckage of the Revolutionary War, Indian disputes, economic fluctuations, and the remains of a quasi-feudal system of government and land-ownership. Suddenly New York was leading all other states by 1825, in population, in business, in speed of settlement, in art, in commerce, and, of course, in variety of occupations among its more than one million inhabitants.

Nothing symbolized New York's supremacy more than the Erie Canal, from Albany to Buffalo, finally completed in 1825. With few resources other than a good idea and thousands of bare hands (for there were no engineers as they are thought of today and no heavy machinery), man took a naturally good system of waterways and with new canals, dams, and locks reshaped it into what Cicero might have called another, superior, second nature.

The Erie Canal represented a state of equilibrium between man and nature. Before the canal, people had been at the mercy of nature. Shortly after the canal was finished, business and other nonagricultural sources usurped farming and a farm-based economy as the leading income producers in the state. After that, the focus was on man.

Before 1800, when nearly all New York State except the corridor of the Hudson River between Manhattan and Albany was wilderness, nature had been nothing less than a dictator. The pioneers who chose to penetrate what were often called "the howling wilds" faced a domineering and dangerous foe in the form of forests, untilled flatlands where fevers lurked, and mountains. So perilous was the journey of the pioneer, trapper, or explorer into that wilderness that phrases like "the all-conquering army," "the march of civilization," and other military-inspired descriptions have been used to connote the difficulties and portray the achievement.

"On a rainy day in October," wrote British journalist Harriet Martineau, who in the 1830s toured New York and much of the eastern United States, "I saw a settler at work in the forest on which he appeared to have just entered. His clearing looked, in comparison with the forest behind him, of about the size of a pincushion. . . . The hard-working father must be toiling for his children; for the success of his after life can hardly atone to him for such a destitution of comfort as I saw him in the midst of."

Such was the lot of most pioneers from New York to California. Their children did reap some added comforts, but they, too, toiled along with their parents. (Some of the pioneer children described in Martineau's book no doubt received great delight from examining her ear trumpet—she was quite deaf—an instrument, she wrote, "which seems to exert some winning power.")

That modern men have looked back to the pioneering days as romantic and rewarding in no way should distort the facts that those forays into the wilderness were back-breaking, death-defying challenges in a natural world that threatened defeat at every turn.

And pioneering was an exacting occupation. Many were not prepared and, in spite of the general success, there is many an untold story of failure. People starved or froze or died of thirst in the wilderness. Few had time to stand back and admire the scenery.

Most American settlers were probably like those the often-quoted French observer Alexis de Tocqueville described. "They may be said not to perceive the mighty forests that surround them till they fall beneath the hatchet. Their eyes are fixed upon another sight: the . . . march across these wilds, draining swamps, turning the course of rivers, peopling solitudes and subduing nature."

Nevertheless, ruminations about the sheer beauty of the land were not entirely absent in the annals of early North America. Samuel de Champlain, trekking the wilderness of Canada and New York State in the early 1600s, noted that the "country becomes more and more beautiful as you advance." Others voiced similar wonder. But to most, beauty lay not so much in the rawness of the wilderness as in its potential. As Champlain's great biographer, Samuel Eliot Morison, noted, "Whilst Champlain appreciated the beauties of the Canadian wilderness, nothing pleased him more than a garden, with flowers, fruits and herbs from France."

Later, Thomas Jefferson and Benjamin Franklin both wrote about the natural wonders and beauties of the new land. But Jefferson's ideal was, like Champlain's, the plowed field, and Franklin's was the city park. They were in favor of nature but within the limits of man's firm control.

By 1825, most of New York's wilderness was well under the control of man. And the accomplishments of New York's citizens were impressive. In addition to the Erie Canal, by 1825 more than four thousand miles of new roads had been built. The port of New York City controlled half the imports into America and more than a quarter of all the exports. There seemed no end to New York's power and supremacy. The coming of the railroads in the 1850s assured continued growth; and even before the Civil War New York industrialists no longer needed to depend upon local natural resources and productivity. They could tap the world (literally, since the China trade was well established in 1860) for the raw materials they could process, if not produce, in New York. Grain, for example, once a leading crop in New York, was by 1860 a relatively minor product. But flour and meal, ground from imported grains, led the list of New York's most valuable products. Men's clothing, the second most valuable product in 1860, along with refined sugar, the third, were processed from materials whose origins were far beyond the borders of the state.

There was a price for all this success, of course. On the farms phrases such as "rural decline" were heard by 1860. Soil exhaustion, the settlement of the plains states, and poor agricultural practices contributed to farmers' problems. In the cities air and water pollution was as much a problem in 1852 as it is today, only its origin was "natural": horse manure and roaming pigs instead of automobiles and factories. "The streets smell like a solution of bad eggs in ammonia," wrote diarist George Templeton Strong of New York City in 1852.

The existence of a vast, pristine wilderness as late as the 1850s was remarkable in such a place as New York State. But there it was, practically unpeopled, unmapped, fully one-third of the state as wild as it had been when Samuel de Champlain saw it (the first white man to do so) in 1609. He and his party of Indians had left in a hurry after a skirmish with the Iroquois, who claimed it as theirs. After Champlain, many others hurried away as quickly, defeated by the wilderness as they were in few other parts of the eastern United States.

Unpeopled and unmapped, the Adirondack wilderness was the East's last frontier. *Photo by W. F. Kollecker, courtesy of the Saranac Lake Free Library, Adirondack Collection*

2

The Final Frontier

U P NORTH, WAY UP NORTH, where the borders of the state surround the Adirondacks, there are more than nine thousand square miles of mountains, lakes, and forest. In 1830, there was no map of the region, for no man had traversed the wild land thoroughly enough even to begin one.

Americans had mapped Pike's Peak in Colorado and the remote Columbia River in Oregon. They had plowed, tilled, and grown rich from the soil in New York and were beginning to abandon the farms for industry, business, and the promise of the city. There they were creating, after they had conquered and forgotten the wilderness, what even Europeans admitted was a new American civilization.

Yet this enormous wilderness to the north remained. To those who knew it was there at all (few indeed), it was known by such forbidding names as the Great Northern Wilderness and the American Siberia. How could such an island of "gloomy solitude which is seldom trodden by the foot of man," as Nathaniel Bartlett Sylvester described it, slip by the ambition, skill, and cunning of Americans?

Frontier life was always rough and rude, but in *this* wilderness, as a few people discovered for themselves, conditions were harsh enough to preclude rewards. "We came through from the head of Lake George on an awful cold day on the ice," wrote Mrs. Adolphus Sheldon, who left Vermont in 1797 for the same reason many persons avoided or left the Adirondacks. The soil was thin, the rock beneath it was hard, the climate was cold, the growing season short, and the terrain rugged. "The whole length of the lake the great pines stood all around on the mountains, one unbroken wilderness," she continued. "Not an axe had been heard and hardly a gun to scare the deer. When we got to Ti [Ticonderoga, the settlement near the northern end of Lake George], it was all bushes."

Mrs. Sheldon and her family found life as rugged as the land-scape. They couldn't keep sheep because wolves, she said, ate them. They could plant only a few, very hardy crops, and even then frosts often endured into June and sometimes reoccurred in late August. For the first five winters she and her husband homesteaded, with temperatures hovering at zero for days and snow waist high all winter, their house had no stone fireplace. They simply burned logs on the dirt floor, and if the wooden walls of the cabin caught fire, Adolphus and Mrs. Sheldon put out the flames and lit another fire on the floor. Nowhere in New York was the natural world more unremitting, more domineering than in the Great Northern Wilderness of the Adirondacks.

As if to commemorate the historical and geographical imprecision with which the term "great northern wilderness" was for so long applied, confusion about the exact boundaries of the Adirondacks continues today. Some refer to the entire northern third of the state as the "Adirondack region," an area covering over seventeen thousand square miles and encompassing the St. Lawrence River Valley, the Mohawk River Valley, and the Tug Hill Plateau or Upland, a stretch of elevated flatland west of the Adirondack mountains, as well as the Lake Champlain-Lake George corridor.

Within this region the Adirondack mountains themselves take up about nine or ten thousand square miles. The excessively "wild recesses" James Fenimore Cooper referred to in *The Last of the Mohicans* are the High Peaks, a cluster of the highest Adirondack Mountains standing to the northeast of the geographical center of the region. It was this central high range of mountains that was originally named "the Adirondack group" in 1837, but the Adirondack region gradually came to include the lower hills surrounding the High Peaks, and eventually the North Country as a whole.

In the Sheldons' day such niceties of definition meant less than the fact that from the banks of Lake Champlain or Lake George it looked as if an impenetrable mass of wilderness spread, so far as anyone knew, forever west.

Average snowfall in the mountains is between 90 and 165 inches each winter. On the western slopes, which decline gradually toward the Tug Hill Plateau, winds from arctic Canada whip up against the hills and may bring as much as 225 inches of snow, giving this western flatland the distinction of being the snowiest part of America east of the Mississippi. The towns of Lake Placid in the High Peaks and Boonville on the edge of the Tug Hill are often the sites of the coldest recorded temperatures in the nation.

A stand of pines and hemlocks at Wolf Pond in the northern Adirondacks.

While the average January temperature is fifteen degrees Fahrenheit, balmy compared to the real Siberia where in places minus seventy degrees Fahrenheit is the winter norm, Adirondack winters can be damp and feel colder even than they are.

Although many called the Adirondacks "Siberian," the term "Alpine" is perhaps more appropriate. Several Adirondack peaks are high and cold enough to support a so-called Alpine environment where special varieties of mosses, flowers, and bushes alone can survive, as they do on the Alps and on the Alaskan tundra.

Only about 10 percent of the mountainous area is suitable for

Collection of the New York State Museum

agriculture of any kind. Fewer than 100 frost-free days in many sections combine with stretches of ground covered with less than an inch of soil to make farming and grazing nearly impossible.

Even for those like the Sheldons who wanted to try life in the Adirondacks, there were (and are) few natural, easy entrances. Navigable rivers flow around, not into the mountain region, and there are few passes.

Once in, however, water, though plentiful, presents problems. Not many of the countless, picturesque waterfalls work up enough force to provide adequate power potential. Those that are powerful tend to be

Winter. *Photo by W. F. Kollecker, courtesy of the Saranac Lake Free Library, Adirondack Collection*

virtually inaccessible, as many settlers and later iron mine operators looking for mill sites, discovered. In one of the most water-rich regions in the Eastern United States, the rivers, lakes, and streams turned out to be good mainly for drinking and recreation.

If with courage, strength, and determination, a settler did manage to walk into the wilderness through thickets and over mountains, the density of the forest might have seemed less forbidding than the fact that much of it was evergreen. A conifer forest of spruce, fir, and hemlock, like that which dominated the mountains above twenty-five hundred feet,

The East Branch, Ausable River, one of hundreds of picturesque but largely unnavigable Adirondack rivers. *Collection of the New York State Museum*

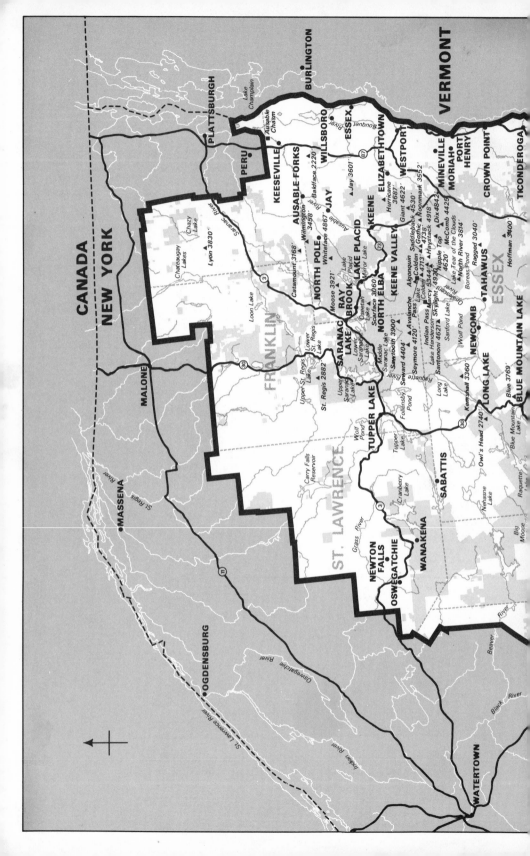

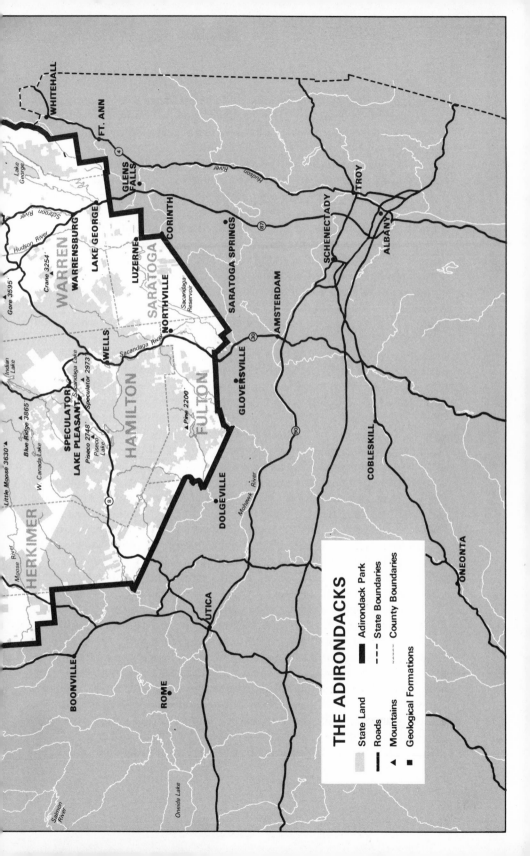

THE ADIRONDACKS

State Land
Roads
Mountains ▲
Geological Formations ■

Adirondack Park
State Boundaries
County Boundaries

tends to be dark, quiet, mysterious, and almost lifeless (or apparently so). Game animals such as bear, deer, and elk were found in the early days, but few of the small animals that make a forest seem warm and lively live on needle-covered forest floors. The howl of wolves, which from all accounts were common in the eighteenth and nineteenth centuries, echoed loudly in such a forest. "You could hear them away off in the night," Mrs. Sheldon remembered, "one would howl, then another would answer—howl, howl—then another, way off, howl, howl, howl— till they got up such a roar that it would almost tear you down."

Nature isolated the Adirondacks. Most pioneers perceived the difficulties from afar and stayed away. Others, less lucky, persisted and died. Those who stayed and survived were among the hardiest of men and women, willing to live simply and work hard, versatile enough to attune their wits to nature without trying to reshape it.

Even the resourceful New York Indians seem not to have built settlements in the Adirondacks although they hunted there, mainly moose probably, and knew how to get through the mountains easily. The earliest Indian groups in the region, the so-called Paleo-Indians (from the Greek "paleo" meaning ancient and indicating the obscure origins and habits of these people), seem never to have gone into the mountains. There was no reason for them to go since the large mammals they hunted were not there. When these people were hunting in the St. Lawrence Valley, around 8,000 B.C., the northern New York climate was still warming up after a centuries-long ice age, and the mountains were slower than the flatlands to warm up enough to support vegetation or animals.

It wasn't until around 2,000 B.C., at the very earliest, that later Indian groups apparently made trips beyond the foothills. These incursions into the mountains were probably seasonal and sporadic hunting expeditions, according to archaeological research. Pottery vessels from later cultures have been found, indicating that during the centuries just before the arrival of white men, Indians made camps if not permanent settlements in the Adirondacks.

Indian legends speak of fierce battles between the later northern Canadian groups (Hurons and Algonquins) and the more southerly Iroquois groups Mohawks and Oneidas particularly) to retain hunting rights in the Adirondacks. But even more vicious, or at least documented, disputes over territorial rights in the Adirondacks came about only when white men, arriving in significant numbers in the seventeenth century, added their claims to the hills. What white men wanted most was fur. The Indians were the most knowledgeable trappers and became increasingly possessive about the beaver-rich recesses of the Adirondacks.

The European explorers of the sixteenth and seventeenth centuries, many of whom forged the Indian alliances and provoked the disputes that later made portions of the Adirondacks battlefields, really added little to the meager store of hard information about the wilderness.

Jacques Cartier, the French mariner, saw the mountains from the heights near present-day Montreal in 1535 but was told by his Indian guides only that the land was bounded by "delightful plains" and otherwise "unexplored," as he reported.

Samuel de Champlain, one of North America's most intrepid explorers, got closer in the summer of 1609 when he ventured south from his base in Canada and discovered Lake Champlain. But his journey was less exploratory than military since his Indian guides, many of them Hurons, had only one reason to go south, to wage war on their enemies, the Mohawks of the Iroquois nation. Champlain learned more about the battle rituals of the Indians than about the blue green forest and hills that formed the backdrop for the skirmish between Mohawks and Hurons. At some point between present-day Crown Point and Ticonderoga, Champlain, on behalf of his allies, became the first man to shoot a gun at other men in future United States territory. The day after the rout, which Champlain's gun assured, the explorer's party left immediately for home.

One of Champlain's biographers, Morris Bishop, reports that, except for the killing, Champlain thought the expedition an "intoxicating journey. He was stirred by the beauty of the summer nights on this lovely lake [Lake Champlain], winding among monstrous mountains." Perhaps Champlain would have liked to have been the first white man known to have gone deeper into those mountains.

The honor fell to another, however, under circumstances far less pleasant even than those encountered by Champlain. A Jesuit missionary from France, Father Isaac Jogues, was captured and enslaved in winter by a group of Mohawks in 1646. He was dragged half-naked, bleeding from serious wounds, hungry, and sick at heart because the Indians had no interest in his religion, into the remote hinterland of the Adirondacks. Father Jogues died in the wilderness. He no doubt would have agreed with another early American religious figure, William Bradford, who came to Massachusetts in 1620 to found a City of God in the wilderness but found his promised land "hideous and desolate . . . full of wild beasts and wild men."

But Father Jogues, though the first white man *known* to have gone into the wilderness, was probably not the first after all. Those who went before left no names or diaries or reports for commissioners or kings back home. Their names are forgotten. They are called Mountain Men today, and they penetrated places like the Adirondacks because the closest thing to North American gold was there: beavers.

3

How a Hat Won the West

F UR TRAPPERS WERE TRAVELING MEN, "pursuers of wild life, always going somewhere, never settling down," wrote Rutherford Platt in *The Great American Forest*. They had no intention of farming or homesteading and no desire to impose their will upon the land or conquer anything except as many fur-bearing animals as possible.

Their territory was that of the North American beaver and other animals such as marten, lynx, fisher, even squirrel. Unlike would-be settlers, trappers were at home in the North Woods of conifer forests and stillness. They were the first white men, often accompanied by Indians, to penetrate much of America's inner wilderness. And they were the first white men to see the recesses of the Adirondacks. They passed through like a net, scooping up nearly all the beaver, mink, otter, and other such creatures, then moved on.

They left little evidence of their presence except perhaps a forest even denser than the one they found, for the demise of the beaver allowed the trees to grow tall and straight and profusely without the constant flooding from beaver dams.

The trappers' invasion of the Adirondacks was swift and relatively short lived. By the time Father Jogues was dragged into the mountains, the trappers were probably on their way out. No one knows how many beavers lived in the mountains or how many the Europeans and Indians took, but based on the number living in the Adirondacks today (since conservationists replenished them) there may have been as many as twenty-five or thirty thousand when white men began trapping more than 300 years ago.

So complete was the trappers' haul that even the earliest

botanists and zoologists who explored the Adirondacks in later years simply accepted the fact that they were gone. "Like the Moose that once roamed these mighty forests, [the beavers] have, excepting a few isolated individuals, been exterminated or driven beyond our borders," wrote Dr. Clinton Merriam, a scientist of the mid-1800s.

As early as 1650 (some say 1640), traders and trappers alike were complaining that few beavers were left in the Albany area. Once the area had been the richest beaver territory on the continent; in fact, Albany owed its existence to the beaver trade. The Dutch who established the town first called it "Beverwyck," from which by 1656, thirty-five thousand beaver and otter skins were shipped to Europe. Eight years later, forty thousand skins were exported from the Hudson River town to Europe, where merchants paid six or eight, and later as much as ten times the original purchase price for each pelt.

Albany and her two rivals, Montreal and Quebec, remained dominant fur trading centers for another 100 years, although local supplies were getting scarcer all the time, and furs were coming not from New York and Pennsylvania but from Michigan, Wisconsin, Colorado, and finally from California by the 1700s.

One of the earliest maps of the Adirondack region was labeled "Couchsachrage, an Indian Beaver Hunting Territory." That was in 1756, after the Indians and Mountain Men had finished their all-out assault on the Adirondacks' beavers. But the name stuck for a while and gave the Adirondacks their first identity besides just plain wilderness.

The greedy thirst for beavers reflected a European demand for the skins. Between 1500 and 1900 and somewhat beyond, only the style of men's hats changed, not the social or physical necessity of wearing them. The big, floppy, plumed Cavalier hats of the sixteenth century, the tricornered American colonial hats of the eighteenth century, the Wellington or stovepipe hats (in which men could carry papers) of the nineteenth century, and all the styles in between, had one thing in common: the best of them were made of felt.

And the best felt was made from beaver fur. So vital was this fur to the manufacture of hats that before about 1850, the word "beaver," was used more often not in reference to the animal but to the hat.

Once beavers were plentiful all over Europe, but by the mid-sixteenth century, nearly all of them had been killed and their skins transformed into hats, or less frequently into capes or boots. By then, fishermen from the Netherlands, France, Britain, and Portugal were accustomed to making yearly journeys to the coasts of North America where they found vast quantities of cod for another of Europe's perpetual

The North American beaver. *New York State Department of Environmental Conservation*

needs—fish on Fridays for the Catholic majority and easily preserved food (in the case of cod, by salt) for everyone. The fishermen who landed on the rocky coasts of Newfoundland, Nova Scotia, and New England to dry their fish apparently engaged in a substantial side-business in peltry trading (or the skin trade) with local Indians. The pelts, one for one, turned a better profit than the fish, although the volume of cod was far greater than that of pelts for many years.

In 1534 Jacques Cartier, the mariner from St. Malo, France, landed on the banks of the St. Lawrence River and became the first white man known certainly to have done so. But the Indians he met seemed not to be surprised or puzzled by his presence or purpose. They greeted him with beaver skins stuck on sticks, like white flags of peace, indicating they knew (or thought they knew) exactly what he had come for.

It turned out that the North American beaver had the world's best fur for felt making. Equipped to survive in harsh climates and cold water, the northern beavers' fur was thick, protected on the outside by long, coarse hairs and insulated near the skin by short, soft, very thick layers of fuzz. (Beavers in the southern parts of North America had less fuzz and more coarse hair. There, deer or buckskin did for the economy what beavers did for the northern cash flow and gave the American language its slang word "buck" for money.)

The northern beavers' fuzz was the furrier's prize. When heated and pressed, the fuzz matted together in such a way as to create a lush, malleable, durable material that could be brushed, molded, and shaped into a dozen or more forms. Other animal fur could be made into felt, but beaver gave the smoothest finish and the most durability.

Beaver was "soft gold." For 200 years after Cartier's encounter with the Indians, white men and Indians forged alliances and fought battles (the so-called Beaver Wars of the 1660s and '70s) over the precious pelts, the territories of their beavers, and rights of various contenders for trapping in those territories.

Amidst all the rumors of gold and treasure in the New World, rumors that circulated about the Adirondacks as well, the only constant bounty was animal fur. Beaver was the most abundant and valuable, but otters, martens, rabbits, fishers, and others were also trapped for their fur in the Adirondacks and elsewhere. A shipload of beaver and other skins could save a company from bankruptcy or a settler from starvation. "The governor," wrote a soldier visiting Trois Rivières, a St. Lawrence River town where one of the earliest beaver trading posts in the New World was established in the 1600s, "would die of hunger if he did not trade with the natives for beavers when his small allowance is out."

The price and quantity of beaver skins from North America rose steadily, both as Indians demanded more than trinkets in exchange for beavers and as European markets tried to keep up with the demand. The big profits normally went to the middle men, those who bought cheaply from the Indians and sold expensively to Europeans.

But the new American land profited too, in a way. A trapper, Indian or white, would make an appointment to meet the middle man at a bend in the river, near a certain tree, or perhaps a hill overlooking a lake. Little by little, more trappers and traders were meeting at the same place, and word sifted down to peddlers who knew they could sell wares there.

Settlers learned that certain necessities for that first hard winter in the wilderness could be bought from the peddlers. Many a trading post turned into a town, then a city, this way: Albany, New York; Springfield, Massachusetts; Detroit; New Orleans; Montreal, Quebec; and hundreds more. The march of civilization seemed to follow the beaver men.

The trappers were heroes or devils, depending on one's point of view. They were the famous French *coureurs de bois* (woodsmen, loosely translated), or frontiersmen of British stock after whom James Fenimore Cooper probably modeled his wilderness characters. Many trappers seemed almost Indian, so faithfully did they adopt the clothing and habits of their frequent companions. Many were crude, rootless men who endured terrible hardship in the wilds of mountains and deserts most of the year in return for a drunken bash at the trading post every few months. Benjamin Franklin called the lot of them the "most vicious and abandoned wretches of our nation," while it was said of others that their love of wilderness was simply ahead of its time.

John Jacob Astor made his first money as a trapper and can hardly be called "refuse," another of Franklin's words for trappers. Astor arrived from Germany in New York in 1785. He had no money at all and worked for a time with his brother, a butcher. But Astor had heard about the fabulous opportunities in trapping and trading, and as soon as he could, he set off by himself into the wilderness beyond Albany, on the western fringes of the Adirondacks, in search of soft gold. He found enough to make his journey worth the hardship for a man without special wilderness skills or appreciation and went, again by himself, to London where he sold his skins for a handsome profit. After that, he left the trapping to the trappers and built his trading skills into the first of his fortunes.

Other famous, rich men of the era did the same thing. Schuylers, Van Rensselaers, de Peysters, scions of New York society, and even John Winthrop of Masachusetts, whose Puritan society in 1643 banned beaver hats as frivolous and vain, engaged in the fur trade. For the pioneer as well as for governors, ready cash was always a problem in early America. Riches indeed there were, but as historian Oscar Handlin wrote, they "were not lying open to the conquerors as they had been in Mexico and Peru." Fur was the only fast-cash crop to be had in North America.

Historians, conservationists, and religious leaders have deplored the "courtly vanity" that provoked the demise of the American beaver and created the only cash flow often available to early Americans. But the fact remains that more people explored the wilderness reaches of America in search of beaver than for any other single reason. By the time beaver hats went out of fashion—around 1832 when silk hats came in—America was almost settled. Its beaver population was nearly extinguished by then anyway.

In the Adirondacks a few remained. Pioneers there were able to get a bit of precious cash every now and then when they could find one of the busy, industrious, energetic creatures.

On the whole, however, the beaver trapping phase of Adirondack history defied the norm. Beavers were plentiful; they were trapped in large numbers; but the Adirondacks did not succumb to the civilizing influences that so often followed the trapping and trading. Wild, isolated, implacable, the Adirondack wilderness resisted the forces that transformed so much of the surrounding land into farms, towns, and gardens. The wilderness absorbed the trappers and may have given a number of men the means for making a temporary living from their traps, but the Adirondacks' generosity stopped there.

4

Dreams of Glory and Times of Trouble

W E ARE NOT ABOUT TO START on a squirrel hunt, or to drive a deer into [Lake George], but to outlie for days and nights and stretch across a wilderness where the feet of man seldom go, and where no bookish knowledge would carry you through harmless." So said Hawkeye in James Fenimore Cooper's novel *The Last of the Mohicans*. The year was 1757; the setting was the Adirondack Mountain region, taken from fact, as were many of the novel's historical details. Hawkeye and his two Indian friends led a search for two English girls who had been captured by the Hurons, and like Father Jogues, taken into the Adirondacks, land of "privations and difficulties" as Cooper described.

One of the many battles for possession of American land had just taken place at Fort William Henry, an undermanned British outpost at the southern tip of Lake George. The natural north-south waterway formed by Lake George and Lake Champlain was so crucial, and so many battles were fought for possession of the route, that it became known as a dark and bloody ground. The 1757 victory of the French over the British at Fort William Henry was a factual event Cooper used to get his story started.

The wilderness looming behind the isolated fort was also real. More than 100 years after Cooper's hero, Hawkeye, was supposed to have summoned all his courage and woodcraft to trek that wilderness, many a part-time woodsman, out for pleasure in the same region, would argue over the identity of the real person after whom Cooper modeled his character.

The Adirondack guides who led nineteenth-century vacationers through the wilderness as efficiently and knowledgeably as Hawkeye led the search for the kidnapped English girls were often the stuff from which legend is made. Theirs was no "bookish knowledge." Their ungrammatical wisdom and their skill with wood, hunting, and fishing were learned from doing and surviving in the wilderness, traits which many an educated, city-bred vacationer found charming for being so different.

But who were these guides? Where did they come from? Why did they stay, when so many others left the wilderness?

Some were descendants of pioneers like the Sheldons. There were never very many of them. Only a few of those who crossed Lake Champlain in search of better, less-crowded land than was left in New England, went directly west into the mountains. Most, and there were thousands of these, turned due north after they crossed the lake, toward Plattsburgh, then west again to Malone or Massena. Or they turned south toward Albany, where the Mohawk Valley led them to fertile flatlands in central New York. As the threat of Indian attack decreased, as rumors of fertile fields further west spread, and as New England became more and more crowded, migration picked up and amounted to what has been called a torrent. "The Yankee Invasion," propelled by what some have called "New York fever," or the mad dash to get land there, astonished observers between 1700 and 1800. But the flood-tide went around the Adirondacks.

Near Armagh, a city in northern Ireland, there lived a young man who aspired above his station in life. William Gilliland was not yet twenty years old in 1753, but he was handsome, cheerful and charming. He seems to have been educated and from a respectable family, and he was popular with the best society. He often dined or went on hunting trips with country gentlemen.

But in that time and place it was one thing to dress up and attend parties at the request of local noblemen; it was quite another to want to marry one of the scions of society. Gilliland, however, proposed marriage to Lady Betsey Eckles and thereby affronted her family and the inflexible social order. Gilliland's biographer, Winslow Watson, described it this way: Betsey's family was forced into the "vigorous application of power and the expatriation of Gilliland." He was neatly disposed of within the ranks of the British army, which in its turn sent him with the Thirty-fifth Regiment to America where the French were forever causing trouble over beaver territory, transportation routes, and possession of the land.

His tour of duty in America gave Gilliland something he could never have hoped for in Ireland, the means to realize his ambitions. The evidence suggests that he was with the Thirty-fifth at the battle of Fort William Henry in 1757, and he no doubt was awed by the great expanse of unoccupied land that seemed to go on forever. Gilliland, it seems, determined then and there to make a part of that land his own.

Immediately after his discharge from the army in 1758, he headed for New York City, which already had the reputation as a place where fast money could be made. Nearly 100 merchants in a population of twenty thousand people were selling everything from native potash, wheat, beef, and pork to lumber, hemp, and flax which was shipped to the West Indies, the southern coastal colonies, or Europe. In return, New York merchants sold imported furniture, clothing, tea, spices, paints, drugs, and other luxury items to a growing and increasingly wealthy population at home.

One such merchant was a Mr. Phagan, who ran a medium-sized operation and was eager for the help of a versatile assistant. Gilliland impressed him and within a year after joining the firm was made Phagan's full partner—and his son-in-law.

Gilliland married Phagan's daughter, Elizabeth, and received a handsome dowry of £1,500. He put this and all his own money into buying a two-thousand-acre tract of land south of the Bouquet River on the western shore of Lake Champlain, about 100 miles north of Fort William Henry. Gradually, he acquired more land, and by 1764, he owned almost four thousand acres stretching half a mile north and six miles south of the Bouquet and for several miles inland.

He knew it was virgin land. It was "howling wilderness," as he wrote in a diary that survives today. Getting to it, he also knew, was a "vexatiously delayed" journey, a "labyrinth of fatigue, anxiety, trouble and expense." Anyone with much baggage was especially "embarrassed." But settling the wilderness was the great challenge and opportunity in the New World. "Many and great advantages . . . must unavoidably rebound . . . from the early settlement of the waste lands in America." Otherwise, those rich resources would serve "no other purpose but to accommodate the savages and beasts of the forest."

There was, of course, something more than the advantage to the land. There was the advantage to William Gilliland. The land he bought was to his mind better than anything in Ireland, a lake and river at his feet, the magnificent Adirondacks at his back. Land, the symbol of wealth, position, and authority, was way beyond the reach of the likes of Gilliland in Ireland, as Betsey Eckles' family had made clear. But in America it could be his, as could the means to "feudal authority," as Watson described Gilliland's ambition, and "affluence and power."

Gilliland set out to fulfill his ambition in the spring of 1765. With an entourage including two millwrights, a minister, a weaver, an indentured servant, a cooper, two farmers and their families, a blacksmith, wagon-maker, tailor, a Negro man named Ireland, twenty cows, a bull, and twenty oxen (but not on this occasion his own family), Gilliland reached the Bouquet River in June. It took him over a month to get there from New York City, and the vexations on the journey were legion. The cattle, having had to swim in places where they could not be driven, hauled, or ferried, were let loose to eat what they could find when at last they reached the Bouquet. But in the fall, when as many as could be found were rounded up, they had reverted to a wild state and were barely manageable.

More serious even than the cattle or the difficult journey was the problem of water power once the cows and men were settled. Gilliland had hoped to build, first thing, a saw mill, but the falls on the Bouquet River were not powerful enough. Instead, he had to build several small mills further inland than he had planned.

Still, by the end of that first summer, Gilliland had made a skeleton of his estate out of the raw land. From oaks, cedars, hemlocks, birch, pine, and spruce he had sawed enough timber to begin a house for himself, "the first dwelling built by civilized man between Crown Point and the line of Canada," as Watson said. It was only forty-four by twenty-two feet, but it was water-tight. He had a road, and he had surveyed the land and marked off the sites for four villages, all named for his family: Bessboro, Janesboro, Charlottesboro, and Elizabeth.

In the autumn Gilliland ventured further into the wilderness he considered to be his own. He took a boat and went north on Lake Champlain, then made a sharp left turn into the Ausable River, the first white man known to have done so. It was a "most curious canal," he wrote. Most curious of all was a great chasm, now known as the Ausable Chasm, a favorite tourist attraction. To Gilliland it was "an admirable sight, appearing on each side like a regular built wall, somewhat ruinated, and one would think this prodigious cleft was occasioned by an earthquake."

He also explored the Salmon River and the Saranac, which he called the Savaniac. The further inland he went, however, the more "ordinary" in terms of farming potential the land became. All in all, he had chosen one of the best agricultural regions in the Adirondacks by staying close to Lake Champlain. The Bouquet River empties into the lake amidst a stretch of good soil. It is not too sandy as it is elsewhere in the lake shore area. The climate is dry, and farmers are spared the scourge of spring mud.

Instead, Gilliland had plenty of sun, an average of 150 frost free days between May and October (more than higher altitudes in the Adirondacks offer as the Sheldons discovered), and an average temperature of 69 degrees Fahrenheit in summer. He was able to grow wheat, tobacco, cabbage, lettuce, turnips, parsley, spinach, peas, flax, beans, cucumbers, squash, carrots, parsnips, radishes, muskmelon, savory, celery, mustard, leeks, potatoes, and corn. Some of these came up "very short," Gilliland wrote, "owing I believe to dry weather." But they came up.

Eventually, enough calves were born to his original herd of cows to make veal plentiful. And, of course, he had pigs, shot deer for venison, and had ample fish from the lake and rivers; on his first fishing expedition he caught sixty.

Only a year after Gilliland made his first assault on the wilds, he had things well enough in order to bring his family to the North Country. In the spring of 1766, he brought them from New York City, but the journey was even more vexatious than his first one.

Getting his mother (probably his mother-in-law), wife, assorted nieces, nephews, and in-laws, and his own four children, as well as more smiths and farmers, servants, two boats, and twenty-two wagons from the city to the Bouquet River was a feat not too much less daring than the trip many thousands later hazarded across the continent in the next century. All paid a very high price. Gilliland's five-year-old daughter, Jane, after whom he had already named one of his villages, was drowned when the boat she was on was caught in a swirling mass of branches on the spring-flooded Hudson River near Stillwater. A minister was drowned, too, and Gilliland himself was temporarily blinded during the accident.

It took the party three months to get to their plantation. Once there, however, prosperity seemed within reach. In the fall Gilliland had enough excess produce and supplies to send three shoats (weaned piglets), several salmon, and a fat calf to the British governor of the colony, who he apparently knew and for whom he later negotiated Canadian boundary disputes.

In January 1766, the climate made itself felt. Twelve inches of snow became fifteen inches by February 7, and twenty inches three days later. Cramped quarters and bad weather aggravated tension among Gilliland's tenants and servants. Several threatened to leave. Others threatened the life of Gilliland's brother, Watson, who had to call on British troops at Crown Point for help.

It was not only weather but Gilliland's increasing tendencies toward authoritarianism that made matters difficult on this outpost of civilization. As his community grew, Gilliland played a more and more lordly role. He was master, chancellor, and aristocrat here. Within ten years of his arrival, several hundred people lived in his private kingdom, which he claimed by 1775 to encompass sixty thousand acres, including twenty-eight homes, forty out-buildings, a school, two grist mills, two saw mills, horse stables which he brought over the ice in winter from Canada, plus assorted herds, flocks, orchards, roads, and bridges. With an income of about £1,000 a year Gilliland thought himself a success. His three villages, Willsboro (named for himself), Elizabethtown (named for his wife), and Bessboro formed a triangle of security for him and propelled him toward even greater ambitions, and in the minds of some of his tenants, delusions of grandeur.

Perhaps a sense of survival equal to Gilliland's own encouraged the tenants in what the chronicler Winslow Watson called their "public sentiment towards democratic institutions, and its bias towards the ideas of self-government." Perhaps Gilliland, remembering his treatment in Ireland at the hands of an insular aristocracy, checked his own tendencies toward feudal authority. Even in the wilderness of northern New York, current events did not escape notice. Revolution was thick in the air. Discontent with Britain and an urge for independence reached Gilliland's colony.

In March 1775, thirteen male tenants convened and drew up what Burton Bernstein in his profile of Essex County, *The Sticks*, called a document that sparked "a diminutive, grass-roots American Revolution." The document was a democratic constitution. Gilliland was recognized as the first power among the people, but the colonists all bound themselves to a covenant dividing responsibilities evenly among them all. Colonists would henceforth vote on "regulations concerning roads, fences, bridges and hogs." The majority vote would "be binding on us respectively, by every tie of honor and honesty." The following year the "constitution" had worked so effectively that nine more men signed it.

Whether Gilliland sensed the turning of the tide in America or was moved by genuinely democratic impulses, he allied himself with the Americans when war became inevitable. In fact, he was quite outspoken about his loyalties and claimed to have instigated the first battle of the Revolution, the raid at Ticonderoga.

History contradicts him, and so did Vermont's Green Mountain

William Gilliland, portrait by Ralph Earl, 1789. *Courtesy, The New-York Historical Society, New York City*

Boys, led by Ethan Allen. But Gilliland did establish his own militia and serve in it as an ordinary soldier, for "example's sake," he said. Some evidence indicates that he envisioned a new state (or nation), of which he would be governor, in northern New York.

But the Revolution proved Gilliland's downfall. It all began with Benedict Arnold, a man filled with his own dreams of glory who possessed a personality every bit as testy and determined as Gilliland's. Arnold, envisioning a glorious military career for himself, had rushed to Ticonderoga the minute trouble started and appointed himself revolutionary leader. Intoxicated with the easy American victory over a poorly protected fort, he and Ethan Allen decided to storm Montreal in 1776 and topple the British government in all North America once and for all.

Gilliland was waiting for them when they returned in rags and defeat. He said he gladly took the miserable, half-starved, freezing, filthy soldiers in, fed them, nursed their wounds, and gave them shelter.

Arnold claimed otherwise. He said Gilliland had fleeced the soldiers, taking advantage of their weakened condition. In self-defense, Arnold said, his men looted Gilliland's property. Many of the tenants, who so recently had signed their democratic agreement, ran away from the colony on the Bouquet River in fear of British retaliation after the Americans' defeat in Canada, leaving Gilliland with little help from what he said was the wanton destruction of his fields, tools, furniture, and buildings.

"You're a parcel of damned robbers," Gilliland was said to have shouted at Arnold and his soldiers. He later accused Arnold of "temerity," "rashness," "impudence," and "error," as well as being "intoxicated with power."

For his part, Arnold retaliated by charging Gilliland with treason. "I am fully of the opinion," Arnold wrote to General Horatio Gates who was in charge of the American-held Fort Ticonderoga in 1776, "that Gilliland [and several relatives and tenants] have from time to time sent expresses to the enemy. Gilliland is a most plausible and artful villain."

If, indeed, Gilliland was a British spy, only feigning American loyalty, the British didn't behave as if they trusted him. They condemned him as an outlaw and issued a reward of £500 for his arrest. Two of Gilliland's children in Canada were placed under house arrest.

Arnold, however, was at the time an important American military leader, and his charge, though never proved, was weighty enough to have Gilliland put behind bars in New York City. Eventually he was released but arrested again in Albany for spreading rumors about American casualties at the Battle of Brandywine. Again he was released, but it was six years before he could get back to the Bouquet River and his home.

What he found, Watson wrote, was "more desolate than when he first penetrated the wilderness. . . . The beauty and grandeur of nature, then redeemed the gloom and solitude of the scene. Bushes and wild vegetation now usurped fields, which toil and expense had wrested from the forests—fences decayed, bridges had fallen, roads were broken up, charred and blackened ruins marked the site."

What Arnold hadn't ruined in 1776 the British finished. They and their Algonquin allies, having recovered their losses at Ticonderoga, burned the few remaining sticks left of Gilliland's world. One wonders if British General "Gentleman Johnny" Burgoyne's soldiers knew they were plundering the possessions of an Irishman, or if Gilliland felt some aristocratic vengeance was punishing the commoner who had achieved such untoward success.

The fire went out of William Gilliland. After the war, when British-held land reverted to the new American government, Gilliland's original deeds were found faulty. The land was nearly useless anyway. He had tried to recoup some of his losses by selling timber, but his shipment was stolen in transit by his own agent. Gilliland went to prison for a third time, for debt.

Finally, he was able to go home. By then he was old, no longer a threat to anyone. Instead, he was said to be quite dotty, muttering and lashing out against fate, a burden to a son-in-law living in Essex, a Champlain lakeside village not far from Willsboro.

He found occasional work as a surveyor for the land speculators who were beginning to buy land—any land at all—in the mountains. The rest of the time he seemed almost to be in another world, ordering nonexistent tenants to mend fences and organizing imaginary expeditions up the Ausable River.

Some say Gilliland was on one of his surveying trips on February 2, 1796. Others say he was on his way to visit a friend. He was found frozen and blood-stained in the snow near Lake Champlain. He was sixty-two years old.

Before the war Gilliland's only potential rival as Adirondack overlord was an Englishman named Philip Skene. He had an estate about fifty miles south of Gilliland's, near present-day Whitehall. Gilliland and Skene were friends and had planned to combine their resources in an attempt, some evidence indicates, to get a royal charter for a North Country colony.

Skene was on the losing side in the Revolution and left the

country. Gilliland, though a professed patriot, lost everything anyway. All that came of these feudal, transient outposts of civilization were the names of Elizabethtown and Willsboro, pleasant communities today but not the realities of William Gilliland's dreams. The site of Gilliland's Elizabethtown is now Westport, and the Town of Jay grew out of Willsboro.

Perhaps, just perhaps, a few of the tenants, hoping for success, doing what the Indians had done when they needed a place to hide, had gone into the mountains. If they were clever and strong enough, they learned how to live there, and their descendants later taught wilderness skills to visiting city-folk.

Gilliland's struggle against nature in the Adirondack wilderness appears to have been successful. He chose a good spot and had all the requisite energy and ambition. His problem was man. But his story and the setting in which it took place left a sour taste. Few tried to follow his footsteps in fear of catching his luck.

5

Land for Sale

ALTHOUGH THE ADIRONDACKS were virtually uninhabited in the early years of American history, they were not without owners. A curious circumstance in Adirondack history is that, while the region remained largely unmapped until 1837, most of the acreage belonged, on foolscap at least, to someone for at least two centuries before that.

The French, Dutch, and British had all claimed ownership at one time or another while they were at each others' throats for most of the seventeenth and eighteenth centuries over possession of the Lake Champlain waterway. Both the French and British had given away chunks of Adirondack land as bounty payments to their army officers. Few discharged soldiers settled, or even saw, the land they received; but some made money from selling their deeds to others, who in their turn tried to resell them.

The American Indians of the region, of course, had a long-standing claim to the Adirondacks. By the time Europeans were established in New York, the Oneidas and the Mohawks, both members of the Iroquois federation, split the mountains somewhere down the middle. The Oneidas claimed the western slopes and the Mohawks the eastern ones, but eventually they ceded or sold most of the land to white men's governments.

After 1759, when the British finally won a decisive battle over the French at Ticonderoga (two years after the battle that opened Cooper's novel, *The Last of the Mohicans,* a battle the French won), all land deals were transacted by the British government. It forbade anyone to deal directly with the Indians.

It was a clever British ploy, for in the eighteenth century land was

Such was often the kind of land speculators bought sight unseen. *Photo by W. F. Kollecker, courtesy of the Saranac Lake Free Library, Adirondack Collection*

the hottest commodity available. Just as the most exalted persons of an earlier era were usually involved in the fur trade, so many of the most famous men of the eighteenth century dealt in land speculation. "Congratulate me," wrote William Cullen Bryant, the American poet, even as late as 1843, "there is the probability of my becoming a land holder."

The longing to own land lasted late and made many a man's fortune, as well as many a bankruptcy. George Washington dabbled in land speculation and was said to have set off a major depression when he sold out much of his investment in 1796. "If Washington is selling," one can almost hear others saying, "there must be trouble. Sell too!"

It wasn't just Washington, of course, or any other single person or event that usually caused the frequent crashes. Much of the land was a good deal poorer than it might have been, and as historian Marcus Lee Hansen wrote, "In the scramble to secure [land], prices rose far beyond any value that Nature would ever justify."

In a nutshell, that is what happened to huge tracts in the Adirondacks. By 1771, much of the region was tied up in private ownership, even though very few of the owners had ever been to inspect their investments. No surveys of the highlands or even the majority of the lowland areas had been completed, and no single name (although as many as thirteen would be used before 1837) had been given permanently to the mountains.

As was the custom of the day, speculators bought first and looked later, if they looked at all. That was what happened in 1771 when, in one of the most mysterious and complicated episodes in Adirondack history, two ships-carpenters acted as front men for a group of more sophisticated financiers in the purchase of what was believed to be eight hundred thousand acres in the central mountains.

The seller was the British government, which had arranged to buy the land from the Mohawk Indians for a little over £1,000 and sold the same for £40,000. (Such was the reason Britain insisted on being a middle man in all land deals with Indians.)

The names of the buyers — both the frontmen and the actual investors — are important for two reasons. First, the buyers' names — Totten and Crossfield—stuck to the mountains. Many years later people still referred to the region as the "Totten and Crossfield Purchase." Another huge tract was known for generations as "Macomb's Purchase," after another fiery Irishman who lent color to early Adirondack history— and a great deal of money to the shipwrights and others.

Alexander Macomb was one of the silent partners behind the Totten and Crossfield Purchase. He had made money in the fur trade and was lured early into the other profitable American enterprise, land speculation. He never gave up hope of making a fortune from northern New York land sales. Though he seems never to have seen the Adirondacks up close, he was strangely faithful to them.

He kept buying more and more land and never accepted the fact that owning it was never to benefit him. Few had wanted to buy plots of land from Totten and Crossfield in 1771. Fewer still wanted to buy later from Macomb.

The second important event that came about as a result of the Totten and Crossfield Purchase was the first survey of the central High Peaks and western regions of the Adirondacks. The survey didn't amount to much. The surveyor, like many who succeeded him, gave up about halfway through the job. The land was too rugged and the rum ran out. His map turned out to be two hundred thousand acres short.

Much later in the 1830s and 1840s, many of these old and badly documented deeds were still causing trouble. It was found that the original Totten and Crossfield Purchase covered more than a million acres, including the now famous Raquette, Blue Mountain, and Indian lakes.

Nevertheless, that 1771 survey established the rough units people called townships, demarcations which divide the region today. Smaller than counties yet far larger than the villages or towns, the term "township" has been shortened in modern parlance to "town." The results today are confusing. William Chapman White notes the "pile-up of language, as in one legal phrase, 'The Village of Saranac Lake in the Town of Harrietstown.'"

The Revolutionary War caused a temporary halt to the feverish land speculation in New York and elsewhere. But it took financiers little time to begin renegotiating deeds and purchases with the new American government after the war. Both the state and federal governments were strapped for cash after the war and eager to sell the land they found themselves with.

Alexander Macomb, undeterred from prewar debacles, was in the thick of the renewed speculation and in 1792 arranged to buy nearly four million acres in the Adirondacks for sixteen cents an acre from the New York State Land Office.

Macomb's dealing was not limited to the Adirondacks. He was involved in several other land deals in New York and some say in some shady operations with state officials. He had drawn up an easy payment plan for his four million-acre purchase; but between 1792, when the first installment was due and the first land patent issued, and 1798, when the final patent was ready, Macomb had gone bankrupt. Since his bankruptcy ruined many of his backers, Macomb was put in jail not only for indebtedness but probably for his own protection as well.

Out of friendship, legal obligation, or the speculative fever, Macomb's tract was divided among his backers and other big-city operators. Those who found themselves with acreage along the St. Lawrence River, the Black River, or near Plattsburgh were well pleased with their investments. Settlement was rapid, to their financial advantage. Decent roads were built, one from Plattsburgh to Malone before 1800, another from Carthage, on the Black River, to Ogdensburg in 1801.

But the roads, like the pioneers and the navigable rivers, went around, rarely *into* the Adirondacks. Those who found themselves with land in the central portions of the mountains were, for the most part, stuck. Some swallowed their losses; others were ruined. And a few managed to pass theirs off, often to unsuspecting buyers.

One such innocent was the son-in-law of a Revolutionary War hero, a fervent Baptist, a millionaire merchant, and an imposing 300-pound figure by the name of John Brown, of Providence, Rhode Island. (Brown University was endowed by and named for the same family.) In fact, in the Adirondacks people still talk about "Brown's Tract," the area in the western sector of the mountains near Old Forge.

John Brown had no sons, so he put great hope in his daughters' husbands, especially one by the name of John Francis. He was pleasant, handsome, and intelligent, and John Brown kept hoping he would catch on to the intricacies of the shipping business, grasp the importance of hard work and religious faith, and carry on the family name and wealth.

In the year Alexander Macomb went bankrupt and to jail, 1798, one of Brown's ships came into the port at New York City with a very valuable load of silks and spices and other merchandise from China. Young Francis was sent to the city to collect the proceeds from the shipment and bring them back to Providence.

He managed the first part successfully. But in a somewhat mysterious series of events, including the consumption of wine and the heady company of some powerful financiers, Francis returned not with cash, but with the deed to a tract of two hundred thousand acres in the central and western portion of some mountains in New York State (now parts of Herkimer and Hamilton counties).

John Brown's fury was matched only by a determination to do the best he could with a bad bargain. Almost immediately he sent a team of surveyors to see what he was dealing with and had them mark off eight townships. To each he gave a name he hoped would inspire his son-in-law: Industry, Enterprise, Perseverence, Unanimity, Frugality, Sobriety, Economy, and Regularity.

The township of Economy was the focus of Brown's all-out effort to make good his "investment." He had a decent road (one of the first into the mountains) built, cajoled a few settlers to follow it, and with the aid of a sawmill and a gristmill, hoped to turn the area into one of those communities with a "virtuous, industrious Christian population" others dreamed about building in the Adirondacks.

When iron ore was discovered, it looked as if Brown might be saved. But the ore proved difficult to work, expensive to transport, and ultimately profitless. The settlers encountered the same difficulties with thin soil, bitter winters, and isolation that those on the eastern slopes had discovered. One by one, they left after a few years. The forest enclosed the remains of houses, mills, the forge, and the road.

By 1811, the Brown fortune was nearly gone. Brown had died and his family was getting desperate. Another son-in-law, an elegant, well-educated German by the name of Frederick Herreshoff, decided in a last-ditch effort to try to revitalize the family fortune by turning the old property up north into a genuinely profit-making community.

With the last of his and his wife's money, Herreshoff rebuilt the road from Boonville (named for another land speculator, Gerrit Boon, who tried and failed to make *his* fortune from North Country maple sugar), studied husbandry and mining, and scouted around for settlers and tenants. The largest cabin on the weed-infested site was patched up and dubbed "The Manor." Herreshoff, who like Gilliland before him, left his wife and children behind while he tried to get things going, then began writing to them the hopeful, detailed letters that told the poignant story of his efforts.

Herreshoff rediscovered the poor soil and harsh climate. The terrain was too rugged for wheat. He found that sheep could not live on the local grasses, and wolves tore the flock to bloody pieces. When he threw the last of his money into trying to revitalize the forges, he had the same problems with the ore his predecessors had. Finally, on a misty, cold winter morning in 1819, he got up before anyone was stirring, sneaked out back, and shot himself in the head.

That was the sort of story one heard about the Adirondacks in the early nineteenth century. Whatever else was being circulated as information about the region was largely rumor or idle gossip.

Revolutionary War veterans, too, heard of the desolation of the land. The indebted, cash-poor, infant Federal United States Government had set aside several thousand acres of land in what are now Franklin, Essex, and Clinton counties as bounty (instead of cash payment) for its veteran soldiers. Not one veteran accepted the offer. A new military tract had to be marked off, this one in the more desirable western part of the state. Just east of the Old Military Tract (as the bounty land in the Adirondacks was called) another huge tract of land was set aside for Canadians who had sympathized with the Americans and had had to flee British-controlled territory after the war. Not one refugee settled there either, and both tracts reverted to the state.

One land speculator whose site-unseen tract fell with the Oswegatchie Township on the northwest slopes of the mountains near Cranberry Lake, wrote after an inspection tour: "The soil of this town is very indifferent, and the settlers few." And his was one of the better tracts.

On the other hand, rumors of gold and silver, quick riches like those the beaver trappers made in the previous century, spread. Some of

Rock-studded Adirondack earth. *Photo by W. F. Kollecker, courtesy of the Saranac Lake Free Library, Adirondack Collection*

the early French explorers had called the region the "Peru Mountains," thinking they would find treasures like those in South America. Iron ore was known to be buried in the rock, and people like Herreshoff kept trying to mine it.

Of the people living in the mountains, there were stories of hermits, criminals, and escapees from society. One also heard of primitive men, half-Indian, half-white, unsullied by society, perhaps, but closer to beasts than to men. There were Paul Bunyan types, too, it was said, supermen, giants who could hold their own with bears and mountain lions and bowed to no other men.

As late as 1857, the impression that the North Country was a kind of woodland desert persisted. A history of Herkimer County published that year described the large section of the Adirondacks within that county (including Old Forge and the Fulton Chain Lakes) as "a region of wasteland visited only by a few amateur fishermen and infested with the musquito [sic] and midge."

Those amateur fishermen, casually mentioned, had every reason

Once such a scene was thought to be "wasteland." *Photo by W. F. Kollecker, courtesy of the Saranac Lake Free Library, Adirondack Collection*

to keep their mouths shut about what some were coming to think of as their own private discovery: a wilderness whose appearance was not repulsive but alluring, a region of rivers whose isolation and ruggedness was their glory, not their curse, and a natural preserve offering not hardship but peace of mind.

A few others were coming to know the Adirondacks not as a wasteland but as a wonderland. Writers and intellectuals especially were beginning to appreciate what had been to their ancestors a hideous place. Washington Irving, the New York tale spinner who wrote a biography of John Jacob Astor, spent some time one summer in 1803 at Oswegatchie and seems to have enjoyed himself. In 1818, an otherwise unidentified "group of Yale men along with the brother-in-law of the president of Columbia College" got a team of horses at Boonville and rode into the woods as far as they could go on Brown's Road, then walked the rest of the way to a place where they could enjoy a little hunting and fishing and the quiet of the forest.

It could hardly be called a trend, this trickle of thinkers and professionals into the North Woods. Few could speculate ahead to the day when nearly everyone—not just the wealthy—had the time off, spare cash, and a yen for the out-of-doors.

Throughout the eighteenth and into the nineteenth century, "few thought of summer, much less winter, vacations in the country; most lived in the country anyway, and a vacation was simply a few days off for fishing or hunting, and even this had to be justified in terms of economic benefit," as the *Guide to the Empire State* stated succinctly in the 1930s.

There was still too much to be done. America's growth centered in regions of proved or at least potential economic benefit. New York's North Country had disappointed too often. Land speculators, would-be farmers, miners, and even surveyors had been unlucky over and over. (A grandson of one of those settlers around Lake Champlain told William Chapman White in the 1950s, "My grandfather wasn't so much when it come to picking farmland.")

The Indians had long been dispossessed, the Oneidas having ceded their territory to the United States in 1788. Even the beavers were so scarce that only an occasional pelt found its way to a dwindling market. Lumbermen were still reaping plenty of timber in Maine, New Hampshire, and Vermont.

In short, the rivers would not be stopped or turned, the seed not planted, the earth not fertilized, as Cicero described man's laudable victory over nature. Man by his best efforts had failed to make another, to his mind, better nature out of the northern wilderness. Americans didn't waste time over lost causes in the eighteenth century. They just moved on.

6

The Rock

THE ADIRONDACKS MEANT TROUBLE to explorers, pioneers, land speculators, and trappers because of the *kind* of mountains they are. Most mountains present barriers and difficulties of sorts to people, but the geological forces that produced the Adirondacks gave them certain unusual characteristics destined to seem onerous to some, delightful to others, and obvious, if inexplicable, to all who have known them.

For one thing, Adirondack rock is extremely hard, and the layer of soil over the rock is very thin in most places. Farmers learned as much when their plows hit bedrock all to easily and often.

Furthermore, it has always been difficult to get into and across the Adirondacks. They are not a range of mountains strung out like the Appalachians. Instead, the Adirondack region as a whole is shaped like a knobby dome with all the highest peaks clustered just to the northeast of the geographical center of the region. Pioneers trying to move west from Vermont or Massachusetts (as many thousands did) encountered this group standing like a giant rock wall on the far banks of Lake Champlain. The land rose from ninety-five feet above sea level at lakeshore to over five thousand feet atop Mt. Marcy, only twenty miles away.

There are few passes—or notches or gaps—as one finds in the Appalachians, Pyrenees, or Rockies. Nor are there any navigable rivers cutting all the way through the Adirondacks. Of the six thousand miles of river water in the mountains, most of it runs down individual mountains.

Moving north and south through the mountains, as the Indians who knew the right trails could show white men in the early days, was somewhat easier than going east or west. Something resembling five individual mountain ranges carved out of the dome lie on parallel, northeast-southwest axes, with something like valleys in between. Even so, no Adirondack surveyor, explorer, or hiker has failed to note how these "ranges" are connected like Siamese twins by cross spurs which cut off many a potential north-south pass. As William Chapman White wrote: "The interconnections of the various ranges are such that a man can climb up and down many peaks, one after the other, without coming down to the twenty-five hundred foot level."

And Adirondack rock from which the mountains were made is everywhere. Veiled though the rock is in many places by the forest, it is inescapable. Great slabs of it are exposed on mountain tops. The clear water of many lakes reveals it there, on the bottom. Patches of bare rock crop up like bald spots all along highways, even in the deepest forests. In places, as on the trail up Mt. Marcy, the soil is less than an inch deep, and sometimes nonexistent where hikers' boots have worn it away. Elsewhere the erosive forces of nature bared the rock, as at Avalanche Pass where walls of naked stone ascend on both sides of the narrow four-mile trail. Explorers in the 1830s named the pass thinking only an avalanche could have created so awesome a gorge. In fact, glaciers and erosion were responsible.

The geological reasons for all these topographical characteristics lie in the way the Adirondacks were born. Actually, the Adirondacks were twice-born. The mountains are what they are primarily because of two major geological events which took place eons apart: one causing a special kind of rock to form, the other making mountains of that rock.

Other American mountains, like most of the Appalachian range, are the result of folding of the earth's crust. Some western American mountains, like the Sierra Nevada, were faulted, that is rock was shifted upwards along cracks or faults in the crust. Still other mountains, such as Mt. Rainier, are volcanic in origin.

But the Adirondacks seem not to have been originally produced primarily by any of these forces, although portions of the rock have been faulted since. Instead, Adirondack rock which now stands as high as 5,344 feet above sea level was first formed *inside* the earth and was then much later pushed upward to the surface.

The phenomenon is not unique to the Adirondacks. The Henry Mountains in Utah, for example, were formed in a similar fashion when magma, or very hot, liquified rock, seeped up from deep inside the planet, embedded itself in the upper layers of the earth, and slowly hardened there, causing the surface rocks to rise like a kind of blister into mountains.

What caused an intrusion of magma beneath the site of the

Bare Adirondack rock at Avalanche Pass. *Collection of the New York State Museum*

modern Adirondacks is not entirely certain. But many leading geologists believe that 1.1 billion years ago, the forces that were building the North American continent—the Grenville Orogeny (or mountain building process, from the Greek *oros*, meaning "mountain") — created heat and pressure powerful enough to rupture the earth and cause the magma intrusion there. The intrusion covered at least as much territory as the Adirondacks now occupy.

Magma is like lava. It is simply molten (made liquid by heat) rock that instead of being erupted at the earth's surface remains embedded in it. When molten material cools and hardens (crystallizes) it turns into igneous rock, so-called from the Latin *ignis* meaning fire. Igneous rock hardened from lava is often porous and light. But igneous rock from magma is usually extremely hard, dense, and erosion-resistant, like Adirondack rock today.

Most of what is called the earth's bedrock or basement rock is igneous. Sixty-five percent of the earth's crust is made of it. The crust is a layer of rock, normally between ten and twenty miles thick, which is the outer shell of the planet. It overlies the mantle and beneath that the core, which are the real bowels of the earth. No one has ever seen either of them, so deeply buried are they by the crust.

Not too much of the igneous crust is visible on earth either. But in places like the Adirondacks, a portion of it has surfaced, and on every continent, at least some of the crust, or basement rock, has remained above sea level during the ages.

In Canada, for example, almost three million square miles of basement rock has been above sea level for about three billion years. This is called the Canadian Shield and has been described as the "embryo of North America," since geologists think that it was the original nucleus onto which the rest of the continent was added.

The southeastern portion of the shield, on which much of eastern Canada now rests, is about the same age as the Adirondack rock that now protrudes as mountains, that is, about 1.1 billion years old. In fact, on geological maps it looks as if this portion of the shield, known as the Grenville Province, has a tail—a rounded appendage extending southward and connected to the main body of the province by a neck that runs under the St. Lawrence River—the Canadian-American border—and is visible in the water as a series of islands, the Thousand Islands as they are called. The tail itself surfaces in New York and is the bulbous mass of the Adirondacks.

In only one other place does the Canadian Shield extend into the United States, and that is in the Midwest where Michigan, Minnesota, and Wisconsin share it and its mineral wealth, especially iron ore. Much of the world's precious ore—gold, uranium, silver, and iron ore—is stored in such crustal, igneous rock. Adirondack crustal rock also has iron ore, a great deal of which, unfortunately has proved to be difficult to extract.

CANADIAN SHIELD

GRENVILLE PROVINCE

ST. LAWRENCE LOWLAND

**THE GRENVILLE PROVINCE
OF THE CANADIAN SHIELD**

Magnetite is the principal source of Adirondack iron ore. Rich deposits all over the mountains once promised wealth and a stable industry. William Gilliland knew about the ores near Lake Champlain as early as the 1700s. In the next century more than 200 mines and forges were opened, and by 1880, 15 percent of all America's iron ore was produced in eastern New York, mainly in Essex County.

But the isolation of many mines, the expense of building roads and dams, and the problem of impurities of the ore itself always made iron ore production risky at best.

The primary impurity turned out to be a mineral called ilmenite. Miners cursed it; businessmen despised it; but around 1912 it was found that ilmenite could be made into titanium dioxide—one of the whitest compounds known to man. During World War II scientists used it for smokescreens and other wartime materials. The iron ore, in a reversal of the nineteenth-century process, became the substance that was discarded.

Titanium dioxide is now highly prized as a white pigment for the finest paints,and the ilmenite mine near Tahawas is today the largest in the world.

Ironically, another extremely white mineral, wollastonite, is also found in enormous quantities in the Adirondacks. Its primary use, however, is as an ingredient in industrial and decorative ceramics since wollastonite is extremely durable and heat resistant and lends these qualities to other materials. Today, the most concentrated wollastonite deposit in the United States is being mined near Willsboro.

Three other more familiar minerals—garnet, zinc, and talc—are also abundant in Adirondack rock. Garnet has been mined successfully since 1878 at Gore Mountain, near North Creek. It is so plentiful that garnet was named as the New York State gem. Most of that mined today in the Adirondacks is used in industry, for sand paper, emery boards, and other abrasive products.

St. Lawrence County, in the northwest corner of the Adirondacks, yields talc and zinc. The volume and value of Adirondack talc are the greatest in the nation, and more zinc is found in the single mine at Balmat than anywhere else in the United States.

Graphite is found along Lake Champlain and was the mineral that made yellow Ticonderoga lead pencils famous in the early 1900s. Marble and limestone are quarried from Adirondack rock, too, as is anorthosite, all used for building stone. Adirondack marble, like anorthosite a metamorphic rock, is quarried mainly near the town of Gouverneur, way up in the northwest. Some of the sidewalks of the town are paved in marble, in fact. Unlike anorthosite, however, marble was originally sedimentary rock. The dark spots characteristic of this lustrous stone may be the metamorphosed remnants of fossils, the only remaining, and at that, extremely tenuous, evidence of possible early life in the Adirondacks.

Adirondack magnetite is still mined today, though in relatively small quantities. Some scientists believe that as other sources for iron become rarer (already the hematite ore in the Midwest is nearly gone), the processes by which iron can be extracted from magnetite will be improved, and so then will the Adirondack industry.

What of Adirondack gold? There isn't any, though early explorers heard rumors that it was there. Some silver has been found, but in very small quantities. And garnet is the only genuine gem the old hills render. One kind of quartz found in Herkimer County looks a bit like diamonds and is sold in gift shops as "Herkimer Diamonds."

But before Adirondack rock could yield its ores and minerals and be seen as a portion of the Grenville Province of the Canadian Shield, it had to be exposed at the earth's surface. The second major event in Adirondack geological history was the uplift, a force that pushed the hardened magma up from perhaps eighteen or thirty kilometers inside the earth. In effect, the uplift made new mountains of the old rock.

Exactly what kind of heat and pressure, or both, caused this to happen and when it began are still unknown. Geologists believe it might have begun as early as 350 million years ago or as recently as 20 million years ago, a time when flowering plants and the modern animal groups were established. One leading New York State geologist, Y. W. Isachsen, believes that the uplift is still in progress, meaning that the Adirondacks are rising still.

While the causes of the uplift are still mysterious, the effects are obvious in the domed shape of the region. Fanning out from the pinnacle of the High Peaks, the Adirondack terrain becomes less dramatic. Hills to the north, south, and west seem to roll as they reach toward the flatter lands of New York State, whose geological history and structure are quite different from that of these northern mountains. Basement rock in the southwestern parts of the state, for example, is now buried under eleven thousand feet of newer rock and soil.

The Adirondacks, then, are a rebirth of a mass of very old basement rock. This was originally created in Precambrian time, the era covering the origin of the planet all the way through to a time about 600 million years ago when life emerged, a total of nearly 4 billion years. But instead of being buried, the old rock has been uplifted. As a result, scientists are fascinated by the Adirondacks. They have, as James F. Davis, former State Geologist, writes, "an opportunity to examine rocks much like those which lie buried . . . in other parts of the state."

One of the things they find is a fifteen-hundred-square-mile mass of anorthosite, two miles thick, underlying the High Peaks. Anorthosite is *the* Adirondack rock. It is thought to be the hardened and much altered remains of the magma that so long ago intruded into Adirondack territory. In fact, there appear to be at least two roots of anorthosite projecting about six miles downward into the earth. These may well mark the paths or fissures through which the magma seeped upward.

While the anorthosite was originally igneous rock, it has changed so much over the millenia that it is now classified as metamorphic rock, meaning it has been transformed or metamorphosed.* It is, therefore, sometimes referred to as metanorthosite or meta-anorthosite.

Once, big, shiny blobs of blue or green crystals may have stood out in the rock. These would have been labradorite, the chief mineral in anorthosite. Today, labradorite crystals are smaller, but in certain lights they shine as brightly. Labradorite is one of the feldspars, a class of

---

*Because of such profound metamorphosis in Adirondack anorthosite, some scientists are not fully convinced that its original form was igneous. Some believe the forces that created it were at work a great deal earlier than 1.1 billion years ago. The theories described here, however, are the currently prevailing ones.

rock-forming minerals, and was named after Labrador, where Moravian missionaries discovered it around 1775.

Some specimens of labradorite are gemlike. One piece from Russia brought £10,000 in 1799 since it was said to be a nearly perfect likeness of the French king, Louis XVI's profile. So striking is the fickle play of color in the mineral that jewelers coined the word "labradorescence" to mean sparkle in any stone. To see the magnificent show of color in labradorite, the sun must hit it at just the right angle, and when it does, a blaze of blue green erupts as if it had been ignited by some internal fire. In Lewis County labradorite is so abundant in some river beds that at least one river, the Opalescent, was named for it since the water seems to glow like opals, which labradorite resembles. In some places on Mt. Marcy, the king-pin of the anorthositic High Peaks, the blue green mineral crystals sparkle in the sun, too.

Labradorite and the other minerals of anorthosite help make the rock remarkably durable. Builders appreciate the tough resistance of the stone, which is highly valued in construction.

Bits of anorthosite were found on the lunar surface recently, which surprised geologists because on earth anorthosite is usually found only in deeply eroded mountain root zones, like the Adirondacks. On the moon, however, practically no erosion takes place. The mineral composition of lunar and terrestrial anorthosite is slightly different too, but the biggest difference is age. Lunar anorthosite is more than 4 billion years old, older than any found on earth.

Today, some Adirondack anorthosite is white and some is black. Whiteface Mountain, for example, thought by Adirondack writer Russell Carson, author of *Peaks and People of the Adirondacks*, to be the "most graceful of all" of the peaks, was named for an enormous slab of white anorthosite exposed on its side. On Mt. Marcy, however, the anorthosite is black.

Concentrations of anorthosite decrease on the mountains surrounding the High Peaks. Other rocks, known certainly to have been originally igneous, such as those called metagabbro, compose large portions of the Central Highlands, the mountains at the center of the Adirondack region. Amphibolite, granitic gneisses, and other kinds of rock appear as well.

Most of these rocks, especially the anorthosite, are extremely erosion-resistant—a trait that assured their survival throughout so many years. But it wasn't only time, wind, and water that had their ways with the rock, testing its endurance. Forces other than erosion and the two cataclysmic events, intrusion and uplift, were at work, too.

Some scientists believe that the old roots, before and possibly during their uplift into mountains, supported other, now-vanished mountains. It seems relatively certain that when the original magma intrusion occurred 1.1 billion years ago, an enormous mountain range was also being created, a mountain range that stood *on top of* the magma. But those mountains were made of layers of sedimentary rock, formed from the consolidation of sand, shale, ash, and other sediments, which when subjected to heat and pressure, are cemented into rock.

Sedimentary rock — which with igneous and metamorphic varieties form the three basic families of rock on earth—is the most common kind that is visible today. Seventy-five percent of the earth's surface is sedimentary rock: it is a little like the planet's skin. It forms constantly, on the bottom of lakes and rivers where water helps consolidate sediments, in valleys, and on mountain sides. But while sedimentary rock is rather more easily formed than other kinds, it is also more easily eroded. And those mountains which encased the Adirondack basement rock eons ago, have long since disappeared as a result.

During the first 500 million years after the magma intrusion, while the sedimentary rock mountains atop it eroded, the rest of New York State was inundated. As the mountains were eroded, the sea crept in and flooded all but the highest remaining tips of land.

Yet beneath the waters, new land was forming even as the old mountains eroded. Deposits of sand, ash, pebbles, and fragments of igneous rock were consolidating into new layers of sedimentary rock which over the second 500-million-year period after the magma intrusion were built into a new mountain range. It seems possible that this second mountain range on top of the site of the intrusion may have reached, at its peak, as high as three miles above sea level.

Had this second mountain range survived, the Adirondacks would probably be filled with fossils, for if sedimentary rock is forming at precisely the moment when plants and animals are growing and dying, conditions are highly favorable for the preservation of plant and animal remains, or the imprints of their remains. And life had emerged on earth by the time New York was inundated and had even made rapid progress by the time the second "Adirondack" mountain range was built. Unfortunately for scientists, the second sedimentary mountain range eroded away as the first one had, taking with it all evidence of primitive forest or prehistoric animal life.

Today the Adirondacks are among the few areas in New York where virtually no fossil evidence of life is found. Metamorphosis would have erased such evidence even if the rock was not originally igneous. More's the pity because just south of the Adirondacks, in the Catskill Mountains, the fossilized remains of the oldest forest known to man were unearthed. A kind of crazy proliferation of giant ferns and mosses, some of which grew to be forty feet high, reached maturity around 350 million years ago. (A recreation of this forest was one of the most popular exhibits in the New York State Museum for decades, and photographs of this diorama of strange, primitive woodland illustrated basic botany textbooks for years.) Such pulpy scale trees, as they are called, with leathery trunks, bulbous bases, and feathery foliage may have grown in the Adirondack region at some point when sedimentary build-up created mountains above sea level. But no one knows.

The very qualities that prevented the anorthosite and other granitic rock from being fossiliferous, however, assured their endurance until the uplift pushed them into today's mountains.

The uplift created the mountains of today, but the glaciers of the recent Ice Age shaped them. Lasting more than 500 thousand years, and ending only about 8,000 B.C., the Pleistocene epoch, or Ice Age, was a time when at least four glaciers, one after the other, crept across much of North America. Since each glacier tended to wipe out the geological evidence of its predecessor, the last one, known as the Wisconsin glacier, is the one scientists know most about. They know a great deal about what it did to the Adirondacks.

At its peak, the Wisconsin glacier covered one-third of North America or 6 million square miles. At its center, in central Canada, the ice was two miles thick. It took ten thousand years to reach its maximum extent, which was as far as Long Island in New York and St. Louis in the Midwest. And it took another ten thousand years to melt away. It has still not melted completely; visitors to Greenland can see it today.

The Wisconsin glacier covered nearly the whole Adirondack mountain region with a blanket of ice that in places, scientists think, was at least six thousand feet thick. Both its arrival and departure had profound effects upon the mountains.

A glacier acts like a snowplow by pushing tons of rock, soil, and other debris in front of it. Wherever the glacier stops, so does the debris. If there had been any sedimentary rock left on top of the uplifted Adirondacks, the glaciers would have ground most of it up and pushed it off. Geologists, in fact, have found what they think is debris (or glacial till) from the Adirondacks as far south as the Catskills and Long Island.

A second glacial effect is called the sand-paper phenomenon. As the glacial ice scrapes the earth's surface, the rock debris lodged inside the ice (having been picked up earlier) behaves as an abrasive. Many of the smooth surfaces of today's Adirondack mountains were sanded down in such a fashion.

Yet the glacier's weight also caused some of the cracks or chasms in the mountains and some of the faulting that resulted in the five distinguishable ranges on the uplifted dome. A nineteenth-century visitor to the Adirondacks, Benson J. Lossing, was awed by gorges whose rocks were, as he wrote, "chaotic in position, grand in dimension, and awful in general aspect. They appear to have been cast in there by some terrible convulsion not very remote." He had not guessed that the "convulsion" was a glacier—scientists only realized the effects of glaciers in the mid-ninteenth century — but the amazed Adirondack visitor was correct in his description.

The glaciers were also responsible for many of the lakes and rivers that today so delight campers, fishermen, and woodsmen. Melting glacial ice was dammed off by boulders or captured in trenches or holes to create lakes. Much glacial water poured down pre-existing river beds or carved out new ones. Once established, many glacial lakes and rivers were continually replenished by rain and snow, thus giving the Adirondacks their reputation as the most plentiful and dependable source of water in New York.

Another reminder of the glaciers is the profusion of enormous boulders. Many of these glacier-dumped rocks, often bigger than summer cottages or "camps," look as if they were the abandoned playthings of prehistoric gods, simply left there, but difficult to remove except by another glacier or a bull-dozer. These boulders, called "erratics," are stark testimony to the harsh geological heritage of these ancient hills.

A more attractive heritage of the Ice Age is the well-known and much loved clarity of Adirondack water. Melting glacial ice rendered fresh water. Since many of the holes, crevices, or cul-de-sacs into which it flowed were simply depressions in the extremely hard anorthosite or other metamorphic rock, which does not shed sediments easily, the water remained unsullied by mud or other sedimentary matter. Such cool, clear water made conditions for lake trout superb, and the thousands of cold rushing streams were ideal for brook trout.

The magma created the rock. The uplift created the mountains. The glaciers created the landscape. And it seems appropriate that geologists were among the men first to bring the beauties of these strange, looming, lovely hills to the attention of thousands of people. The first surveyor to conduct a genuinely scientific exploration of the Adirondacks was a geologist, Ebenezer Emmons. The man who had the good idea to display specimens brought back from that survey (and thereby started the

An Adirondack boulder, or glacial erratic, dwarfs the nearby trees and a photographer, at far left. *Collection of the New York State Museum*

New York State Museum) was also a geologist, James Hall. The Swiss-born geologist who presented the then-astonishing theory that glaciers once covered northern America was a man who enjoyed the Adirondacks as a superb site for wilderness recreation, Louis Agassiz.

Generations of people have noticed how different the Adirondacks seem from their neighbors the Green Mountains in Vermont, the Berkshires in Massachusetts, and the Catskills further south in New York. They are "more mysterious, grander, more interesting," wrote Edmund Wilson, the literary critic who spent his summers on the western flank of the mountains. They seem wilder, more spread out, more varied in landscape, offering drama and gentleness both. At different times, these characteristics have repelled or attracted men and women. Always, they have invited comment.

Only in the last seventy-five years or so have scientists pieced together what they believe is the story of how the Adirondacks really are different and how their dual birth made them what they are. Few chunks of the planet have been through so much and have survived to reveal such valuable secrets about how the earth works.

If any single force must be credited with determining the destiny of the Adirondacks, it has to be the rock. And in the Adirondacks, its rock is truly of the ages.

7

The Forest

FOR THE LAST CENTURY, millions of people have been going to the Adirondacks at least as much because of what the forest offered as for any other reason.

Many have climbed all forty-six High Peaks just for the opportunity to admire rolling, endless carpets of trees below and to analyze the subtle or dramatic differences between a view of the forest from Haystack or Nipple Top Mountain. Some have gone to the mountain forest in search of improved health, said to be engendered by the evergreen-filtered air. Some, like the modern writer and ecologist Anne LaBastille, have chosen to "sit in my cabin as in a cocoon, sheltered by swaying spruces from the outside world."

As there must be music for song, these and other Adirondack experiences have been possible only because of the forest. And no hiker, picnicker, camper, hunter, fisherman, front-porch rocker, or Adirondack tale-swapper would disagree that the Adirondacks are as much forest as they are mountains.

In the 1890s an enterprising forester tried to estimate how many trees there were. He came up with a figure of 193 trees (not counting very young trees or bushes) per acre. If such an estimate is at all valid, it means that today there may be more than a billion trees in the Adirondack Park alone.

The very characterization "wilderness," for so long a synonym for the mountains, sprang as much from the presence of so many trees as from any other single factor. And certainly all creatures in the Adirondacks—animals, man, fish, and birds—have behaved as they have as a result of the forest.

The great Adirondack forest surrounding Heart Lake and covering Algonquin Peak in the background. *Collection of the New York State Museum*

Men and women, of course, have tended to be rather fickle in their opinion of the forest, now wanting to cut it down, now wanting to preserve it. But there is one thing most humans have shared in their perceptions of the Adirondack forest: it seemed ancient.

Ever since, and long before, the most famous Adirondack buff, the Reverend William Henry Harrison Murray, wrote in the mid-nineteenth century that "the forest stands as it has stood, from the beginning of time," people have caught the sense of eternity that seems to emanate from the forest. The great stands of evergreens and broad-leafed trees have always seemed not just old, but primordial, as if they had been witnesses to all earth's history.

In fact, this cherished, traditional belief is all wrong. The Adirondack forest looked like something it wasn't. Extreme age, once thought to be the miracle of the forest, turned out to be only a misconception on the part of awe-struck observers. But there *is* a miracle, and there are a few surprises, too.

First the misconception. For all its primeval appearance, the Adirondack forest that covered the mountains when the first white men saw them was not ancient at all. It was quite new, or as foresters say, young. What Father Jogues, Samuel de Champlain, the fur trappers, and William Gilliland saw was a forest that had only begun to grow sometime between twelve and ten thousand years earlier — a short time indeed, geologically.

The real miracle of the Adirondack forest is that it got there at all. It established itself, after thousands of years of preparation by lesser plants, on rock that had been scraped nearly bare by the glaciers.

Consider the Adirondack landscape of twelve thousand years ago. The glaciers had melted very slowly on the cold, remote, high terrain, more slowly than elsewhere in the state. But when they finally disappeared, they had taken all of the topsoil with them. A few pockets of the old sedimentary rock, which once covered the bedrock anorthosite and other granitic basement rock, remained, as naturalist George D. Davis points out in *Man and the Adirondack Environment: A Primer.* One such remnant near Chimney Mountain fascinates geologists today, but these sedimentary remains were so rare after the glaciers as to have little or no effect upon the total environment.

The very qualities that enabled the erosion-resistant Adirondack basement rock to endure for over a billion years also provided a challenge to new vegetation. Soil, the vital cradle for plants, forms only exceedingly slowly, and sometimes not at all, on such terrain.

Soil is essentially a simple compound. It is a mix of ground-up rock and decomposed vegetable matter, or humus. On soft, crumbly rock like shale, for instance, primitive plants like lichens and mosses can establish themselves, die, and add humus to a gravelly surface. Eventually, soil is formed and more complex plants can grow, die, and increase soil depth.

Thin soil, low shrubs, and erosion on Mt. Van Hoevenberg in the High Peaks.
Collection of the New York State Museum

Adirondack rock, however, cannot easily be cracked, eroded, or ground up. Such qualities make it an excellent building stone. But as a home for plants, it is quite inhospitable. Not surprisingly, native Adirondack rock did not contribute much to the new Adirondack soil.

Instead, most of the soil in which the Adirondack forest now grows is "foreign." The glaciers, having robbed the Adirondacks of their own layer of soil and sedimentary rock, pushed rocks, soil deposits, and other geological debris—or glacial till—down from Canada onto the New York mountains even as they snowplowed Adirondack matter onto the Catskills and as far south as Long Island.

As a result, most of what potential soil there was came from this foreign till that eroded, crumbled, and mixed with humus from dead lichens, mosses, and other simple plants whose hardy, pioneering characteristics had enabled them to grow there. (Several scientists, comparing the Adirondacks to more northern portions of the Canadian Shield, have noted that however poor Adirondack soil is thought to be by New Yorkers, it is generally better than that which is found in many parts of Canada.) Today, though, "no simple and direct correlation between the soil and the underlying bedrock exists," George Davis writes, a condition which subjects the forest to certain hazards, which are explained later.

But before the forest could begin to grow, armies of pioneer plants had first to establish themselves. Leading the way were the lichens, which can grow where nothing else can since they live on air and rock. Some scholars think that lichens may be the "manna" mentioned in the Bible; soup and a kind of jelly can be made from them. They can survive on otherwise lifeless land because they contain highly acidic chemicals which dissolve even granite or anorthosite. By creating tiny crevices, lichens can then poke their roots, which are really minute threads, into the rock, and in effect, fracture it. Decayed lichens add a few specks of dead matter to fractured rock grains and thus produce a kind of soil, or duff as it is called.

Following the lichens, mosses—the second hardiest plant among the pioneering species—can find a foothood in the scant leavings of their predecessors. While many mosses love shade, there are several varieties of so-called cushion moss that can stand full sun. They spread, prevent erosion of precious till and duff, die, and add their humus.

There are still quite a lot of lichens and cushion mosses in New York, especially on the High Peaks of the Adirondacks, where climate and altitude combine to simulate the bleak environment of twelve thousand years ago. Many Adirondack lichens belong to a species called Iceland moss, a name indicative of the kind of climate these hardy natural hybrids, one part alga and one part fungus, inhabit. Another species, the ring lichen, named because it grows radially, represents the long life which these plants can attain. On Mt. Marcy, there is a two-foot circle of ring lichen that scientists believe has been growing, on its outside edges anyway, for thousands of years, making it one of the oldest living things in New York. It may have been around as mosses reclaimed the land and prepared them for bushes, then small trees. For such, basically, is the sequence of a forest's progress.

But the Adirondacks provided more than one nursery for an infant forest. The second legacy of the glaciers—water—was as promising for new life as the new soil.

Glacial water formed lakes and rivers all over the mountains, but it was within the still ponds where the potential for bogs developed and within these bogs was also the potential for more soil.

Just as lichens and mosses began the reclamation process on dry land, microscopic cellular life appeared in ponds and lakes. Green algae, for instance, and what looked like plain scum, which was really many varieties of bacteria and fungi (all of which are airborne matter and were thus brought in by winds), gradually spread over small bodies of water and along the edges of larger lakes. Sphagnum moss and other water-loving plants grew over the water like a coverlet. Recently, a team of scientists studied a lake in Antarctica, a land as apparently devoid of life as the Adirondacks may have seemed twelve thousand years ago, and found that as many as sixty species of organisms lived there. Certainly as many would have thrived on Adirondack water and as they died, mixed with dissolving minerals from the rock bottom of lakes and ponds, and formed mud. Bit by bit, in shallow water, a mud layer on the bottom and an alga-fungus-moss layer on top thickened, growing closer together. Eventually, what looked like solid earth resulted. And rich, hospitable earth it was, friendly to more complex plants, bushes, ferns, and even small trees.

All over the pond-pocked Adirondacks, bogs thickened. Marshes, too — bodies of shallow, standing water where grassy plants grow—and swamps made inviting beds for other plants. Today, bogs are often good places to watch for unusual wildlife. Two rare birds—Lincoln's sparrow and the spruce grouse—are often seen near Adirondack bogs, as is the water shrew, a frantic creature that is quite rare in the eastern United States. Unfortunately for spring fishermen, bogs and swamps are also the breeding ground for the Adirondack scourge — the black fly — and the equally annoying mosquito.

The bog process never stops. Scientists predict that one day, Lake Tear-of-the-Clouds, the small pond near the top of Mt. Marcy where the Hudson River has its source, may one day become dry land. More accessible, a boy's camp on the edge of a lake near Old Forge offers a dramatic example of how bogs grow into dry land. Counselors point out the bog-earth where campers' tents are pitched and are quite secure. Yet the

An Adirondack bog. *Photo by W. F. Kollecker, courtesy of the Saranac Lake Free Library, Adirondack Collection*

closer one goes to the lake, the spongier the earth feels. Only a foot or so beneath the surface, water gurgles. Only halfway to its conversion to land, the bog is still accumulating humus and turning it into soil as countless others did after the glaciers.

The miracle of the Adirondack forest is that from two such basic glacial leavings—till and water—a magnificent woodland grew so well that men and women could look at it and believe it had been there forever. The Adirondack forest of the seventeenth century, the one called primeval, was really new and fragile. Far from being eternal, the forest was, if anything, especially susceptible to the destructive forces of nature. The relatively thin layer of soil all over the mountains gave precious little depth in which trees could sink long, supportive roots. High winds, like those of the severe Blowdown of 1950, could knock over thousands of mature trees as if they were matchsticks.

Since the nonporous bedrock is so close to the surface and has no direct correlation with the soil on top of it, poor drainage is a problem. It means that during floods many trees simply drown at the roots. It also means that during droughts there is little accessible reserve water deep in the earth. In very deep soil a tree can send its roots ever further downward in search of water and can thus often survive long dry spells. Such is not the case for many Adirondack trees. Also, trees without the resources of deep soil can be hard-hit by disease and insects. Both have, at times, taken terrible tolls in the Adirondacks. Thus a young forest that has not had time enough to build up soil depth is really quite vulnerable.

Since the Adirondack forest is neither eternal nor primordial, it is perhaps more wonderful even than the petrified redwoods of California or the hardened remnants of genuinely primeval fern trees found in the Catskills. The Adirondacks have no such botanical mummies. While the mountains have been existing in New York for more than 1.1 billion years, the only *known* forest was the one that began to grow after the glaciers. It was not, for all its ancient appearance, a relic, but a part of the new world, as fresh, inventive, and surprising as the events of human history that would have so profound an effect upon it.

Some observers of the early American settlers and pioneers believed they perceived a new breed of man coming alive in the new land. Likewise, the Adirondack forest had new breeds of trees, for that forest was not just new, it was modern. In places species of trees and bushes sprang up that had not, so far as paleobotanists know, grown before the glacier, anywhere on earth. And today the trend toward modernity — encouraged both by man, who is planting nonnative species, and by nature, since a shift in the balance of the kind of trees growing seems evident—continues.

But, where did the postglacial trees come from? Wind, birds, and animals all carry seeds, and wherever conditions are right the seeds will grow. Adirondack trees came primarily from two directions, the north and the south.

From the north, the great Boreal forest (named after a Greek god, Boreas, who was said to be proprietor of the North Wind) of evergreen trees—spruce and fir mainly—had crept southward during the Ice Age, growing on the Appalachian mountains and wherever the cold-loving species could survive. As soon as the glaciers released their hold on their native northern habitat, these evergreens returned.

Once most Adirondack trees were evergreen, like those further north in the North Woods of Canada. But not all were, for from the south the other distinct expression of tree life on earth, as botanical historian Rutherford Platt defines the forest of leaf-dropping or deciduous trees, crept northward to populate the lower slopes and protected valleys of the

Adirondacks with maples, beech, yellow birch, white ash, northern red oak, black cherry, and other broad-leafed trees.

Since the two types of forest — evergreen and leaf-dropping — meet in the Adirondacks, the region is called a transition zone, or a hemlock-hardwood forest. The hemlock stands in for the Boreal forest, and the hardwoods represent the deciduous forest of the temperate regions. The Adirondack territory is the original home of few, but comfortable for many species of trees.

The Eastern hemlock, once the most common conifer in new York, represents the Boreal forest since it looks so much like the spruce and fir that are the true northern species. In fact, the hemlock, blue green and northern-looking though it is, is really a tree of the northern transition zone and is one of the few conifers (with white pine and junipers) that is entirely at home among deciduous trees. It likes cool, not frigid, weather, moisture, and high humidity, conditions readily available on the slopes of the Adirondacks. In the nineteenth century hemlock was an important resource since its bark contains tannin, the crucial ingredient for tanning, or turning animal hide into leather. As a result, hemlocks were cut with abandon, so today the tree that gives the Adirondack forest its categorical name is somewhat less common than might be expected.

Yet the hemlock, like conifers as a group, is tenacious, hardy, and tolerant. An infant hemlock can grow in the deep shade of a mature forest and survive long enough, without direct sun, until a break in the forest canopy gives it a chance to grow as tall as the rest of the trees.

While different species of conifers have different needs — some cannot grow in shade at all — the evergreen is, on the whole, one of the sturdiest, most versatile trees on earth. It is also among the oldest kinds of trees growing on earth. There was a kind of pine growing more than 300 million years ago, and conifers grow in extreme climates all over the world.

The key to their endurance is in the way their seeds are clustered in hard, naked, woody, durable cones, called gymnosperms (from the Greek word meaning "naked seed"). The cones can lie dormant for decades, waiting for a chance to spring to life. In all, there are more than 300 species of conifers on earth. Only about five grow to dominating positions in the Boreal forests, and in the Adirondacks varieties of hemlock, as well as pine, tamarack, spruce, fir, and cedar, represent them most commonly.

The conifers have soft, light-weight wood, a trait that allowed loggers in the nineteenth century to float them down rivers to markets and sawmills. Pine, spruce, and fir were the most valuable lumber trees from the Adirondacks, the pine being logged first, since it grew on lower slopes; to get the spruce and fir, loggers had to go further up the mountains.

Just as the Adirondack forest as a whole is called a hemlock-hardwood type, there are within this general region several sub-zones. What divides the zones is altitude since it dictates climate, and the higher one goes on any Adirondack mountain, the more Boreal the forest becomes. Thus the Adirondacks offer a kind of museum of eastern American trees. On the lowest land, around Lake Champlain, for instance, trees that grow in southern temperate zones can thrive. As altitude increases, New England natives take over. And on the highest peaks, Canadian trees dominate.

Above twenty-five hundred feet, for example, the hemlock cannot grow healthily; it's simply too cold. Instead, denizens of the Boreal forest—spruce and fir—thrive, as they do further north in Canada and northern New England. Since these two conifers are so predominant in the famous High Peaks region of the Adirondacks, people argue fiercely over which can be called *the* Adirondack tree.

The balsam fir, which composes about 80 percent of the forest above forty-five hundred feet, is perhaps the more beautiful of the two. Its shapely symmetry, its blue green foliage with hints of silver, the pungent, long-lasting fragrance that gave it the reputation as "the healer," since many believed the odor to be healthful, all enhance its reputation. In a region where unemployment plagues the population, the balsam fir supports a minor Adirondack industry. Pillows stuffed with its aromatic needles are sold in gift shops, and many a transplanted New Yorker can take a scent of home with them, wherever in the world they go.

The most characteristic Adirondack spruce—the red—was, on the other hand, more widespread than the fir, accounting in earlier times for 35 percent of the entire forest. (Spruce was heavily cut when paper-making operations found that its wood could easily be turned into pulp.) The red spruce is less hardy than fir; it is its cousin, the white spruce, that accompanies fir in true Boreal forests, as in Canada. But in favorable locations the red spruce can hold its longevity over that of the fir. In fact, the spruce is the longest living tree in New York. One was found to have 325 annual rings, another to have a diameter of 41 inches, and the species has spawned individuals that are known to have lived as long as 350 years. While firs dominate the tops of many Adirondack mountains, it is the red spruce that gives the hills their wide waistband of deep pure green.

These upper spruce slopes are part of the great North Woods of North America. Stretching from Maine to the Yukon River, four thousand

The boreal forest at Lost Brook. *Collection of the New York State Museum*

The tree line. *Photo by W. F. Kollecker, courtesy of the Saranac Lake Free Library, Adirondack Collection*

miles away, the North Woods are, in Rutherford Platt's words, *the* "prime continuous coniferous forest on earth," comparable only to the forests of Siberia. Since the Adirondacks offer climate and altitude that welcome a southern extension of this forest, visitors get a taste of wilderness they would otherwise have to go to Russia or Canada or northern Maine to see.

Visitors are also able to see an environment whose native location is more than 300 miles further north. The Adirondacks have a "tree line," beyond which even white spruce and balsam fir cannot grow. The tree line in Canada is less a line than a region as trees gradually get smaller and more scattered. But on steep Adirondack slopes, the demarcation is quite distinct. On one level there are trees, though they are stunted; on the next level, perhaps only a few feet away, there are none.

At about forty-three hundred feet on Mts. Marcy and McIntyre, for instance, even the firs are dwarfed. They look like miniatures here where wind and cold prevent them from growing bigger. A few feet beyond, only the hardiest bushes can grow.

Dwarfed trees signal the beginning of the so-called sub-alpine zone. Above it, at altitudes around forty-nine hundred feet, is one of the most fascinating and unusual environments in the eastern United States. It exists on ten Adirondack peaks and is called the alpine zone. Only lichens and very rugged dwarf berry bushes, some plump wild flowers and mosses grow there, mimicking the Alaskan tundra, except that permafrost does not exist on Adirondack peaks.

At about forty-nine hundred feet (and in some places as low as forty-five hundred feet) only these wind and cold resistant plants can survive. On Mt. Marcy and on Haystack Mountain, to name two alpine-tipped peaks, many of these so-called cushion plants, as George Davis writes, "strike one as tiny reproductions of the herbs and flowers of our gardens. In many cases this is exactly what they are." Their fat leaves and stems allow them to retain water and fight harsh wind. And, of course, lichens and mosses, clinging to the rock like ship-wreck victims to lifeboats, flaunt their survival traits. In Canada and Alaska the caribou live on lichens, the one plant that can grow abundantly and constantly in the bleakness.

These far northern zones of the Adirondack forest have the most claim to a kind of eternity. Though the plants are fragile—large numbers of hikers threaten in some places to destroy them — their lineage is as ancient as their persistence is awe inspiring. In fact, these plants promise eternal life on earth as few other things can. Scientists believe, as Rutherford Platt noted, that "as long as a microscopic speck of vegetable matter is left on earth to nourish bacteria, the evolution of life can start all over again." And that evolution will almost certainly begin with lichens.

But there is a price for survival. However fascinating the far northern Adirondack forest may be, it lacks variety. On the lower slopes of the Adirondacks, where the hemlocks and hardwoods take over, the forest seems richer, lusher, more interesting. Here, many more than a few species thrive. Almost twice as many species can grow to dominating positions than on the more elevated slopes; and most of the wildlife of the mountains lives below four thousand feet or so.

The deciduous, hardwood tree is today as characteristic of the Adirondack forest as the evergreen. In fact, there are now more deciduous trees than conifers in the Adirondack Park; over 50 percent of the forest is made up of sugar maple, yellow birch, beech, northern red oak, white ash, black cherry, and other northern hardwood trees. Winter in the Adirondacks reveals dramatically how very many deciduous trees there are since their dormant bareness stands out against the relatively fewer evergreens. (Evergreens drop only a few needles at a time but do so all year long, thus making them seem always green. Deciduous trees, so-called from the Latin verb meaning "to drop," shed all their leaves at one time, in the autumn.)

But in the spring, summer, and autumn these trees show off their color and lushness in ways that make the conifers seem staid. Some people think this northern branch of the temperate zone forest is the most wonderful part of the Adirondacks. Whereas the conifer forest tends to be dark, silent, even ominous, with a needle-covered floor and little under-growth, the more southern portions of the forest support a thick tangle of undergrowth and allow more sun to stream through. Here violets, trillium, and berry bushes grow profusely. Nearly fifty varieties of ferns make the forest floor seem as rich and soft as velvet. Sometimes the plant life is annoyingly abundant. The thick, tangled, low-growing hobble-bush, or witch-hopple, can be so dense as to trip hikers repeatedly, and at least once, witch-hopple played an important part in military strategy. During the Revolutionary War, American troops had to abandon Fort Ticonderoga when superior British forces appeared in the summer of 1777. Fleeing south, the Americans blocked the road with trees, forcing the British to hack their way through dense, unfamiliar wilderness on their way to Fort Edward, only fifty miles away. That journey cost the British nearly a month while the Americans were free to recoup strength.

The British suffered in the tangles of undergrowth, but dozens of animal species love such a forest. Deer, rabbits, squirrels, beavers, otters, bears, fishers, foxes, skunks, woodchucks, muskrats, and many more thrive. Most of the more than 200 bird species characteristic of the Adirondacks flit about, making the wood seem bursting with life. The contrast with the "virtual woodland desert," as Hugh Fosburgh describes the mature, still evergreen portions of the forest, has startled many a woodsman.

The sheer variety of hardwood trees that gives the forest such a lush, rich mien makes description difficult. But among them are the stately, sprawling beeches whose smooth, pale gray bark has always tempted initial carvers. Beeches, though recently threatened by a fungus, are more common now in the Adirondacks than they were 200 years ago. They were of no use to loggers and so were left alone to spread and attract bears, squirrels, and other creatures who love the beechnuts.

As fragile as the beeches are solid, spindly, quaking aspens announce their presence with their rustling leaves to the ear before the eye discerns them.

Birches come in three varieties and like the aspens grow fast in clearings. Abandoned farms and logged-over acres attract these sun-loving, swiftly maturing trees. Extensive stands of birches, in fact, tell the observant woodsman that not too long ago, fire, wind, farmers, or loggers had been at work removing trees of more stature. The three common Adirondack birches are the paper birch, which has white, easily peeled bark; the spindly gray birch, smallest of the three, which has chalk white bark that does not peel; and the aristocratic yellow birch, whose amber or golden-hued bark encloses valuable hardwood timber, and which grows taller than either the paper or the gray.

Sugar maples give not just syrup (much of which is sold to Vermont and thus helps make another state's reputation), but gorgeous fall foliage. These along with northern red oak, American mountain ash, two varieties of cherry, the American elm, and dozens more form northward-reaching fingers of the great American deciduous forest that after the glacier burst to life most spectacularly in the temperate zone of eastern North America. This temperate zone forest grew in an area smaller than that of the North Woods. Stretching roughly from southern Massachusetts to northern Florida, across from the Atlantic coast to the Ozark Plateau and north again to Michigan, the forest that originated here after the Ice Age was a genuinely modern one.

While the ancient species re-established themselves in the north, reclaiming what was probably even poorer soil than had existed before the glaciers, the trees of the temperate zone found conditions better than ever. They grew to be enormous, healthy, and incredibly diverse. And along with them new species, especially shrubs and bushes, appeared for the first time on earth.

The main reason for such exuberant growth was that southward-flowing waters from melting glaciers washed millions of tons of rich till onto the land as far south as Mississippi. Around the James River in Virginia, for example, the soil, having formed largely from till, today measures more than one hundred feet deep; around portions of the Susquehanna River in Pennsylvania, glacial till was twice that deep.

In the mature deciduous forest that sprang up in these regions, as many as twenty-four species of trees may dominate compared to the five or so in a Boreal forest. For all their variety, deciduous trees tend to be frailer and more demanding of climate, soil, and moisture than conifers. Their seeds (called angiosperms, from the Greek word meaning "vessel") are soft and juicy, enclosed in flowers instead of cones, and produce the fruits, berries, and nuts on which so many animals depend. Their wood is hard and represents a relatively late botanical innovation: the earliest trees on earth had pulpy wood (similar to that of the sycamore which is a living relic from very early forests), and the ancient conifers have soft, fibrous wood.

Those deciduous trees that adapted to the Adirondack climate are now known as northern hardwoods. People who refer to the Adirondack forest as "warm" or "friendly" or "inviting," often have these many-branched, colorful, and varied species to thank. And wherever a white ash or sugar maple excites admiration, a woodsman can be sure that sheer time, which allowed the development of deep, rich soil which these trees must have, is deserving of a nod or two as well.

But what of the most famous Adirondack tree, the white pine? Great stands of these spear-straight, towering wonders awed early American explorers and settlers. Many trees were 150 feet tall and looked for all the world like the masts of the earth; they were, of course, ideal ships' masts and were cut with abandon. As early as the 1770s, the British, worried that these precious assets might be going too fast, issued an ordinance limiting the number that could be cut each year. Later, the white pine provided the finest lumber money could buy and has since been credited as the tree that built the nation. (In Jared Van Wagenen's account of pioneering life in upstate New York, *The Golden Age of Home-spun*, the value of the white pine is dramatically clear; for nearly every-thing made of wood—and such was nearly everything the pioneer used—the white pine was almost always rated the most desirable.)

Growing alone, the white pine sends out long, graceful branches that make it the climbing tree *par excellence*. The pines, however, grow more typically in groups, where the branches cannot survive below the canopy. Instead, the straight, naked trunks, whose diameters can be four feet, ascend in dense profusion from the forest floor. To stand among such woody columns is indeed to worship in nature's cathedral and under-stand why trees have been called its very buttresses.

But the white pine is not a true northern tree. It is not even excessively happy among hemlocks and rarely grows in altitudes above twenty-five hundred feet. It likes protected regions and grows along rivers and lakes where water moderates the temperature. Many Adiron-dack white pines once grew within sight of Lake Champlain, where altitude is the lowest of the Adirondack region, and where, of course, the British and French and later Americans could easily get at them. But for all its fame and stand-out beauty, modern botanists estimate that the white pine probably did not comprise more than about 10 percent of the Adirondack forest of the eighteenth century.

Part of the reason for that was that 200 years ago, the Adirondack forest was in a climax state. That is, it was in a mature condition where certain characteristic trees have assumed dominant positions and con-tinue to propagate their own kind to the exclusion of others. George Davis defines the climax stage as one where a plant community is "in equilibrium with the environment," having, in a way, gone as far as it can go so long as a major catastrophe, like fire or logging or hurricane, does not disturb things. But since catastrophe is common and inevitable, one botanist prefers to think of the climax state as a "long pause." In a Boreal forest, for example, spruce and fir are the climax trees, as are hemlocks and certain hardwoods in the transition zone.

And the white pine is not a climax tree. It will at least partially be crowded out in a true climax forest. Instead, the white pine is among the pioneering species, or sub-climax trees. It grows very quickly, more quickly than any other conifer in the eastern United States, and since it can grow in sandy, dry soil, will take over a field, clearing, or windswept acreage in a relatively short time and prepare the ground for later, dominant, climax trees. So while the white pine may be the king of the forest, its presence has never been as widespread as loggers would have liked or as nature lovers long for. (The white pine is also very susceptible to a nasty blister-rust and weevil, whose fierce attacks have made recent replanting efforts fail.)

As the Adirondack forest grew and changed, its inhabitants changed with it. Deer, for example, would have been healthy and numerous during stages when low-growing bushes were common. The so-called hemlock shrub (or American yew), and arborvitae, a kind of cedar with flat clusters of succulent needles, were once abundant. Few of these species grow today in the Adirondacks, mainly because deer have eaten them all. As voracious vegetarians, deer must have lots of such mouth-level food, the kind which does not grow well in climax forests. Deer populations will normally decrease as a forest proceeds toward maturity.

A forest that cannot support deer will often support moose, the mammal prehistoric Indians probably hunted most energetically during their sojourns in the Adirondacks. They may have hunted deer on the lower slopes, although deer were plentiful elsewhere in the state, but they cannot have been after both at the same time. Deer carry a parasite that is harmless to them but fatal to moose, who get the "blind staggers," as the brain disease is called. As a result, the two species rarely live near each other. Once moose inhabited the higher slopes of the Adirondacks where deer could not live happily anyway. Today, some scientists believe that moose might be able to return to these northern, high altitude sections where dwarf balsam fir and some of the very hardy northern hardwoods and viburnums would provide ample food, the kind of food that grows in a forest that cannot support deer.

While man was indirectly responsible for the increase in the deer population — since he logged climax forests and thus encouraged the

One of a group of white-tailed deer from a diorama in the New York State Museum's Adirondack Hall. *Collection of the New York State Museum*

sub-climax, bushy foliage that welcomed deer — and the concomitant decrease in the moose population, and while man has rightly been called the "super-factor" of major change in the forest, there is one creature that may be said to rival him: the beaver. Their dams kill acres of forest land by drowning trees, thus reinstigating the bog and swamp process. Yet without the beaver ponds, muskrats, otters, and many birds could not live. The forest became a much less lively place when the beavers disappeared so long ago after the trappers swept through. Today, since the beavers have been returned, their ponds are often the most entertaining outposts for wildlife watchers.

Wolves, cougars (or panthers), ravens, bald eagles, ospreys, elks, lynx, and wolverines once tramped the forest or skirted it from above, as if they owned the place. Today foresters lament the extinction of at least seven species (timber wolf, moose, elk, panther, lynx, wolverine, and woodland caribou) and worry about rare species such as bald and golden eagles, ospreys, and the water shrew. They constantly work to keep the lakes and rivers stocked with the trout (four species of them: the brown, the brook, the rainbow, and the lake) and to maintain a balance among the other sixty-six species of fish that can live in lakes and rivers. The Adirondacks still provide a wildlife sanctuary that has no peer in the state. Certain species may be rare and threatened, but perhaps the essential quality of Adirondack wildlife is, as the Canadian scientist Dr. D. H. D. Clarke wrote, its "persistence."

Two hundred and twenty species of birds live in the Adirondacks, and while only about forty-one winter over (accounting at least in part for the marked silence of the forest in fall and winter), there are a large number of birds that visitors come to the Adirondacks expressly to see. Among them are the loons, whose number has been cut in half in recent years since boating disturbs their lake shore nests and even mild water pollution harms them seriously. Nevertheless, their high-pitched, eerie squeals are frequent enough to remain an emblem of the forest, and those who are enchanted by their dramatic take-off flights from ponds, their apparently faithful "marriages," and their courtly mating behavior have a better chance of observing them in the Adirondacks than almost anywhere else. The same is true for spruce grouse, ladder backed three-toed woodpeckers, Canada jays, ravens and Lincoln's sparrows, and perhaps the grandest of birds, the eagle. Both bald and golden eagles, though rare (as evidently they always were in the Adirondacks), do still nest high in trees and on cliffs.

Two mammals characteristic of northern mountain forests are the pine marten and the fisher. Both are small creatures, and both have commercially valuable fur, which of course subjects them to the same hazards suffered by the beaver. Yet both are abundant in the Adirondacks as they are nowhere else in the state. And the fisher, whose tracks look like long series of equal marks, and whose shiny black fur makes it resemble a black panther, is probably more abundant, in terms of density per acre, in the Adirondacks than anywhere in the United States.

Some people lament and are trying to restore the "original"

wilderness, the one they call primeval. Yet even if the cougar, the elk, and the caribou (which are thought to have wandered in the High Peaks, eating lichens, soon after the glacier receded) were returned, the forest could never be a replica of one that went before. New species of trees have been introduced for one thing. The scotch pine, for example, was brought from Europe and has adapted extremely well in places where native white pine has not. The scotch pine was never part of the virgin wilderness, but it can hardly be said to detract from the contemporary wilderness.

Wilderness has perhaps certain unchallenged characteristics, but since change, natural change, is one of them, overly precise definitions and requirements can only prove confusing and counter-productive. The forest wilderness of the Adirondacks is difficult enough to analyze since exceptions to neat descriptions of zones, even the qualities that separate deciduous and evergreen trees, abound like clumps of witch-hopple to trip up would-be codifiers. For example, while it is true that the red spruce is the denizen of the Boreal portions of the Adirondack forests, it also grows on the lower slopes and forms the attractive spruce swamps that offer deer privacy and protection, though not food. Standing in the swamps below twenty-five hundred feet, spruce can thus accompany maples and elms—a gathering that would seem contradictory.

It is technically correct to say that deciduous trees are rather more fragile than conifers. But in the Adirondacks the pioneering species that prepare hostile ground for the sturdy evergreens are usually deciduous trees. And although it is safe to say that deciduous trees drop their leaves all at once in the fall, whereas conifers drop theirs a few at a time all year long, at least one Adirondack conifer—the tamarack (or larch)—behaves as if it were an aspen or oak and drops its needles, all of them, in the fall. Furthermore, a shrub that so delights gardeners and forest trampers in spring — the rhododendron — is both evergreen and an angiosperm! (Some botanists think it may be a transition plant between gymnosperms and angiosperms; its bud resembles a refined pine cone.)

The miracle of the Adirondack forest, contradictions and all, continues wherever there is a bare spot revealing the naked rock below. And every spring, the humans who anticipate the revival of sugar maples, beech, birch, aspen, white ash (now the most common decidu-ous trees), and the new growth on the old faithfuls—red spruce, balsam fir, and hemlock — can envision that first centuries-long spring that followed the Ice Age. When the "live green [of lichens and mosses] flashes in the morning sun," as William Chapman White writes of an Adirondack April, it recapitulates the appearance of the pioneer plants, the first live green of any kind to flash on the mountains.

Then the so-called weed trees, often reviled by loggers and ad-mirers of climax trees, flaunt their feathery new growth as if to remind detractors that they were probably there long before firs or spruces. And the well-beloved (at least in the spring) shadbush, flowering fully before anything else, its abundant white flowers recalling "the snowdrifts so recently gone," describes White, is saved from its summer obscurity. So is the cherry, whose blooms come next.

E. H. Ketchledge, whose studies of the Adirondack forest have made him a kind of dean of North Country botany, writes in his handy *Trees of the Adirondack High Peak Region: A Hiker's Guide*, that the short-lived Fire Cherry, which must have full sun and grows only "where there has been some severe disturbance," is one of those transients whose intolerance and quick rejection by more dominant successors is most regrettable. "It is one of our most attractive trees," he writes, "and would otherwise make an excellent ornamental." While man has been dubbed the super-factor of (often disturbing) change in the Adirondacks, some-times nature's own process of change is unfortunate.

The Adirondack forest today is different from the "virgin" forest of 300 years ago. But after at least two major upheavals in recent earth history—the glaciers and the hand of man—the trees have proved their powers of survival and have returned. Probably the post-glacial forest was richer, more diverse and beautiful than whatever may have grown in earlier eras. And it seems possible that man, by replanting, careful tend-ing, and a commitment to "forever wild" may add even more richness and diversity.

The Adirondack forest, as new as a seedling and as old as a lichen, vulnerable, persistent, recalcitrant, and adaptive, is not just the crown of the mountains and the buttress of the wilderness. It is the most tangible bridge in New York between man and nature. Ironically, it was imminent destruction by man that alarmed New Yorkers and made them act upon a deep appreciation of the threatened woodlands. Since then, a concern over the forest has been the strongest article in a tentative but surprisingly successful truce between man and nature in the Adirondacks.

THE WILDERNESS IN TRANSITION
(1830–85)

8

Timber!

THE PIONEER FEARED IT. Perhaps at times when he had another forty acres to clear, he hated it. But for all the difficulties, complaints, and even terrors associated with it, no one could live without it: the forest.

"America," wrote Rutherford Platt, a historian of the natural world, "was the biggest surprise in the history of man." And the topper was the forest. It covered one-third of the land, taking up an estimated 1.1 billion acres in 1600.

"The country is all covered with great and high forests," reported Champlain in 1604. His comment seems nonchalant, especially from a practical man like Champlain. He must have known of the disappearance of the European forests and the increasing demand for wood there. It was almost as if the first person to land on Mars radioed back to Earth and said without enthusiasm, "The country here is filled with oil."

For men and women in the seventeenth, eighteenth, and nineteenth centuries, wood, no less than oil in the twentieth century, had a part in nearly everything they used and needed, from soap and clothing to fire, tools, houses, and roads. And the Adirondacks' portion of the great American forest was the closest thing to oil wells or gold mines the region ever yielded.

It took nearly a century after the Revolutionary War for people to exploit fully the sylvan riches in the Adirondacks. When they did, they were desperate. America's appetite for wood was immense. That hunger, growing all the time, had as much to do with the story of logging in the Adirondacks as did the techniques and traditions of the era itself. And like so much else that affected the Adirondacks, the need for wood and the forces that propelled men into the mountains originated from outside, not from within the mountains.

A mountain of Adirondack logs ready for the mills. *New York State Department of Environmental Conservation*

The intimate relationship between man and the American forests began with the pioneers. The moment they saw their plots of land they could make certain judgments about them from the kind of trees growing. As William Cooper, who settled Cooperstown in western New York in the late 1700s, wrote in a book for and about pioneers, a person was lucky indeed if he found bass and butternut trees, interspersed with sugar maples, elms, and beeches. A good, rich soil from which to grow grass and grains was almost certain.

If, however, spruce and birch prevailed, that meant trouble. The soil was likely to be thin or clay-bound. In the Adirondacks, of course, more than 15 percent of the forest was once spruce and birch. That was one among many reasons why the land was "the last taken up," as Cooper said all such land was.

Whether promising or discouraging indicators of the soil's worth, the trees on a pioneer's property had to go. They could be burned down and their ashes boiled into potash, the basic ingredient for soap and fertilizer. Potash was the first and absolutely essential cash "crop" on the frontier. The trappers had reaped most of the soft gold in the form of beavers; the pioneers often made it through the first seasons from the proceeds of black gold or potash. It was one of New York's primary exports as late as 1822.

In the 1600s, the prospects of abundant potash from the American forests were part of the British incentive to get and keep the new land. Back home, where forests were rare even then, huge quantities of soap, made from potash, were necessary for the cleaning of new wool, and wool was one of England's economic staples.

For the large land-holder facing many acres of trees and not needing quick cash from potash, girdling was another means of getting rid of the forests. The agriculturally inclined Seneca Indians in western New York taught settlers how to notch trees so that the vital liquids seeped out.

Whether cut or girdled, trees left stumps—a problem under any circumstances. William Cooper advised that they be allowed to rot. Only the Germans in Pennsylvania bothered to clear them methodically, achieving the clean fields for which they became famous. Most people felt that sort of fame was foolishly acquired: there was too much else to do.

The log cabin, then its successor, the frame house, then *its* successor, the brick house, all had to be built. Wood, of course, was vital. Almost every roof was made from wooden shingles. Furniture, clocks, buckets, baskets, the plow, the harrow, the pipes for leading water, wagons, bridges, fences, and most early roads were wooden. The lavish use of planks for roads astonished many a European visitor whose diminished wood supply at home made a plank road seem outlandishly extravagant.

Leather for clothing and saddles was tanned by means of the tannin in hemlock bark. Fuel was universally and almost exclusively wood. Every pioneer was an expert on which wood was better for cooking and heating and making charcoal.

It took an acre of forest a day to keep a large iron furnace (or smelter) going with charcoal, the only fuel for forges until coke, then coal were found to be better. Forges were common all over early America, accounting for the relative frequency of places names incorporating the word: Valley Forge, Old Forge, and many others. One Adirondack mining company used an estimated 1.5 million cords of wood for its forges during thirty years.

But the pioneers' domestic use of wood was nothing compared to what the cities and towns needed. Everything was heated and powered with wood. Fireplace fuel was so scarce as early as the 1780s that Benjamin Franklin set to work on his famous stove which was designed to get twice as much heat from wood as an open fireplace. All urban buildings were built from wood or from brick, which was made in wood-fueled kilns. Fires were a part of life, and more wood was always in demand.

America was built, literally and figuratively, with wood. While the all-out assault on the American forest at the hands of pioneers and lumbermen has been called baleful and worse, there was little choice. The most eloquent pardon comes from Jared Van Wagenen, historian of what he called the "golden age of homespun."

"Realizing," he wrote in his book of the same title, "something of the conditions confronting the pioneer, I have no single word of censure for him because he was an anti-conservationist. . . . Trees were the enemy that stood between him and smooth fields, and he who removed a tree was to be esteemed a public benefactor." For the cities, the lumbermen were the public benefactors.

Besides, nature seemed incredibly lush, dangerously so. People expected the trees to grow back at about the rate they were chopped down. The forest was an "incumbrance," as Robert Beverly in Virginia reported in 1705. Even in the twentieth century, one logger's most vivid memory about the forest of northeastern America was its "persistence." Trees, wrote Stewart H. Holbrook in *Yankee Loggers*, "merely hide in the soil until the man with the axe or hoe has turned his back for a moment, instantly to send up their first shoots and to advance in astonishing number and size until all signs of man's efforts have been obliterated."

Until the 1850s, the New England forests met, though often barely so, the Northeast's needs. But demand grew frighteningly quickly. In New York City at mid-century, a resident had to pay a dime—out of what was for many less than a dollar a day in wages — for enough firewood to cook one meal. Heating needs were even greater. Coal stoves had been patented in Troy, New York, in 1815 but were slow to catch on even among the wealthy, and they remained extremely expensive for years.

Loggers were moving further west in search of wood, and in 1850

New York achieved the distinction of being the leading lumbering state in the nation, surpassing Maine. The Adirondack forests, for so long contributing to the reasons man circumvented the region, at last provided the incentive for men to come in, and thousands did. Suddenly the Great Northern Wilderness was coughing up desperately needed resources to a nation ravenous for wood.

Chopping down trees—as distinguished from logging on a grand scale—in the Adirondacks was as old as the first settlements along Lake Champlain. The British and French both used the magnificent white pines, some of them 150 feet high, for ships' masts and lumber. (Wood for shipbuilding was so diminished in Europe as early as the 1550s that the Spanish had to go all the way to the forests around the Baltic Sea to get timber for their three-hundred-ship Armada; the English had to do the same thing for their ships which fought and defeated the Armada.) All the forts along the lakes' edges and inland had used quantities of wood in the early years. Lumbering on the Lower Raquette River began as early as 1810 and on the Schroon River in 1813.

For a long while, however, such efforts were exceptional. Local needs, for which most of the trees were logged, remained relatively low. It was the national need that provoked the all-out assault.

By 1850 the assault was under way. Lumbermen after white pines, the premium lumber logs, were working in the eastern and central portions of the mountains. More than seven thousand sawmills in the state and nearly two thousand in the Adirondacks still could not get enough wood. Deeper and higher into the mountains the lumbermen went, moving along the upper reaches of the Raquette River and around Tupper Lake. The white pine was always their first choice, and it went fast.

Meanwhile, the hemlock, whose bark supplied tannin for many of the more than one thousand tanneries in the state, was also being cut in enormous quantities. By 1840 there were already 270 tanneries in the Adirondacks alone. Workmen didn't need the trees themselves, only the bark, so they simply stripped millions of hemlocks and left the logs to die and rot.

The red spruce came next when it was discovered in 1867 that the best paper pulp (heretofore made from rags and straw) could be made from the fibrous wood of the spruce. The best piano sounding boards and mandolins had been made from spruce for a long time, but the need for paper was the greatest incentive to cut it. In 1899, over 200 million board feet of spruce for pulp were cut in the Adirondacks. By the early 1900s the once plentiful Adirondack spruce was almost a rarity.

Loggers needed towns. Villages like Tupper Lake and Saranac Lake sprang up out of the wilderness as quickly and haphazardly as gold mining towns did in the West. The 1860 census listed thirty names in the entire Township of Waverly, where Tupper Lake Village eventually grew up. Thirty years later more than a thousand people lived in the village alone. More than 100 buildings had been built, including Hurd's sawmill, "said to be the largest ever erected in New York State," according to Louis J. Simmons, Tupper Lake's recent chronicler. Thirty-three million board feet of softwood lumber could be sawed there in a single season.

A generation earlier the region around Tupper Lake had been so remote and uninviting, the "labor of converting the forest into farms being found too strenuous," as a newspaper article put it, that several would-be settlers fled. By 1890, however, everything had changed. The land was still poor, but it wasn't the land that mattered any more. "It is the poorest country I ever saw!" wrote a surveyor. "They are cutting the timber all off, leaving it one big slash as far as one can see."

"All the life here . . . radiates to the spruce tree," a journalist visiting an Adirondack lumber camp in 1902 wrote. This, he added, was "the story of our progress in the last century." The journalist identified himself only as the "Spectator," for a magazine called *Outlook*. To him, as to many others, wood was a living not just for the loggers but for the entire nation. "Between this density of spruces walling in the camp and paper which records this winter picture are the great forces of the world, turned—after what an interval!—to man's advantage: wood, coal, steam; mechanical and chemical appliances; the accidents of winds, storm, drought; the danger and hazard of human life; common sense, judgment, education."

The Spectator's article, like many accounts of Adirondack logging, is a masterpiece of ambivalence toward the question of man and nature. Turning nature to man's advantage was a Ciceronian "great force," yet the rugged individuals whose lives were so close to the trees, to nature, were seen as romantic figures, "becoming hopelessly assimilated in these surroundings." Such men would have made Jean-Jacques Rousseau happy. They were "Shakespeare's rustics or Hardy's woodlanders," the Spectator wrote. Their songs, their "easy nonchalance" in coping with natural hardship, their health and strength, their "direct pointed humor," their versatility and apparent intimacy with nature made them seem not only superhuman, but noble, better than ordinary men. Their surroundings were filled by "sights and sounds in nature," "Thoreau's smoke-cloud," the "little brook tinkling underneath its palace of ice," all the things "a woodsman truly appreciates and knows in their manifold relations."

Whether or not the loggers were supermen or instruments of

destruction, whether they were pitted against nature or somehow welded
to it, their habits and experiences came down in American legend with as
much clarity and flavor as those of the cowboys. Loggers' hard work and
harder play, their crude, but specialized language, their clothing, the
typical red and black checked wool shirts, suspenders and long underwear, all helped shape the image, embodied in such characters as Paul
Bunyan.

Photographs of camps and lumbermen from the heydey of
Adirondack logging — the 1870s through the early 1900s — show lean,
serious-faced men, dressed with remarkable scantiness as they stood
outside amid icicles and snow.

Most of the logging process took place between October and
April, the coldest months, and a logger had to be healthy, strong and a
master of many trades. As an Adirondack song describes:

> The choppers and the sawyers
> Lay the timber low;
> The swampers and the skidders
> Haul it to and fro.

The first chore, after the logging site had been selected, the
housing for men built hastily, and the workmen hired, was to "lay the
timber low." A good axman or chopper could fell as many as sixty trees a
day in decent weather, although forty trees were thought to be a good
day's work for a man. Some legendary figures were said to be able to fell
seventy trees in a single day.

Until the 1890s, most loggers used only the ax. The cross-cut saw
did not come into widespread use in the Adirondacks until then. When it
did, a good sawyer could average over 100 logs a day.

Until the machine age of the 1920s, all logging tools were simple
and wielded by hand. But loggers were so skilled with their primitive
tools, the best of them could fell a tree in such a way that its crash to the
ground would hammer previously positioned stakes deep into the earth.
Such stunts, traditional in logging camps, provided much needed
amusement.

Skill in aiming a falling tree was not just an amusing stunt,
however, but an important talent. It avoided lodging, the unhappy event
when a falling tree hit and lodged in the branches of a standing one. And a
good aim averted death for anyone standing nearby. The shout of
"timber!" was only a warning that a tree was coming down. Both the

axman and those in the way had to know exactly where a tree was going to fall in order to avoid it.

After the tree was felled, it had to be moved or skidded to one central place. Skidding logs was often done with the help of a team of oxen whose yoke had a large iron ring. The logs were tied together with a chain, and the chain was attached to the ring. "I have hauled as many as 200 logs a day in this manner," reminisced a retired logger by the name of James Truman Hayes, who in 1876, at the age of thirteen, ran away from home to try his luck in northern Essex County as a logger. "It may be readily understood," he continued with pronounced understatement, "that this was not an easy's day's work, especially for a boy."

> Then comes the jolly teamster,
> Just at the break of day;
> Up he loads his teams;
> To the river he hastes away.

When the pile of logs filled the skid, the stand on which felled trees were stacked, the next task was given over to the drover or teamster. A team of oxen, or in the 1860s of horses whose footing on steep grades was surer, was hitched to a sled or wagon which could pull fifty or so logs tied together with chains. The destination was the banking ground, usually a frozen pond or artificial lake which had been dammed. There the logs waited for spring.

One of the toughest jobs was clearing the way for the sled-loads of timber. The routes between the skids and the banking grounds had to be as hard as macadam. The snow had to be packed down and steep inclines had to be regraded into gentle slopes, often with straw or ever-green boughs. On flat surfaces, where a slick roadbed was necessary to keep the heavy loads moving, water was sprinkled into the ruts of the trails so that ice assured a smooth journey. On steep grades the problem was just the opposite. If a load of timber behind a horse team began to slide like a toboggan, gaining speed all the time and heading downhill, the animals and men driving them could be crushed beneath the career-ing load of logs. "Taking a ride down the mountain," was the expression used in the Adirondacks to describe such an accident, and it wasn't the sort of free ride one looked forward to.

The loggers had to be skilled in river craft as well as road building. When spring came, and the frozen water of the banking grounds melted, the most dangerous and exciting phase of logging began. The masses of timber had to be floated down rivers to the markets and mills.

A log sled leaving the skids for the banking ground. *Photo courtesy of The Adiron-dack Museum, Blue Mountain Lake, New York*

The practice of driving thousands of single logs down rushing, spring-swollen rivers and streams originated in the Adirondacks. In 1813, a few logs were sent floating down the Schroon River to its confluence with the Hudson and thence to Glens Falls. Previously, in other logging operations in New England and elsewhere, logs had been tied together into rafts for water travel, but it was cheaper to forego the tying process. Adirondack logging, though it took another thirty years to become exten-sive, was given its vital boost when those first logs were sent successfully downstream without being tied in 1813.

Drivers, both those who literally walked the logs downriver and those who manned the boats along the way, were usually paid more than teamsters or choppers or skidders. When the dams and sluice gates were opened and the giant logs released from the thawed banking grounds, a few hundred at a time, into the rushing waters in April, a man had to summon all his energy and courage for the nearly twenty-four-hour working days that followed for weeks until the logs made it to the mills.

A short drive, from Schroon Lake to Glens Falls, for example, took about a week. As loggers went deeper and higher into the mountains, the drives got longer, often lasting several weeks. Never sleeping, only catnapping, in and out of icy water all day long, the log drivers worked until they dropped. Time was short. The rivers were wide, deep, and fast enough for only a few weeks in the spring, and competition was fierce between logging companies, all of which wanted to get their logs on the rivers first. On the Raquette River, for instance, "rivalries often developed roughness and ill temper on the part of the driving crews, their purpose being to get one drive down the river ahead of the other, as the first flood waters made the river drive less expensive," recalled one logger.

Sometimes the rivers were too fast. They could swell to twice or three times their normal size if heavy snows had fallen or if spring rains were unusually torrential. Log jams were more likely then. At other times not enough snow or rain fell, and water routes were tortuously narrow and shallow.

On the job, the men never changed their clothes. Many a logging memory featured dozens of men, steam pouring from their breeches and jackets like smoke from a chimney, standing around the open fires and stoves at camps. On long drives portable camps followed the men like the chuck wagons on cattle drives out west.

At any stage of the process, the loggers got up before dawn and ate their immense breakfasts. A dozen eggs a man, as many flapjacks, a loaf of bread and quantities of coffee composed the typical meal that, as Harold Hochschild, Adirondack chronicler and author of *Lumberjacks and Rivermen in the Central Adirondacks*, noted was "not yet complicated by vitamin calculations and balanced diets." The point, as one retired logger remembered, was simply to "cram in enough calories to last until [the loggers] got back to camp at night." The evening meal was huge and starchy too. Stews, potatoes, and more bread were common. The camp cook was a man to be respected and left alone since he did all the baking, stewing, and coffee making.

After breakfast, work began by lantern light until the slowly brightening sky was clear. For his labor, the logger received almost ninety cents a day in the 1870s, the peak years of Adirondack logging in the eastern sections, plus food and lodging. The pay scale compared favora-

A bunkhouse kitchen. *New York State Department of Environmental Conservation*

bly with that in the cities, where in the mid-1800s a laborer might receive fifty to seventy-five cents a day, and that without food or board. Log drivers got as much as $1.50 a day in 1900, and the boatmen, thanks to their special skills, sometimes got as much as $3.00.

Occupational liabilities were high. Many men suffered from rheumatism as a result of constant exposure to cold and water. One sure sign of a logger was a gnarled hand or the absence of a couple of fingers, a leg, or an eye. Accidents were frequent at every stage of the logging process. Many a man walked or limped on a badly patched leg, once, twice, or more often broken.

Loggers, like their predecessors the fur trappers, have sometimes been portrayed as rootless men, unmarried, unattached to society, free to drift from camp to camp ever westward as the eastern forests, like the eastern beavers, receded. In an 1824 gazette the lumber trade was described as "always ruinous to the morals . . . associated as it usually is with a prodigality of store trade, strong drink, a profligacy of manners and morals, extravagance in prices and expenses of living, debts, elopements and squalid misery."

Many loggers were, indeed, drifters and hell raisers. Their experiences in the wilderness were as crude and toughening as those of the trappers but were relieved perhaps by the camaraderie and companionship of teamwork, something the trappers didn't often enjoy.

At the end of the week (Sundays, except during the river drives, were traditionally free), or at the end of the job, with money in their pockets and a taste of freedom, the loggers' exploits in town were as notorious as those of the trappers at the trading post. But many loggers were also serious men, hard workers with definite plans. They could work in the woods for a few years, save money, then finally collect enough cash to get married and buy a farm. Thousands of French Canadians, reputed to be the best lumbermen, came south into the Adirondacks for just such a purpose. Many stayed, and their French names sprinkle the mountains today giving many an Adirondack place name a cosmopolitan flavor, especially compared to the Anglo-Saxon places names of New England.

As the nineteenth century progressed and as logging became more regular and specialized, complete with loggers' associations, specific work hours, and compensations, more settled, stable men turned to logging for seasonal work. Some say the main reason cutting traditionally began in autumn was that farmers were free to work only after their crops were in. Few Adirondack residents were ever able to earn a living from a single occupation, be it farming, trapping, logging, or guiding. Combining talents and incomes always has been a part cf life in the mountains. The men who left their farms and families in October to put in a winter's work on the skids and rivers were often men with heavy responsibilities and serious economic worries. As their number increased, stories about binges and squalor decreased.

Tales about past sprees, supermen, the daily dramas in the forests and on the rivers accumulated into a rich folklore which loggers often translated into songs and myths. Interestingly, essentially the same tunes and plots were spun in logging camps from Maine to Oregon. Only the place names changed or a verse or two added about specific loggers or forests:

In the Adirondacks, where logging on a large scale began only after the forests of Maine, New Hampshire, Massachusetts, and Connecticut had been exploited, loggers for the most part simply adapted old songs and stories to new circumstances, perhaps adding a bit more pathos, since Adirondack territory quickly acquired a reputation for being the most difficult in the East.

Rugged, experienced loggers from New England were awed by the harsh conditions, terrain, weather, and recalcitrant rivers of New York's North Country. "I used to hear them talk," wrote Stuart Holbrook in *Yankee Loggers*, "and they made a trip to Tupper Lake and back sound much like a tour of the known world, though right at home most of them had ridden logs on the longest drive [the Connecticut River, two hundred miles from Canada to Massachusetts] in the entire region."

Part of the danger had to do with the trees themselves. They were enormous. A word that seems to have originated in the Adirondacks was "market," a log thirteen feet long. Circumference measurements varied between twelve and nineteen inches, but the standard by which most Adirondack logs were judged as fit for market was the thirteen-foot measure. Such was the length the market would accept, thus the presumed origin of the word. The chopping, skidding, banking, and driving all involved trees that were, literally, as tall as a house.

Millions of these huge logs roared down the rivers each spring, churning up the water, scraping the bottoms of streams, dragging fish along with them. The loggers charged after the logs in rough spots and sat almost leisurely smoking pipes as they rode easily along smooth, straight stretches.

River routes were established and declared "public highways" by state law: the Bouquet, where William Gilliland had built his estate, the Moose, Black, Indian and Beaver rivers, the Ausable, the Grass, the Oswegatchie, the St. Regis, and the biggest ones, the Raquette, the Saranac, and the Hudson. In the southeast sector of the mountains, where the watershed is south toward the Hudson, most of the logs were destined for Glens Falls or Albany, where sawmills lined the river's edge.

About four miles north of Glens Falls, the Hudson River makes a sharp turn. In the nineteenth century the turn was called the Big Bend, and there in 1851 a kind of corral, called the Big Boom, was built. A boom was a log with a hole drilled through its center, lengthwise, so that a chain could be passed through. In this way, logs could be strung together like beads and used as a floating fence to enclose other, loose logs. Once in the boom, the logs, each with a company mark like a brand etched on its ends, could be sorted and rerouted. Between 1851 and 1900, 102 brands were registered by as many companies working in the Adirondacks.

At the Big Bend in the Hudson, near Glens Falls, the Big Boom was built in 1851. By the 1870s, over a million logs were corralled there each spring. *Courtesy, The Chapman Historical Museum of the Glens Falls-Queensbury Historical Association, Inc.*

The year the Big Boom was built, 26 million board feet of lumber collected there. Eight years later, just before New York relinquished first place and became the second leading lumber-producing state in the nation, 500,000 logs, possibly as much as 100 million board feet (if all the logs were markets; one market log equalled 200 board feet) accumulated. That year, 1859, the sheer weight of the logs combined with heavy spring rains and flooding to cause the Big Boom to break, sending all the logs shooting like torpedoes down the Hudson as far as Troy, New York. The Boom was rebuilt and expanded and in its peak year, 1872, corralled over a million logs. New York was not even the first lumber producer at that time, an indication of the truly voracious demand for wood in America.

River routes leading to the Big Boom or to other booms and mills in the Adirondacks all had their special dangers. The Hudson had a difficult turn just below the town of Blue Ledge, for example. A nest of sand bars always caused trouble near Warrensburg. The Boreas River was bad all the way, it was said. And one of the worst places was a spot called Deer Den, where the Hudson doglegs south at its confluence with the Boreas. Wherever there was a bend, a narrow or shallow or rocky stretch, a sand bar or falls, there was the potential for a "jam stretch," where one or another impediment could cause one log, only one log, to be hung up in midstream. Every log behind it, like automobiles behind a single stalled car, would pile up in the churning waters.

The logjam was the driver's nightmare and some said his most thrilling challenge. Many loggers had a reputation for harboring a "passion for their wild and toilsome life," as one commentator wrote, and the jam was the ultimate in wildness and toil. As the logs began to pile up, like matchsticks spilled from a box (in fact, the log that jammed was often called a "jackstraw"), someone had to go in and chop it loose. By the time the man got to the key log, part of the way by boat (and that was where the boatman's skills were so crucial) and part of the way on foot over quickly mounting logs, a thousand more thirteen-footers might surround the eye of the jam. Often dynamite was used to break jams, but even then the river men still had to go in to chop the jackstraw free.

If the logger managed to negotiate the jammed logs successfully and got to the key or jackstraw log, his trouble began in earnest. The greatest danger was the exploding tidal wave of freed logs lurching forward from their imprisonment. If the logger was not quick and light on his feet, "like a bird in flight," as one writer noted, and the boatmen were not equally speedy, all were crushed or buried or drowned or clubbed to pieces by the onward rush of flowing timber. The list of loggers who died in jams was long. If the bodies were found, they were likely to be washed ashore somewhere far downstream like stray logs.

It was tough work from dawn to dusk during the coldest times of the year. Winter, so hard an enemy to so many Adirondack residents, was to the logger an exacting but loyal friend. Enduring the below-zero weather was the least of his worries usually. He knew that logging would be much harder in summer or spring when mud clogged roads and thick

Logjam on the Moose River. *Collection of the New York State Museum*

undergrowth impeded movement through remote forest regions. Winter made the woods manageable and enabled many a man to earn a living the summer woods denied him.

Logging in the Adirondacks reached a peak in the year 1905, when over 700 million board feet of timber were cut. That meant about 3.5 million trees felled in a single year. The kinds of trees loggers went after had changed over the decades. First, they wanted soft wood, pines, firs, cedars, and other conifers that were used mainly for lumber and had to be as tall and straight as possible. A kind of natural selection was in operation since loggers passed up those trees that were not suitable for lumber, thus leaving smaller trees and giving them a chance to grow and replenish the forest.

Until the 1890s, the yellow birch, maple, ash, elm, cherry, and poplars were left alone for the simple reason that these hardwoods were too heavy to float. There was no way of getting them out of the forest except by water until the railroads came and provided the means of transporting them.

After 1905, softwood logging took a sharp decline from which it did not recover until the mid-1940s. Gradually, the loggers had been moving west from the eastern sections of the mountains, where the upper Hudson watershed area had been logged over by the 1870s. In the 1890s logging in the Cranberry Lake area, on the northwestern slopes, was widespread.

Meanwhile, the hardwood trees began to be cut since railroad lines were being built. Their proportion of the total take continued to rise, and in 1908 over 100 million board feet of hardwood timber were cut. Almost immediately after that peak year, operations declined precipitously for the obvious reason that the trees were nearly gone.

The pulp industry was far less selective about the trees it needed than was the lumber industry. Spruce of any size or shape was good for making pulp. Almost anything green and woody would do. Even young softwoods other than spruce, trees lumbermen had left alone, were cut. "They're cutting straws. And there go the Adirondacks," as one logger predicted as early as the 1870s. Clear-cutting left little. Loggers no longer needed to fear that new trees would spring up immediately. A clear-cut acre on Adirondack soil was prey to fire and disease and erosion before it welcomed new forest growth.

Yet for all the devastation of the Adirondack forest, the outside world was demanding more and more wood. Americans had become ravenous consumers of paper, for example. Newspapers alone required millions of tons of paper, and as the number of published journals jumped from 800 to almost 3,000 between 1830 and 1850, paper was ever more in demand.

That was one reason researchers worked very hard to find new sources of pulp: rags and straw were expensive and hard to transport. The discovery that fibrous spruce wood could be mixed with chemicals to make pulp was a godsend to newspaper and book publishers. Within twenty years of 1867, the year spruce pulp was developed, the paper industry doubled. The Adirondacks kept the New York paper industry going in the 1890s and early 1900s. In fact, more than half of all the pulp mills in the state were operated entirely with Adirondack wood in 1900.

Yet even the Adirondacks could never supply enough. By 1904, even before pulp logging reached its peak in the Adirondacks, much of the spruce for the mills had to be imported from Canada.

It was the increasing clout of pulp interests that changed the standard thirteen-foot Adirondack log to a four-foot length. Length, size, shape, and even quality were of minor importance if the wood was to be mashed up into pulp instead of sawed into lumber. The four-foot measure was adopted in 1924, the same year the last river drive of market logs was sent down the Hudson. By then railroads had replaced the river, and trucks and decent roads were on their way to making the railroads obsolete. The romantic logging days were over.

Within the lifespan of one person, a mere seventy years, logging in the Adirondacks began in earnest, reached a peak, and declined sharply. In 1847, for example, a lumberman by the name of Orson Richards supervised a run of fifty thousand markets through the Saranac Valley to Lake Champlain. According to historian Maitland Desormo, Richards' drive "triggered an era of extensive logging in the very heart of the Adirondacks." In 1904, the last year the Big Boom published records, somewhere in the neighborhood of two hundred thousand logs were received around the Big Bend in the Hudson. Midway between the two dates, in 1870, it was not unusual to see more than a million logs corralled there. A year after the Big Boom stopped recording its logs, logging in the western portions of the Adirondacks reached a peak, then speedily declined.

Loggers swooped in and out of the Adirondacks as quickly as the beaver trappers. Their work was the key to New York's supremacy as a logging state because the Adirondack stands of timber, alone of all the state's forests, went almost entirely to industrial purposes. So few pioneers had preceded the lumbermen that fences, houses, firewood, and charcoal had not consumed the trees first. Von Wagenen's pardon to pioneers needs to be stretched a bit to apply to loggers. Their efforts were a kind of public service, too, but to cities and towns and the people who could not have built them, or their homes, or libraries or fortunes, without Adirondack trees.

Adirondack trees saved Glens Falls, a sawmill town which was nearly dead in 1813 when those first logs were floated down the Schroon River. Adirondack lumber made Albany, just fifty miles south of Glens Falls, one of the leading lumber towns in America for a time. In 1865, there were 3,963 sawmills lining the banks of the Hudson at the state capital.

The lumber industry in New York, however, like a swollen Adirondack river in spring, was potent but shortlived. Few lumbermen made genuine fortunes either. A running battle between loggers and vacationers was already under way in the 1860s and '70s, a time when both the peaks of the lumbering industry and the tourist business were converging in the wilderness.

The sportsmen, hotel owners, and guides, wrote an irate official of one of the large lumber companies in 1874, who, he said, "do not claim any shadow of title to the lands and waters," were waging an all-out war on the lumbermen. Logging camps were burned, timber stolen from skids and banking grounds, even stands of forests were set on fire, according to the official, all because the "sportsmen felt the woods belong to them!" They were nothing more than "interlopers and trespassers . . . a nuisance and a curse to any county they invade."

Essentially the same charges were leveled against the lumber companies, of course. Sportsmen and nature lovers accused them of denuding the hills with ruthless carelessness, of creating fires, of killing fish and wildlife, and of destroying the character of the wilderness. State officials suspected that loggers were trespassing on state land for timber, too.

By 1885 at least two-thirds of the entire Adirondack forest had been logged at least once. Some said more like 90 percent or close to 100 percent of the region had fallen under the loggers' axes.

New York State lost its place at the top of the list of lumber producers in 1860 but remained in second place for a decade. By 1900, however, it was declining fast as the great forests of the upper Midwest and West also succumbed to axes and saws. One measure of the decline was that in 1900 there were only 150 sawmills left in Albany.

Much of Adirondack history is keyed to the ups and downs, supplies and demands of the rest of the state and nation—from "outside," as natives say. But Adirondack lumbering, though initiated as a result of outside demand, had a direct effect upon "outside" when the trees were exhausted. When timber production in the North Country began its decline in 1905, the state's fortunes in wood followed. The depletion of wood in the Adirondacks was the final blow to New York's supremacy as a producer of paper, furniture, tools, and other products.

What was left after the seventy-year logging orgy was a vastly altered environment. Without stands of timber or a forest floor of pine needles and leaves, water from rain and snow-melt evaporates more quickly or runs off steep hills. It is no longer released gently, and what soil is left erodes quickly, diminishing the possibilities for fast second growth trees. Streams, once modest, become rushing torrents or mere trickles depending upon rain and snowfall. The habits, food supplies, and distribution of many animals are seriously disrupted. Log driving, for example, so dependent upon water, tends to take with it many fish, and the courses of rivers are changed when dams are built. All this happened in the Adirondacks.

Forest fires became endemic. Tired men in logging camps were careless, as were vacationers. Woodburning train engines sent sprays of sparks behind them and set many a fire.

In no era of Adirondack history has man been pitted so directly against nature. Yet at the very moment trees were crashing to the ground, many people were beginning to appreciate the forests for their beauty as well as for their usefulness. The feud between lumbermen and sportsmen, hotel owners, and guides pointed up the conflict, and the tug-of-war over the forests got more fierce all the time.

Nevertheless, the forest had strange effects even on the loggers who, as the Spectator observed, were sometimes made better men as a result of their close, if exploitative, association with nature. The bestial and the beatific sides of nature and of man seemed hopelessly mixed up.

Later, as people tried to sort out the two, many moved toward a position that emphasized the sacredness of nature and the rapaciousness of man. Others, as they sat warmly in tight houses, read newspapers and books, enjoyed fine leather saddles and furniture, remembered that if America was built and blessed with wood, much of New York State was built and graced with Adirondack wood.

9

There's Ore in Them Thar Hills

EXPLORING THE RELATIONSHIP between man and nature leads to all sorts of ruminations about trends, attitudes, and philosophies. But consider for a moment the lowly nail. A quarter will buy a handful of nails in any hardware store. But before 1840 each nail had to be made by hand. The iron for each one had to be smelted laboriously, and acres of forest were necessary for charcoal, which until the 1830s was the only known fuel for forges or blast furnaces in which ores had to be smelted. A nail was a thing to be highly valued.

In the 1840s, machines that could turn out thousands of nails made a difference that can be seen today in buildings all over America. If a few planks of lumber could be nailed securely together into a frame, almost anything—plaster, stucco, lath—could be used to fill the gaps and create walls. Instead of log cabins, notched together like pieces in a jigsaw puzzle, or brick or stone structures, both requiring massive beams, extreme precision, and hours of painstaking labor to erect successfully, buildings could be put up in half the time and having twice the strength.

American architecture came to depend upon nails, millions of them in all sizes, and an ever increasing demand for them sent iron on its long ascent toward becoming not just a minor expensive appendage to wood construction, but an essential ingredient to building of all kinds.

Builders began to experiment with other iron structures. It was found that ships' hulls, for example, could be made from iron. The strange, monsterlike ships, the *Monitor* and the *Merrimack* of Civil War fame, "ugly, black and irrestible," as historian Bruce Catton describes them, were sheathed in iron.

Eventually, architects found they barely needed wooden frames for buildings at all. Iron and its alloy steel were stronger and more durable and by 1890 readily available in such forms as iron lattices, grillwork, iron buildings, and steel underpinnings for nearly everything that stood or floated. By then the Iron Age in America was in full bloom, and everyone who knew anything knew there was iron ore in the Adirondacks.

The Iroquois had fashioned simple implements from the ore. William Gilliland had built a forge in Willsboro before the Revolutionary War. Benedict Arnold, it was said, procured iron ore for cannon balls from Port Henry on the shores of Lake Champlain when he was plotting his bold but ill-conceived assault on Montreal in 1775. Not far from Port Henry, at a place called Mineville, a small mining community was built as early as 1804. In a little town called North Elba, near Lake Placid, iron ore was found in 1809. On the southwestern slopes of the mountains near the Fulton Chain Lakes, the town of Old Forge was established in 1817 when a forge was built. In 1822, a blast furnace—one of the first in the nation— was built at Port Henry. In the northern mountains iron ore was discovered in St. Lawrence County, near Star Lake, sometime around 1812, although mining did not begin there until 1889. The iron sheathing for the *U.S.S. Monitor* came from Essex County.

Villages that didn't originate as a result of logging operations were often built around forges. The population of Crown Point, for example, on Lake Champlain, doubled in one year thanks to a mining operation there. By the time of the Civil War, the Adirondacks were famous for their iron.

But there were problems. Many operations failed. The North Elba Ironworks faltered in 1815. The proprietor at Old Forge, Frederick Herreshoff, committed suicide after years of failed attempts to make the ore turn a profit.

Part of the problem was the ore itself. It was abundant in the mineral magnetite, and some of it was of such high quality that it was thought to be excelled only by the ores of Sweden. But much of it was richly laced with ilmenite, the mineral used much later to make titanium dioxide, the highly prized white compound.

Another problem was the old one of topography. Few roads existed in the nineteenth century, and those that did wend their ways up and down and around the hills were often impassable in winter and spring, first from snow, then from mud. Building new roads was an agonizingly slow process. What ore could be extracted from the Adirondacks presented nearly insoluble problems when it came to getting it out.

Still, men kept hoping to find *the* ore bed whose possibilities would overcome the transportation problems and separation difficulties: "speculators in Essex County running wild for ore beds," as one hopeful

An early blast furnace at Ft. Ann, N.Y., similar to the one built at the McIntyre mine in 1854. *Collection of the New York State Museum*

The modern ilmenite mine at Tahawas, N.Y. *Collection of the New York State Museum*

put it in the 1820s. More than 200 forges were built throughout the Adirondacks in the 1800s, and while many of these closed soon after they opened, thousands of tons of cast and pig iron were produced.

In 1826, a group of well-to-do businessmen from New York City and the Albany area thought they had struck it rich at last. "It was a most extraordinary bed of Iron Ore," that vein found near Sanford Lake, about fifty miles due west of Port Henry and not far from the headwaters of the Hudson River. But what lay between Lake Champlain—and civilization—

and the vein was "as wild a place as I ever saw," wrote one of the men who discovered it.

His name was David Henderson, and like many explorers, he and his group of six companions were looking for something other than what they found on that October day in 1826, when an Indian showed them that "most extraordinary bed."

Henderson was a Scotsman. He was good looking, a man with a long, aristocratic nose, curly hair, and slender fingers. He was not unlike another Adirondack personality, Frederick Herreshoff, who tried to revamp the Old Forge community in the early 1800s. Both were Europeans; both were musical; Henderson was a skilled artist. Both wrote long, detailed letters about their experiences in the Adirondacks. And both put their hopes and their money into Adirondack iron.

Henderson had been involved in the unprofitable, six-year venture at North Elba. The chief proprietors and investors of that ironworks were, as so many other Adirondack landowners would be, men of considerable means and standing in New York State. One was Archibald McIntyre, another Scotsman and the principal investor. He had been a state assemblyman and state comptroller. Another principal was Duncan McMartin, who had been an assemblyman and a judge.

McIntyre and McMartin were related by marriage as well as by business interests. In fact, the men who put so much effort into Adirondack mining near Sanford Lake were so intermarried that the connections were complicated. McMartin was married to one of McIntyre's sisters. McMartin's brother, Malcolm, also a large investor, was married to another of McIntyre's sisters. David Henderson married one of McIntyre's daughters in the first of a spate of second generation marriages among sons and daughters and nephews and nieces of the original investors. The patchwork of marriages and mutual business interests gave the impression that a Scottish clan had been transported from the Northern Highlands to the Adirondacks, an appropriate transplantation. The beauty of the two regions has often been compared, and the Adirondacks have been called America's bonny lake country.

Shortly after the Revolutionary War, McIntyre and his associates had acquired part of the Totten and Crossfield Purchase, that giant plot of remote land whose exact boundaries had never been accurately fixed. The McIntyre speculation had at first seemed promising. Iron was found. But the ore could not be worked easily. Miners, at the end, had to bring ore from other places since they were determined to continue processing even if they could not produce iron ore. But the insurmountable transportation problems finally put a stop to the venture.

It was silver, long rumored to sparkle in the remote valleys, that Henderson and his companions were looking for when they stumbled upon a new bed of iron thirty miles south of North Elba.

Henderson wrote immediately to McIntyre, who was in Albany. McIntyre wrote immediately to McMartin who, though he was involved in an election campaign to the senate, began proceedings to purchase the land. It was a complicated procedure. The state was the official owner and required a survey before any land could be sold. The following October, in 1827, the survey of six thousand acres was completed with the usual difficulties. The surveyors' report described a "very high, rocky, sprucy [region] of the worst kind." The terrain was so rugged in places that it was impossible, they said, to fix a border. And to boot, "no oar [sic] in sight," was the surveyors' opinion.

McIntyre and McMartin were not disturbed in the least. They were actually grateful that the place looked bad for they worried constantly that someone else would get to the iron before they did. At last the Scotsmen could breathe easily when their new tract of land, adjacent to their original one, was secured in their names.

But getting in to take a look at the new holdings was even more trying than obtaining them. Sanford Lake is buried in the heart of the Adirondacks, just south of the High Peaks. There was no road within twenty miles. The only access from Port Henry was by canoe, and even a canoe took them only to within four miles of the ore. The only shelter within ten miles was a tiny community called Newcomb's Farm, and the nearest town of any consequence was Moriah, many miles away. Between supply sources and shelter and the "extraordinary bed" were miles of that rocky, sprucy wilderness.

The first priority was to build a road, a project that caused McIntyre much anguish. Between the natural difficulties of the terrain and what McIntyre perceived as recalcitrance on the part of the builder ("The foolish scoundrel . . . the wretch," McIntyre wrote of him), the new road, thirty miles of it from the ore bed to Crown Point, was not completed until 1839. Even the parts of it that were finished by 1831, when the first ores were finally extracted, were often impassable. The very first batch of ore, six tons of it, had to be abandoned along the way to Moriah since December snows dumped three and a half feet onto the mountains overnight. Even the sleighs couldn't get through. Only the men and the horses made it to shelter. They had to go back several days later for the ore.

Traveling remained a constant problem, rivaled only by the "black fleys," as the Scotsmen called the black flies that swarm in the early spring. McIntyre, while visiting the operation, was often in "blotches." Some of the workers were so tormented they ran away, a problem William Gilliland had had with his settlers 100 years earlier. Even if someone did run away, the running could be as treacherous as the staying. In winter the workers were snowbound. In fall rain and quickly melting early snow created a mire of slush and mud. In spring more mud accumulated, and in summer the flies and mosquitoes were worse in the forests than in the clearings.

Barring these natural hazards, wagons were prone to toppling over on the dirt roads. David Henderson and two of McIntyre's sons once were all tossed out of their conveyance with such force Henderson's face was slashed and John McIntyre's leg cut so badly his boot was filled with blood. Such accidents were frequent, and the injuries suffered on this particular journey were considered "nothing serious," Henderson reported. (Later visitors to the Adirondacks, en route to some backwoods, rustic but fashionable hotel, were sometimes strapped into the seats of buggies and wagons to prevent the kind of injuries Henderson suffered.)

Work at the mines went on, and the abundance of the ore ("There is little doubt but the whole valley and sides of the mountains are masses of ores," Henderson reported in 1833) kept everyone's spirits high. A little community, known simply as McIntyre, grew up along with the hopes and plans of the Scottish proprietors. They talked of a dam to produce water power. In 1838, a blast furnace was built to replace the old charcoal forge. In 1840, the word "railroad" began to flash though the minds of the Scotsmen, and plans were made to build one.

David Henderson by then had taken over the day-to-day administration of the ironworks. McMartin had died in 1837, and Archibald McIntyre, though he continued all his life to be passionately concerned with the operation, was growing old and frail.

So many Adirondack projects seem to get just so far, then something happens: the weather changes, an economic depression downstate hits, a road becomes impassable, a war overseas alters demand patterns, attitudes shift and fads change, or just plain bad luck intervenes. For all their potential, the Adirondacks can be exceedingly inhospitable.

David Henderson, so optimistic, energetic, and imaginative, ran up against at least four of the possible problems listed above, and one other that seems astonishing in a region noted for its abundant water. The McIntyre mine had trouble getting enough water, as well as water power, from the beginning. The large lakes in the area were not close to the actual mines. Henderson kept buying new machinery, including a new-fangled magnetic separator which was supposed to draw out the iron ore from the (magnetic) magnetite. Each machine required more and more water.

In 1842–43, a general depression plagued all the East. In June 1843, Henderson was disconsolate. Prices for iron had fallen, and the iron was proving to be more and more difficult to work. He began to add up the money he had poured into the McIntyre mine and concluded he had spent at least $36,000, which he was compelled to consider lost, as he wrote to McIntyre. The next year was even more *"vexatious* (a word Gilliland used about the Adirondacks) *and expensive,"* he emphasized. The lack of water was getting to be extremely serious.

It was on a trip through the surrounding woods to look for a possible channel through which water could be brought to the mines that David Henderson, at the age of 53, encountered the most intractable problem, bad luck. It seems that while a group of five people, including Henderson's ten-year-old son, was making camp, Henderson took off his back pack and while putting it down, accidentally discharged a pistol. He doubled over in pain. Fifteen minutes later he was dead as a result of the bullet wound in his belly. "This is a horrible place for a man to die," he managed to say. Today the pond where Henderson died is called Calamity.

Operations at the McIntyre mine limped along for a while after Henderson's death. It remained a family business for many years with another of McIntyre's sons-in-law acquiring an interest. Another family connection was forged when Henderson's son and daughter married the daughter and son of one Duncan Gregory, who had acquired shares in the mining company. In the late 1840s and '50s, the ore from McIntyre was used in the production of steel, and the Adirondack Steel Manufacturing Company was formed to direct the steel factory in New Jersey, which used Adirondack iron. Some of America's top quality steel was first produced from that ore in the New Jersey plant.

In 1854, the town McIntyre, whose name had been changed to Adirondac shortly after the mountain region itself was so named (using a different spelling), was still a community. In addition to the forges and furnaces, sawmills, and other industrial buildings, there were boarding houses, stables, an ice house, a school house, and at least a dozen other buildings bearing the unmistakable marks of civilization. To the south, another town, named Tahawas, had been built when Henderson's long hoped for dam had been finished. Surrounded by 300 acres of cleared and cultivated fields, Tahawas and Adirondac between them had the look of a permanent, promising outpost of man in the midst of the wilderness. Explorers, surveyors, and hikers knew they could count on a bit of civilization there. The shops even had a few luxuries such as sugar and raisins.

But appearances were deceiving. Negotiations were under way for the sale of the company, and in 1853, an agreement was drawn up and a down payment made. But when it came time for the second payment, the buyer, like Alexander Macomb nearly 100 years earlier, couldn't make it and the deal was off. Again, in 1863, another buyer made a down payment but never made up the balance. By then, there wasn't much left to buy.

A major flood wiped out the dam. A general financial panic, the worst in New York's history until then, took place in the same year as the flood, 1863. Two years later when Archibald McIntyre died, Adirondac and Tahawas were deserted ghost towns.

Workers had always been hard to cajole into staying. To McIntyre's constant irritation they demanded wages higher than anywhere else in the East, a factor contributing to the notoriously high cost of Adirondack iron. McIntyre's ore sold for nearly twice that of other producers. However cozy the settlements looked, their inhabitants seemed to need little encouragement to leave when they sensed the enterprise sinking. They left, in fact, almost overnight. By 1858 only a skeleton of the two towns, like deserted islands in a sea of trees, remained. The McIntyre mining company had gone bankrupt.

There were many children, grandchildren, nieces and nephews among whom the remaining shares of the company were divided. Like the deeds to land in the previous century, untangling who owned what was a long-term chore.

The McIntyre failure was one of the most poignant in the Adirondacks and one of the most fully documented because an Adirondack devotee, Arthur H. Masten, published much of Henderson's and McIntyre's correspondence and their story in a book called *The Story of Adirondac*, first printed in 1923. But the McIntyre story was far from unique or even unusual. Other mines encountered the same difficulties. It was just that few had the same persistent (or articulate) proprietors.

One of the most remarkable facts in Adirondack history is that in 1880, despite repeated failures of individual mines, 15 percent of all the iron ore in America was mined in the Lake Champlain area bordering Essex and Clinton Counties. The ore beds were among the best in the Adirondacks, and the sites had the additional advantage of being near water transportation.

It is often said about the Adirondacks that much American iron was produced there in the late nineteenth century. But the figures, while impressive, are misleading since they indicate general, prolonged success.

In 1880, relatively little iron ore was produced and processed in the United States: England produced twice as much. Nails, however abundant by 1840, did not require huge quantities of iron. Shipbuilding and construction consumed larger quantities, and the demand was high enough to require the United States to import a large proportion of its iron. Before the Civil War, imported iron accounted for twice the value of the American product.

The events that transformed the iron industry into a major economic factor culminated *after* the 1880s. The Bessemer process, developed in the 1860s, by which steel could be manufactured easily, was not used extensively until the 1880s. The discovery of huge beds of hemetite ore in the Midwest and the ease with which coal (which did not exist in the Adirondacks) could be shipped from Pennsylvania and Ohio across the Great Lakes to power the furnaces in Michigan, Wisconsin, and Minnesota gave mining concerns in the region a boost they translated into a booming industry. The exploitation of iron in the South, where Birmingham, Alabama, for example, became a leading producer, also served to usurp the Adirondacks' position in the industry. By 1895 the United States led the world in the production of iron. Before 1900, 10 million tons of steel, the hungriest iron consumer, were produced here, a 500 percent increase in less than thirty years. Alongside steel, the amount of pig iron alone doubled between 1885 and 1897, and doubled again every twelve years until 1915, when it began to double every ten years.

The iron contributed by the Adirondacks remained relatively constant during those years, but its percentage of the total declined to a tiny faction by 1900. Of all the mines opened in the 1800s, only the one at Mineville, blessed by its locality and rich ores, remained continually in operation from the time it opened into the twentieth century, and its proprietors seem to have had as many bad years as good ones.

The national demand for iron served to open the Adirondacks as surely as did the demand for wood. More than one thousand people were working in the iron industry in the 1840s, and their number increased in later years. For the first time, the North Country was attractive to newly arrived Italians and Poles who worked as smelters and miners.

Yet just as the state and national need spurred people to go in, the national need, as it became not just big but immense, left the Adirondacks as a primary iron producer far behind. The greatness of the American iron industry unfolded elsewhere.

But mining changed the Adirondacks for good. Thousands of acres of forests were burned for fuel to power the forges and furnaces. In 1841 alone, over twenty thousand tons of fuel were used. One company

The Crown Point Iron Co. Railroad and the denuded countryside, middle 1800s.
Photo by S. R. Stoddard

estimated it needed a thousand cords of wood each year for each kiln in
which charcoal was made. The mines themselves, which were mainly
deep shaft, not open pit, didn't alter the environment as much as the
miners' and smelters' need for wood. Thus mining contributed to the
"burned over" look of the mountains, to the dangerous defoliation, and
eventually to the deep concern over the fate of a once "sprucy" but by the
late 1890s nearly denuded wilderness.

     Archibald McIntyre stumbled on part of the reason for that grow-
ing concern even while he was trying to make his fortune from exploiting
Adirondack iron ore. He seemed to feel better, despite black flies, each
time he made a trip to the mountains. Outdoor life in the Adirondacks
bucked him up. "I wish we had suitable roads to, and suitable accommo-
dations at 'McIntyre' for our families to go there. I have no doubt it would

be beneficial for them to spend a month or two there annually," he wrote in the winter of 1833.

And David Henderson, sharp businessman that he was, noted four years later, "The *territory* is getting into so much notice, that I verily believe, were a railroad to be made from the lake, and a large public house erected—it would become a fashionable resort for the Summer months."

Had Henderson's fate not been tied up in Adirondack iron, his fortune might well have been made in another, more enduring Adirondack enterprise: recreation.

10

How the Adirondacks Got a Name

D AVID HENDERSON called the region "the woods," or the "Essex Mountains." Archibald McIntyre, writing to Judge McMartin, spoke of "the wilds where you are buried." William Gilliland spoke of the "howling wilds." "Beaver Hunting Territory," "The Black Mountains," "Macomb's Mountains," "The Peru Mountains," and, of course, in the plainest language of all, "The Wilderness": these were among the dozen or more names people called the Adirondacks over the centuries.

Until 1836 there was no official name, though such an omission on a map like New York's was something of a scandal. But other things contributed to the acute embarrassment among state officials. In 1836, many a face was red when it became clear that New York's reputation was lagging behind Pennsylvania's, even North Carolina's, in the increasingly important field of scientific research, especially natural history.

In nearly everything else New York was an undisputed leader. To be bested by Pennsylvania, a traditional rival, was too much. In order to redress the balance, the state legislature decided to do in spades what at least fifteen other states had already done. More than $100,000 was set aside in 1836 for the most extensive, comprehensive, expensive survey ever planned or executed in any state. The most detailed scientific data about native rock, soil, and animal life were to be collected and analyzed.

Between the possibilities of discovering valuable mineral resources and new stretches of fertile soil and the prospects of attaining unparalleled prestige, the state survey was the result of a combination of idealism and practicality. And it led to one of New York's most famous achievements: its first Geological Survey.

When the initial surveys were completed, many of the reports were gathered and published in 1842 as the *Natural History of New York*. The multivolume work, lavishly illustrated in color, received enthusiastic acclaim from the scientific community and from the public and remains a source of pride.*

The same combination of high-mindedness and downright greed was to re-emerge forty years later among a new generation of New Yorkers who created the Adirondack Forest Preserve. But the earlier compromise, leading to the surveys, had an impact of nearly equal importance on the mountains.

Northern New York was one of four sections of the state to be surveyed. This "Northern District" was assigned to one of the most famous geologists of the day, Dr. Ebenezer Emmons, a scholar who was trained in many fields, including chemistry and medicine as well as geology. He was teaching at Williams College in Massachusetts when he was offered the job of exploring New York's rugged, mysterious northern hills.

Emmons was young and strong, fortunately, for "to tread the almost roadless Adirondacks, sleeping under clear or rainy skies, was no light task for Emmons and his young assistant, James Hall," wrote historian Dixon Ryan Fox a century later. Hall was later pulled off the Adirondack job to take over the western section of the survey, and he became even more famous than Ebenezer Emmons as a geologist and as the founder of the New York State Museum.

Occasionally, man and nature collaborate as if they were the most devoted allies. Emmons and his small party, including a local guide (one of the first to receive mention in Adirondack history) had an opportunity to witness a nearly perfect instance of that occasional alliance. Both the few men they encountered in the back woods and the endlessly difficult natural hazards of thick underbrush, dense forest, rivers, mountains, and weather greeted them with equal hostility. The rugged mountain men suspected the team of treacherous schemes to raise their taxes and often refused to answer questions or give directions. And the natural hardships threatened the health of all the surveyors as they had frustrated others in the past.

The team used the facilities at the mining town of McIntyre,

*One of the offshoots of the survey was the creation of the American Association of Geologists, suggested one evening in the home of one of the surveyors as a means by which the survey team could share problems and solutions with other outstanding scientists. So successful was the organization that it led to the formation of the American Association for the Advancement of Science a few years later.

Geologist Ebenezer Emmons. *New York State Science Service, Collection of the New York State Museum*

where the first ore was being extracted in 1836, as a base. Several proprietors of the operation, including David Henderson, even accompanied the surveyors on exploratory trips. Emmons named one of the mountains he "discovered" after Archibald McIntyre, another after Judge McMartin.

Emmons had the opportunity Champlain and others missed, to name mountain after mountain, lake after lake. Most were nameless when he found them buried in "a country as little known and as inadequately explored . . . as the secluded valleys of the Rocky Mountains or the burning plains of Central Africa," Emmons reported.

It was Dr. Emmons who chose the name "Adirondack" for the High Peaks region. He was told that a group of Indians by that name had once hunted in the region, had thought of it as their own, but had been expelled by later groups. Emmons wished to commemorate the earlier group. He believed the name "Aganushioni," the Iroquois word for Long House and the name they used to identify their tribe, was smoother than Adirondack, but he felt a tribute to "historical fact" was more important than euphonics: so "Adirondack" it was.

The exact meaning and origin of the word "Adirondack" is unknown. A long-standing tradition has it that the word meant "barkeaters," or "they who eat trees," and was used derisively by Iroquois Indians to insult the Algonquins who were forced in winter to survive like deer by eating buds and bark. Linguists and historians dispute this. There is only one thing on which every interpreter seems to agree, and that is that "Adirondack" is a word of Indian origin, probably Iroquois, and may have applied to one or more groups living near the mountains at various, very early periods.

The New York state legislature was happy enough with Emmons' suggestion and approved it in 1837. The Great Northern Wilderness had an official name at last. Although Emmons' "Adirondack" originally applied only to the High Peaks, that "cluster of mountains in the neighborhood of the Upper Hudson and Ausable rivers," the name soon came to apply to the entire region. Emmons contributed other names, too. For example, he called the highest Adirondack peak, which he climbed and measured on August 5, 1837, "Mt. Marcy," after the New York governor who authorized and supported the geological survey.

Emmons found more than unexplored mountains, lakes, and forests, however. He found a region as wild and beautiful as any in the eastern United States. Even the local mountaineer guide who led the surveying party to the top of Mt. Marcy was overcome with the scene below. John Cheney was the guide's name, and he became one of the most famous characters the mountains produced. He typified the orneri-

Emmons' drawing of the High Peaks, the region he named the Adirondack Group
in 1837, including Mt. Marcy and Mt. McIntyre. *New York State Assembly, Assembly
Document, Vol. 200 (1838)*

ness, independence, woods wisdom, and ungrammatical yet pungent language for which Adirondack guides became known throughout
the nation.

Cheney's remarks while he stood with Emmons on top of Mt.
Marcy are perhaps the most often quoted sentences uttered about the
Adirondacks. "It makes a man feel," he is reported to have said, "what it
is to have all creation placed beneath his feet. There are woods there
which it would take a lifetime to hunt over, mountains that seem shoul-
dering each other to boost the one whereon you stand up and away,
heaven knows where. Thousands of little lakes among them so light and
clean. Old Champlain, though fifty miles away, glistens below you like a
strip of white birch when slicked up by the moon on a frosty night, and

the Green Mountains of Vermont beyond it fade and fade away until they disappear as gradually as a cold scent when the dew rises."

What Cheney, Henderson (who was with them), Emmons, and the others saw that day in 1837 was genuine wilderness. Loggers had not yet reached the High Peaks. Mining operations were small. Tourists were nearly nonexistent. Man had intruded very little upon nature's domain, leaving a virtually untouched landscape. The sight of that wilderness inspired in the men who saw it a surprising impulse of appreciation. They had come to look for minerals, soil, animals, and trees. They had come to measure mountains and to analyze and catalog their findings. But they found someting more than the particulars, something their surveying equipment could not measure. They stumbled upon mystery, awe, and wonder and in so doing may have reckoned with a hunger they had not identified before. Wilderness evoked not fear or the urge to settle or intimations of hardship. It evoked pleasure, adventure, peace, and comfort of spirit.

Many of those who followed Emmons and his group into the mountains and woods did so with a conscious desire for such wilderness benefits. They were as hungry for these as the loggers and miners were for wood and ore. Few places in America would satisfy the need for wilderness so much as did the one Emmons saw and named and appreciated years before many Americans diagnosed their growing appetite for natural beauty.

New World Cathedrals

EMMONS' "DISCOVERY" was a sensation. The news that there was such a place as the Adirondacks, a stretch of nearly unbroken wilderness the size of the State of Connecticut only 200 miles north of New York City excited financiers, entrepreneurs, and aspiring immigrants anew.

But other people, like the one-legged New York City journalist, Charles Fenno Hoffman, were elated not at the thought of material resources, but because they had come to believe that America's most precious resource was in her magnificent, untouched natural scenery. To men like Hoffman, news of the Adirondacks was an addition to the chain of natural wonders that made America a special and superior nation.

Almost as soon as Hoffman read about the Adirondacks and Emmons' survey in the newspapers, he got in touch with guide John Cheney and arranged a tour. Only a month after Emmons had climbed Mt. Marcy, Hoffman was on his way to see if all that wilderness really existed. It did, and like the mountains, valleys, plains, and rivers Hoffman had seen in the West, the Adirondacks convinced him even more persuasively that all the human history of Europe was nothing compared to the grandeur of nature at home. The crumbling cathedrals of the Old World, Hoffman thought, were corrupt, perishable artifacts, while natural scenes such as Indian Pass, Ausable Chasm, and Mt. Marcy mirrored the innocence, goodness, and morality of the New World.

Since it was in the presence of the wildest spots that Hoffman developed his notions of the real American heritage, the natural wilderness, he logically began to link the rawest portions of nature with the purest of American principles. For him, the Adirondacks were among the most precious of all America's assets precisely because they were so primitive and wild.

117

On his first trip to the Adirondacks, Hoffman got as far as Indian Pass, the gorge Richard H. Dana, the American author, ten years later compared favorably to Yosemite Valley. Hoffman wanted very much to climb Mt. Marcy but reluctantly decided his single leg was not up to the task. There were other tests of skill and endurance though, and Hoffman's account of his trip was a first in what became a virtual industry, adventure stories about sojourns in the Adirondacks.

In addition to admiring the gigantic pines, Hoffman experienced the agonies and pleasures of camping out. There was the fresh aroma of evergreen trees, the hush of the forest, the sparkle of lakes. There was also rain. One night the fire would keep going out. Then, when a good blaze was achieved, thanks to John Cheney's skill, the wind would shift, blowing great clouds of smoke into the campers' faces and forcing them to run from the fire. They all shivered "as if in an ague" during long, damp, cold nights. But that was part of the adventure and the fun, or at least it became so in the telling.

Hoffman's book about the Adirondacks, *Wild Scenes in the Forest*, was published in 1839 and was followed by others. An ailing minister, Joel T. Headley, praised the healing powers of the forest as well as the beauties of nature in *The Adirondacks: or Life in the Woods*, published in 1849. Such books and dozens of magazine articles by others who shared Hoffman's almost religious belief in American nature helped spread the gospel of nature and the Adirondacks' plentiful share in it.

By the summer of 1858, when a group of nine middle-aged men carrying bags and books arrived at the tiny settlement later known as Keeseville, only about five miles from Lake Champlain, visitors were no longer a novelty. The few farmers on the fringes of the High Peaks had taken to putting up visitors in their houses in exchange for a few extra dollars. Men like John Cheney could count on summer jobs guiding sportsmen, finding deer and trout, and making camps for them. There was, by 1858, nothing especially unusual, though as yet nothing routine either, about sportsmen or nature lovers seeking out the Adirondacks as an excellent place to hunt and fish and relax.

But this one group was different. The most eminent scientists of the day were included. Ralph Waldo Emerson was there. James Russell Lowell, the poet and essayist, came, too. And most startling for being the most famous, Louis Agassiz was there. Agassiz was the Harvard geologist who turned down lucrative and prestigious positions in his native Europe to stay in America where he lectured and collected birds and rocks. The whole community turned out to see and honor Agassiz.

"The figures are small, nature large," William Verner wrote of Sanford R. Gifford's 1864 painting, *Twilight in the Adirondacks*. The art and the attitude marked a shift in Americans' view of nature and the Adirondacks. *Photo courtesy of The Adirondack Museum, Blue Mountain Lake, New York*

A journalist and artist, William James Stillman, who had recently moved to Cambridge, Massachusetts, and was in the habit of spending summers in the Adirondacks, had invited these eminent Bostonians and Harvard professors to share his discovery of the wild mountains. He had gone to a great deal of trouble for his friends, hiring the best guides—eight for the ten men in the group—renting boats and other camping equipment for each person, and choosing what he believed to be the best spot, near a remote lake, "out of the line of travel," where the group could experience the most genuine wilderness and escape from the "daily groove."

Emerson had written *Nature* nearly twenty-five years earlier. The book had been reprinted in 1849, and his ideas that man and nature were joined by some "occult relation," and that "nature is a language" through which man could gain intimacy with God and knowledge of self remained firm in his mind. Furthermore, Emerson had been spreading these ideas across the country when he lectured to lyceums, schools, and community groups. (His primary source of income came from lecturing.) Stillman was especially eager to witness Emerson's reaction to the Adirondacks where nature, being at its wildest, was doubtless most eloquent.

Emerson was enchanted. The laws of nature, which had no rival in the great forest, seemed to make humans as free as the birch and pine trees, "All dressed, like Nature, fit for her own ends," as he wrote in a poem about his Adirondack adventure. "To feed this wealth of lakes and rivulets,/So Nature shed all beauty lavishly/From her redundant horn."

These sophisticated, worldly men were stripped of all pretension, all masks, as Stillman hoped they would be. Released from all society's constraints and responsibilities, the "pure personality" of each man, in Stillman's words, was revealed.

No personality shone forth with such purity as Emerson's, in Stillman's opinion. "He rises above all his contemporaries." He was insatiably curious, "the great student." He explored the woods and lakes as if not to miss a ripple or leaf or breeze that might be another clue to spiritual information or understanding. He several times asked to go out in a boat in the evening to see again how the tops of the pines bent eastward from the constant pounding of wind. That aspect of nature, no less than any other, was bound to be instructive. Every tree, every worm, every flower, every man, especially perhaps the guides who fascinated Emerson, was potentially an intermediary between God and man.

That such transcendence seemed most possible in the presence of wilderness was confirmed in the minds of Emerson and Stillman during that meeting of what came to be known as the "Philosophers Club," on the shores of Follensby Pond. "In the woods we return to reason and faith," Emerson had written in *Nature*. "There I feel that nothing can befall me in life . . . which nature cannot repair." The Adirondack wilderness renewed that sense in Emerson, lifted and inspired him as love or religion does in other men. "This image of Emerson claiming kinship with the forest stands out alone," Stillman wrote. "To *be*, as Emerson was, is absolute and complete existence."

The urge to *be* and to experience such existence in the presence of wilderness grew among millions of other people in the years after 1858. Many vacationers did the same thing the Philosophers Club members did. They chose an isolated spot in the mountains, settled by a lake or pond or stream, walked, fished, hunted, read, and relaxed. Groups of people bought land and built "camps," as both lean-to's and lavish mansions were called in the Adirondacks. "Going up to camp," became almost synonymous to "going to the Adirondacks."

One prominent Boston family, for instance, built a camp in the High Peaks region in the early 1900s. Their little enclave grew to include six roomy buildings, a main lodge for dining and gathering after dinner, separate bed cottages for each family member and guest cottages, too. Their summer vacation entourage always included at least two servants to do the cooking and washing. Yet they always spoke of "going to camp." Later, after the property was sold and the family scattered, one of the sons built a summer cottage in New Hampshire. Although he was in New England and in a setting quite different from the old one in the Adirondacks, he never broke the habit of calling his New Hampshire cottage a "camp" and of planning repairs or improvements "up at camp." Removed from the Adirondacks, the words seemed strange.

What this and many other families sought was fulfillment of the need Emerson and his colleagues had defined so many years earlier, "the love of nature." It was part of the profound "influence of liberalism [that] went far beyond those who embraced it as a faith," historian Samuel Eliot Morison wrote of Emerson's transcendentalism. Indeed, Emerson was often accused of being an atheist or worse. Yet transcendentalism, a word which other scholars imposed upon Emerson's ideas (he himself never used it), was onto something its originators anticipated and to a large degree guided. Ordinary people discovered a need to escape the streets and cities, noise and clutter of the culture they had worked so hard to build. They wanted to renew a sense of pioneering, to pit themselves against nature perhaps as their ancestors had done, but by so doing, achieve a closer relationship to nature.

However, the urge to escape, if only for a few weeks each year, while sanctioned by America's most respected philosopher, remained for many years an uncomfortable if powerful yearning. To want to return to wilderness so soon after it had been conquered required some logical compromises. Nature had for so long been an enemy. To befriend it, people needed some good, practical reasons.

Most Americans in the middle of the nineteenth century were noted not for their love of nature, but for their energy, enterprise, and inventiveness. Even those who could afford it seldom indulged in luxuries like vacations. Pleasure was in doing, signs of relaxation were practically nonexistent. Perhaps this was what Charles Dickens, touring the United States in 1842, noted as the "prevailing seriousness and melancholy air of business." Dickens felt that Americans needed a "wider cultivation of what is beautiful, without being eminently and directly useful." European visitors commented on the astonishing absence of recreational facilities in the United States. Even sports were virtually unknown. Only horse racing and cock fighting could be considered typical pastimes, and these indulgences compensated enthusiasts by providing the illusion of profit potential.

In an age when usefulness was the purpose of nearly everything —even science before the Civil War in the United States was devoted to invention, not to pure research or the advancement of knowledge for its own sake—recreation for its own sake entered the minds of only a few. But if a good reason for travel or vacation could be put before people, many were likely to acknowledge that, after all, one did need a rest now and then and a change of scenery, if only to be propelled to greater industry and productivity upon one's return.

In the late decades of the nineteenth century, many persons began to want recreation. However, they had to find a way to square their new emotional embrace of nature and their desire to understand it with the older, practical necessity of subduing nature for survival and profit.

One bridge between a lingering need to subjugate nature and a burgeoning need to appreciate it was the idea that nature could bring people closer to God. Growing numbers of people were thus able to justify trips to wilderness areas and to acknowledge the possible benefits derived from leaving such areas alone rather than using them as commercial resources.

Some may have realized that people like Emerson had been trying to say all this for a long time. But just who said it mattered less, perhaps, than the fact that more and more people had time and money enough to take vacations and indulge in what was once considered to be unconscionable frivolity.

In 1858, the year the Philosophers Club met for the first time at Follensby Pond, more money was deposited in American savings banks than at any previous time. Within two years, the amount had more than tripled—one sign among dozens that growing amounts of money were accumulating in the nation.

The Civil War, devastating in so many ways, prodded northern industry into undreamed-of levels of productivity. Instead of slacking off at war's end, industry simply kept going. Even given the ensuing boom-and-bust cycles of the postwar era and the cruel reality that the rewards of increased productivity were not spread evenly over the population, the fact was that there was more money around in 1865 than any time before. During the next ten years, the money grew at an unbelievable rate, and so did the ways of using it.

In 1869, for example, the golden spike was hammered into the ground near Salt Lake City to connect East and West via the Central and Union Pacific railroads, and Jay Gould cornered the gold market. (While he nearly bankrupted the United States Government by buying up almost all the gold there was, he managed a cool $11 million profit in one day.) Cornelius Vanderbilt acquired every inch of the New York Central and Hudson River railroads, making him king of the extremely valuable route between New York City and Buffalo. The United States Government instituted an eight-hour workday for federal employees, and the Noble and Holy Order of the Knights of Labor formed with the purpose of helping "all those who toil," both events that led to improvements in working conditions and better wages for average Americans. Between 1859 and 1869 there had been nearly 80 percent more factories built than in any previous decade, and approximately one hundred thousand new businesses started.

Philosophy, for those inclined to it, had time and space to spread, and philosophy and practicality converged on the Adirondacks. Despite Emerson's own fears and distrust about "things and too much money," it was the abundance of both that enabled more and more people to take his advice and see nature. New York's prosperous decades after the Revolutionary War, when the rush to conquer the wilderness took off, had actually discouraged movement into the Adirondacks. Nearly 100 years later, the post–Civil War boom inspired many thousands of people to go into the Adirondacks, both for profit and pleasure. Money gave people the opportunity to love nature, sometimes even while they were exploiting it.

Into this situation entered the Reverend William Henry Harrison Murray. In 1865, he was a young, handsome minister in Connecticut, not far from the town of Guilford, where he had grown up on a farm. As a teenager he had conquered a disconcerting stammer, and by the time he was twenty he was noted as an electrifying speaker.

His oratory and zeal, his direct manner and his legendary energy —he could go on a hunting trip for two days, without sleep and show up at the pulpit to deliver a sermon that had everyone in the church alive with religious conviction — made him famous in New England. His language was filled with metaphors and similes drawn from the natural world, as would have pleased Emerson, whom, in fact, Murray was later to know.

But if Emerson was an armchair philosopher, Murray was a doer. Good preaching, he wrote, depended not on books or intelligence or culture but on "personal force, power, sympathy, authority individualized." In a sense, Murray was a sort of religious Jay Gould, who in the business world symbolized the era when unfettered individualism was almost universally applauded.

Murray was definitely a go-getter and an individualist. "A church under good preaching," he wrote in a volume about how to succeed as a minister, "is like a pond of water when a breeze is on it; it is full of movement and ripple. Timid preaching makes stagnant churches."

Murray was accused of many things, but timidity was never one of them. If his parishioners wondered at his knack for making the natural world seem somehow a model for Christianity, they probably didn't know that in the early 1800s—at whose suggestion is not known—Murray had taken to visiting the Adirondacks. There his personal authority and energy, his farm-taught skills with guns and fishing rods, and his deep love of nature could be exerted to the full in an atmosphere more challenging than any pulpit. In turn, he brought his memories and his renewed energies from the wilderness to his pulpit.

Like Emerson before him, Murray was enchanted by the Adirondacks. He was more a sportsman than Emerson and did not hesitate to kill deer or bear. In fact, little brought him more pleasure. But true to his profession and time, Murray always made a point of emphasizing the spiritual refreshment received in the wilderness.

So thrilled was he by these weeks each summer in the Adirondacks that he began to publish vivid articles about them for a local Connecticut newspaper. His stories, descriptions, and tall tales were in the tradition of Headley and Hoffman and described lofty mountain scenery and a thousand lakes, an atmosphere as pure as Eden's, "refined and bracing." He wrote of the restorative qualities of the air. Almost any ailment could be cured, he claimed, if only a person could breathe the air of the evergreen-clothed mountains.

The adventures he wrote about were exciting, too. He told of narrow escapes running rapids in slender canoes, of silvery ghosts who appeared on moonlit lakes, of fish almost jumping out of the water into one's boat, of colorful native guides who carried canoes and cooked and made camps, and of the peace within uninhabited stretches of virgin forest.

Murray's articles, often printed with his sermons, portrayed the Adirondacks as a paradise. Just how revolutionary such a portrayal was, in terms of American history, is hard to express. But compare it to the

The Rev. W. H. H. "Adirondack" Murray in 1871. *From William H. H. Murray, Adventures in the Wilderness (Syracuse: Syracuse University Press, 1970)*

account of Father Jogues, the seventeenth-century missionary who suffered desperately in the wilderness and turned to God who he believed was above all nature. Murray experienced renewed life and firmly believed God was *in* nature.

Although Murray did not speak of Emerson's "occult relationships" between man and nature, with his vigor and all the overstatement of successful revivalist preaching (to which school Murray was proud to belong), he imparted essentially the same idea.

Murray said that the wilderness brought God close to the human heart in ways the plowed field or the city street could never accomplish. The soul, in direct contact with a mountain or a remote lake, a storm or a brilliant sunrise, "escaped the bonds of formal worship, [and] for the first time tasted of freedom and tested [the soul's] capacity to soar." In short, Murray wrote, "in the mountains . . . you see Him."

By 1868 Murray's reputation as an orator had spread to Boston. He was invited to become minister to one of the city's wealthiest and most socially prominent congregations, the Park Street Congregational Church. It was one of the highest honors available to a Protestant minister, and Murray, still fairly young, accepted happily.

Bostonians liked him, and he made friends with many of the rich, eminent citizens. He came to know a publisher with the prestigious firm of Ticknor and Fields (Emerson's publisher) and on the spur of the moment one day, gave him copies of his Connecticut newspaper articles.

At first, the publisher was cool. But after rereading the collection of tales about the woods in northern New York, changed his mind and told Murray that he could "not recall . . . anything just like" his descriptions of nature and wilderness adventure. The next spring, 1869, Murray's slender volume *Adventures in the Wilderness, or Camp Life in the Adirondacks* appeared.

If Emerson's book of about the same length, *Nature*, articulated what was a smoldering, even elite revolution in an American attitude towards nature, Murray's book, published thirty years later, was like a good advertisement, exactly in step with its time. Sprinkled with outspoken, conventional religious messages and, most of all, vigorous, informative tales—quite simply a good read—*Adventures* hit the bookstores just when citizens in the eastern states, still depressed from the emotional turmoil of the Civil War, longing for recreation, more affluent than ever, but still needing a darn good reason for vacations, seemed almost to be waiting for it.

Murray's book gave them that reason. Hundreds of copies sold within a few weeks, despite the fact that the better reviewers condemned it as silly. *Adventures in the Wilderness* was reprinted ten times in three months. Within two months of its publication, the book's popularity was translated into fact: literally thousands of people, from places like Boston, New York City, Rochester, Providence, and Buffalo, were packing up in preparation for their own adventures in the Adirondacks.

One of the most extraordinary events in Adirondack history took place that summer of 1869, only two months after Murray's book appeared. The year before perhaps a few hundred people had gone into the Adirondack woods. In 1869, though no statistics are completely reliable, the number apparently tripled, perhaps quadrupled. Murray himself estimated three thousand visitors.

At the time there were about fifty places where tourists could stay in all the mountains. People fought each other for beds and meals. Those who made it into the remote sections, found others had gotten there first, reaping the trout and grabbing whatever shelter could be found. In addition, that summer turned out to be particularly rainy. Many visitors found not stretches of virgin forest, but burned out, logged over hills. Murray had managed to leave out descriptions of such depressing pockets left over from human enterprise.

Those who managed to hire the infrequent and irregular wagons to get to Saranac Lake, Lake Placid, Long Lake, or other spots Murray recommended, often did not find the rough, mountain guides helpful or cheerful or cheap, if they could find anyone at all to steer them through the wilder parts of the mountains. Others found they didn't especially enjoy the out-of-doors after all, or the black flies or mosquitoes. Their imaginations were prepared for appreciating the wilderness and finding God in the trees, but their desk jobs, comfortable homes, their growing dependence upon certain luxuries left their bodies unprepared for carrying canoes between lakes, stalking deer in the woods, building fires and surviving in the wilderness, never mind enjoying such labor.

Many spent a miserable summer. Drenched in cold rains, exhausted from rides in crude carts over ruts in the rock (the paths could hardly be called roads), they were furious that someone like Murray had managed to allow them to waste their precious time and money. Many roundly condemned the author who had promised so much. Their cash thrown away, their lives reduced, not uplifted, a horde of disappointed, angry people poured out of the Adirondacks the same summer they had gone in so hopefully. Many wrote letters to their newspapers complaining.

For the second time in history the Adirondacks hit the news. Thirty years earlier, the Emmons survey had been big news. In 1869, the Adirondacks were news again, this time controversial. It was an era when newspapers thrived on sensation. News had to be "terse, colorful, entertaining, dramatic," as social historian Arthur Schlesinger described it, and "withal, afford the reader a romantic respite from the daily grind."

Millions got such satisfaction from reading about the Adirondacks. Attacks on Murray and counterattacks appeared. Articles and letters protesting Murray's dishonest enthusiasm for what some regarded as a mosquito-infested, black fly-ridden, damp, inhospitable jungle of the north were answered by defenders who saw a natural paradise. Many sportsmen who had been going to the wilderness for years were appalled by the arrival of new people who frightened the deer and threatened the trout. They wrote equally vituperative letters and articles about the un-prepared, unappreciative hordes invading their precious wilderness. Nearly everybody, it seemed, was mad at Murray, except for the railroad companies whose lines went near the mountains. They had never had quite such a season.

The controversy stayed hot for a year, feeding tempers and editors who milked it for all it was worth. Murray never really recovered from it all. He resigned his Boston church, established his own congrega-tion, lost his money, and drifted from Texas to Montreal. Though he lived to be quite an old man and died in Connecticut in the house where he had been born, he became another Adirondack personality, with Gilliland and Henderson and Herreshoff, to meet an unkind fate as a result of a close association with the Adirondacks.

But the episode in Adirondack history he precipitated brought the northern New York mountains to the attention of millions of people. While "Murray's fools," those whose unrealistic expectations of the Adirondacks were dashed, may have been disappointed, others were not. They came better prepared and discovered, if not God, a certain quiet and happiness in the woods. And before long they had available increas-ing comforts. Within six years of 1869, the number of hotels had grown four-fold. By 1875 there were 200 hostelries, including elegant inns, big hotels with wide porches and sweeping lawns, efficient staffs, and plenti-ful food.

If Americans needed people like Murray to give them a justifiable reason for going to the Adirondacks, many, once there, found reasons for staying and for going back. "Murray's fools" may have received a lot of publicity, but they didn't discourage what eventually became a torrent of visitors.

By the 1880s the Adirondacks had become one vast resort. The mountains both inspired people to appreciate nature and provided a magnificent means by which ordinary and well-to-do people could fulfill their need for wilderness.

In 1836, Emerson had complained that "to speak truly, few adult persons can see nature." Seventy years later, in less than a generation, more than two hundred thousand people went to the Adirondacks dur-ing the summer of 1900 for just such a purpose. If they didn't make a spiritual connection with Emerson's "Universal Being," or share with Murray his Christian rejuvenation, they did begin to learn how to have a wonderful time, at least most of them.

12

A Pound of Flesh

AN EXTRAORDINARILY LARGE NUMBER of the people who have written about the Adirondacks have been invalids. So were a great many of those who began visiting the region during the middle and late 1800s when fresh air and altitude were thought to be restorative.

Alfred Donaldson, a successful but ailing banker from New York City, for example, was sent to the Adirondacks when he was twenty-nine years old to try to defer a sure and early death from tuberculosis. He lived in Saranac Lake to be fifty-seven and in the early 1900s wrote the first comprehensive history of the Adirondacks, two volumes still in use today. But at the end of his life, he was, according to a friend, "the frailest human being I have ever known."

Earlier, Joel Headley, the ever-ailing minister who nevertheless poured out popular volumes on Napoleon and George Washington, as well as articles and books about the Adirondacks, wrote not only some of the first stories of Adirondack wilderness adventure but was also one of the first to publicize the curative powers of the air. Headley's diseases were only vaguely identified. One was called "an attack of the brain," and it was this particular illness that sent him in 1847 to the Adirondacks.

One famous and also frequently ill writer who did not write about, but in, the Adirondacks, was Robert Louis Stevenson. Having heard how healthful the atmosphere was, he decided to spend a season at Saranac Lake in 1887. Immediately upon arriving there in October, despite a "long drive in the rain," as his mother reported, he proclaimed that "he already feels the air of Saranac doing him good."

Eugene O'Neill, the playwright, Christy Mathewson and Larry Doyle, the baseball players, William Morris, the theater agent, and many other famous persons spent time in the Adirondacks for their health.

Illness and accident, as much as enterprise, characterized the nineteenth century. Tuberculosis alone killed one out of every seven people and afflicted even more. Yellow fever, typhus, typhoid, cholera, diphtheria, scrofula, cancer, arthritis, and even ringworm, chillblains, and blisters were all potentially deadly. All baffled the medical profession which was, ironically in an era of fast technological growth, at a distinct low in the half century after the 1850s.

Doctors had once learned from doing, apprenticing at the sides of experienced practitioners. After 1830, however, when American medical schools began to flourish and at the same time founder in a morass of semiscientific quackery and faddism, the quality of medical training and treatment actually declined.

Faith in education had grown. People concluded that since classroom instruction was useful for farmers, businessmen, lawyers, and teachers, then surely it would be beneficial for doctors. In a misguided attempt to be scientific, most medical schools limited their one-to-two year courses to lectures, drawings, and oral quizzes featuring such questions as, "What is pain a symptom of?"

One young doctor, Edward Livingston Trudeau, who later became famous for his precise laboratory work (but not because he learned the skills in medical school), remembered that when he took his first job, as head of a hospital in New York City, "I had never before that time had the slightest practical experience in seeing and treating illness and injuries at the bedside." His training was typical.

Superstition, cultism, and mystical theory were the foundations for early nineteenth-century medicine. Even among the Transcendentalists, who were usually devoted to science and learning, health fads were as contagious as diseases. Bronson Alcott, who grew up with Emerson and was one of his colleagues in Concord, Massachusetts, and was Louisa May's father, believed firmly that no one should eat hot or cold food, only tepid fare, without seasoning. Catherine Beecher, another New England intellectual and Harriet Beecher Stowe's sister, advocated in her many books on how to be healthy and upright the presentation of only one dish at any meal, and the one dish should be eaten slowly, without seasoning.

Clothing as well as food was often chosen for its health value instead of for comfort or pleasure. Beecher, for example, believed that flannel underwear was a good preventive measure against malaria and other "unhealthy miasmas" since it absorbed perspiration and "matter thrown off by the body which would otherwise accumulate on its surface." Some mothers took her a bit too literally. In autumn they put their children into suits of flannel and stitched the last seams where buttons otherwise might have been; hundreds of youngsters spent all winter swaddled in the same unwashed flannel.

Vegetarians (in an age before vegetables could be preserved), exercise enthusiasts, even architects proclaimed the virtues of all sorts of methods for keeping fit. Bathing in salt water, living in octagonal houses built with cement, and other "cures" for illness were widely practiced.

Good health was everyone's dream, but few could boast it. When Thomas Jefferson was born, his father's first and most fervent prayer was that the boy be healthy. Rugged, vigorous farmers and pioneers as well as sedentary ladies were equally prone to illness, and millions of people understandably latched onto any hope—from sleeping porches to herbs —that might make them feel better.

Two of the most enduring panaceas for disease control were mineral water and fresh air. Fresh air treatment, though, was controversial. Many felt too much air, especially cool air, was bad, particularly for consumptives who, as a result, were kept cooped up in windowless rooms. Some, however, like Sylvester Graham, a health reformer who invented the Graham cracker, advocated open windows at night so that the sick and healthy alike could get enough oxygen.

Thousands remembered the ideas of Dr. Benjamin Rush, one of America's most active, versatile figures of the eighteenth century. Among other things, he was a signer of the Declaration of Independence, author of the first American textbook on hygiene and the first on chemistry, an advocate of the abolition of slavery and a publicist for the abolition of capital punishment, and a crusader for women's rights, universal education, sympathetic treatment of the mentally ill, and temperance. Rush recommended vigorous exercise, especially horseback-riding, since he thought the inhalation of horse odors was beneficial to diseased lungs. He also believed fresh air was good for tuberculars.

Mineral springs were a less controversial treatment for ill health. Europeans had long been in the habit of spending time at springs such as those at Baden-Baden in Germany, where people both drank and bathed in sulphurous or carbonated water for every conceivable kind of complaint. In America, patronizing certain springs was an important colonial activity. In Virginia, Georgia, South Carolina, Pennsylvania, Rhode Island, and New York, mineral springs became meeting places for influential (and often ailing) persons. In his *The Americans* J. C. Furnas notes that some observers believed that the very popularity of spas enabled persons from all over the colonies to meet and exchange ideas and establish a solidarity of purpose which ultimately led to the Revolution. The spas were bridges between otherwise isolated, provincial populations.

In 1767, Sir William Johnson, a British agent who forged alliances with many American Indian groups, discovered the healing qualities of a spring only fifty miles or so north of Albany, New York. He was supposedly taken there by his Mohawk friends who called the spot "Saraghoga." In 1802, a shrewd pioneer by the name of Gideon Putnam built a hotel near the springs, and Saratoga became one of the most popular and prestigious spas in the East.

Some say that Saratoga was the gateway to the Adirondacks. Businessmen, bored by the social frivolities of the season, noticed the endless acres of lumber stretching northward behind the hotels and inns. Sportsmen, feeling constrained in their black broadcloth frockcoats, stiff, boiled shirts, tightly wound silk ties, wool-lined capes and high beaver hats — the appropriate dress of gentlemen on vacation in Saratoga in summer—looked longingly beyond the porches of fancy hotels to where the freedom of the wilds beckoned. Women, bound in stays and encircled with hoop skirts, shared the fantasy that in the mountains they might be free to dress and behave more casually.

Invalids, taking the Saratoga waters or cooped up in stuffy rooms, heard from people like Sylvester Graham that fresh air was actually good for them, especially fresh mountain air. A few heard about a daring physician in Elizabethtown, who in the late 1700s had left the Lake Champlain area for the higher mountains and had recovered from tuberculosis, "the T.B.," as many North Country people called the dread, incurable disease.

But it was Murray's book that spread not just the Adirondack gospel, but the promise of health in the air. Murray's idea was that the air in the Adirondacks was not only clean, but special. It was his contention, one shared by some others, that the thick evergreen trees, especially the balsam fir, filtered and cleansed the air of impurities, much as certain air conditioners today remove smoke and cooking odors. He also believed the very fragrance of the conifers possessed "healing odors [that] penetrated [a patient's] diseased and irritated lungs."

The Adirondacks could also soothe what Murray called "that dire parent of ills," what others called dyspepsia, a kind of general ailment usually having to do with stomach and bowel trouble. The air, the exercise, and peace restored intestines to good working order, Murray thought, and the appetite to healthy hunger. Starch and fats composed the bulk of the American diet in those days. And since Americans tended to gobble up their johnny cakes (cornbread), pies, and potatoes with notable speed and cheerlessness, often encouraging their children to eat as quickly and silently as possible, it does not seem surprising that indigestion, constipation, and other digestive problems were common. Another common disease of the digestive tract was dysentery, the only known cure for which was stuffing the bowels with ice. If breathing clean air was an equally effective antidote, anyone with even a few cents to spare was likely to choose the air over the ice.

While the typical Adirondack menu was hardly more varied or healthful than anywhere else, consisting as it did largely of meat and fish, mainly venison and trout, the region did acquire the reputation for fattening people up.

Excessively thin people were thought to be sickly and often were in the days before thin was chic. One of the illustrations in *Adventures in the Wilderness* showed a before-and-after image of a young man. He arrived emaciated, pale, bent over, and sickly. After a summer in the Adirondacks, he left with glowing pink cheeks, erect posture, and at least fifty new pounds,.as well as a fishing rod and a smile.

"The American conscience," the writers of the WPA-funded *New York: A Guide to the Empire State* noted "accepted ill-health as a basis for compromise with leisure, and when nature withheld this excuse it had to be spuriously affected." Those who couldn't quite justify going off to the woods and mountains for pleasure or in search of God *could* cite the promise of improved health. Others, genuine invalids, undertook the journey in crude carriages over rough roads in search of relief, often as a last resort.

After 1869 more and more people were brought to the Adirondacks on stretchers for the summer. Before the 1890s, tuberculosis and other diseases were not thought to be contagious so few worried about infection from the pale, coughing, feverish visitors.

In October 1875, one of these visitors shocked those who were accustomed to the stream of invalids by deciding to stay in the Adirondacks for the winter. That person was a desperately ill doctor, weak, depressed, and hopeless after a two-year struggle with tuberculosis. He had spent the summer at the hotel of Paul Smith, a guide who had opened an inn near St. Regis Lake. When it came time to go home, the physician, knowing better than anyone how serious his illness was and how futile it was to hope for a cure, decided he was "tired of going from place to place" searching for health. He loved the Adirondacks, and he proposed to forego the long, uncomfortable journey back to New York City and to stay in the mountains winter or no winter.

Everyone thought he was crazy. Paul Smith and his wife were

Cartoon captioned "Before and after going to the Adirondacks," from *Harper's New Monthly Magazine*, August 1870. *From William H. H. Murray, Adventures in the Wilderness (Syracuse: Syracuse University Press, 1970)*

sure he would die toward the middle of February when the ground would be too hard for burial. The medical profession, though divided on the usefulness of fresh air for consumptives, was nearly unified in its fear of cold air as sure to kill a sick person.

But the ailing doctor was convinced he was dying anyway and wanted to be where he could die in congenial surroundings. He had been better after two summers in the Adirondacks. At least he would be happy if not better there in winter.

The doctor was the now-famous Edward Livingston Trudeau whose experiment as a winter patient was a success. He stayed in the Adirondacks, regained enough strength to return to work, set up a practice in the mountains, and devoted much of the rest of his life to developing new methods of treating tuberculosis. He built the world-famous sanatorium for tuberculars at Saranac Lake, first called the Adirondack Cottage Sanatorium (later the Trudeau Sanatorium), which was the first of its kind in the United States.

Advances in medical science in the 1800s were usually accidental. Doctors did not know what germs were or even that they existed. In fact, after Louis Pasteur, the French chemist, discovered the existence of germs, few doctors immediately accepted his theories that diseases were living organisms or bacteria. Trudeau had never heard of germs or the word "pathology," the study of the cause and nature of disease, until his middle age. Effective treatments were often used for the wrong reasons (as were, of course, the more typical, ineffective treatments). It was a matter of "long-term benefits from misbegotten science," as social historian J. C. Furnas described the process of trial and error and accident by which medicine inched its way along.

One of Trudeau's most profound insights into the treatment of tuberculosis was the theory that *rest* helped. It sounds simple and obvious, but the conscious inclusion of rest in a regimen for the tubercular was completely overlooked until Trudeau introduced a theory based on personal and purely accidental experience.

He loved to hunt and had what he called "hunting blood." One of the reasons Trudeau had chosen to go to the Adirondacks when his disease was diagnosed as hopeless was that he wanted to spend his last days doing what brought him the most pleasure, hunting deer, loons, rabbits, foxes, almost anything. Only a day after his arrival at Paul Smith's hotel for the first time, in the summer of 1873, exhausted, thin, and racked with coughing, Trudeau was out in a boat, rigged up as much like a bed as possible. With the boat spread with balsam boughs and blankets and with a gun at his fingertips, Trudeau was delighted to be able to shoot a deer from his boat-bed. He never passed up an opportunity to go hunting, and the guides managed to devise wheelchairs and stretchers, special boats, and easy journeys so that he could be carried into the woods when he couldn't walk.

Once, when Trudeau felt especially weak and feverish, but unable to resist a foray into the winter woods to hunt fox, he noticed, in his own words, "I could not walk enough to stand much chance for a shot without feeling sick and feverish the next day." He also observed that if he did *not* walk much, but rested instead, he felt much better. "This was the first intimation I had as to the value of the rest cure."

Much of Trudeau's future success in treating thousands of patients was based on that simple deduction: he did not feel feverish and weak if he did not walk or exercise much. Abstinence from exercise, he concluded, must be helpful.

Trudeau continued to believe, too, that the air in the Adirondacks was healthful. It was better to sit quietly and breathe Adirondack air than to breathe just any air. He thought that large doses of ozone, a component of oxygen, existed in the wooded atmosphere and that the resinous fragrance of the evergreen trees was beneficial to diseased lungs.

Trudeau, once he was well enough, began to take care of many of the summer patients who came to the Adirondacks for relief. He opened his sanatorium at Saranac Lake in 1884. At first it consisted of only one cottage, big enough for two beds. Here he planned to help those who couldn't afford to pay for their room and board at hotels or boarding houses. His first patients at the sanatorium were two factory girls.

The "Wilderness Cure" became famous. Other sanatoriums opened near Saranac Lake, and the Adirondacks came to symbolize, if not a certain cure, at least definite hope for those afflicted with tuberculosis. Trudeau's methods — fresh air, rest, restrained exercise, decent food — enabled about a quarter of his sanatorium patients to recover. Others, wrapped in blankets, sitting in the deck chairs that came to be called "Rondeckers" on the porches of the cottages, winter and summer, survived a great deal longer than they might otherwise have. And, of course, many others, far advanced in their illness, had to ask themselves hard questions about the future. The poet Adelaide Crapsey, who spent her last years at Saranac Lake before she died at the age of thirty-six, spoke for many when she contemplated the graveyard on the sanatorium grounds. She wrote: "Why are you there in your straight row on row/Where I must ever see you from my bed/That in your mere dumb presence iterate/The text so weary in my ears: 'Lie still/And rest; be patient and lie still and rest.'"

This portrait of the Beloved Physician, Edward Livingston Trudeau, was taken at Christmas, 1903. *Photo courtesy of the Saranac Lake Free Library, Adirondack Collection*

Trudeau was a pioneer in the treatment of tuberculosis; he was not the originator of the most successful cure. His idea about rest was indeed scientifically valid, but it turned out that he was off the mark about the air. In fact, the older idea that air was dangerous was closer to the truth since the discovery of bacteria led to the knowledge that many bacteria are airborne.

Trudeau did accept the germ theory, however, and in 1882 was elated to learn that a German physician by the name of Edward Koch had isolated the particular bacterium that caused tuberculosis, the tubercule bacillus. Trudeau set up a tiny laboratory, at first only a closet in his Saranac Lake house, and spent every free moment he had experimenting, looking for a cure for the disease. He never succeeded, to his profound disappointment. Indeed, two of his own children died of tuberculosis before Trudeau finally did in 1916.

But his laboratory experiments enabled him to diagnose tuberculosis in its early stages and with complete accuracy. He improved sanitary conditions at the sanatorium and later founded the Saranac Laboratory for the Study of Tuberculosis, one of the first and best research centers of its kind in the world.

Until the twentieth century and the introduction of powerful drugs, however, Trudeau's methods were by far the most successful of any used. By 1920, only four years after the good doctor's death, his sanatorium was treating more than 2,000 patients in 150 cottages, some large, others small, on grounds with landscaped gardens, an ornate front gate, administration buildings, a well-equipped infirmary, and an up-to-date laboratory. Trudeau's hospital gave mountain air *and* the best scientific research an equal chance to aid the sick. And Americans, once inclined to see nature as the arbiter of evil and danger, turned willingly to nature in the Adirondacks in search of succor and health.

Few dilemmas have been so confusing to those dealing with the problem of man's relationship to nature as disease. Should nature be placated or altered? Is disease as natural as health? Or is it an aberration from natural processes?

The rise of modern science seemed to give man an answer at last. By discovering accurate, effective means by which to control disease, scientists were often inclined to think man had proved himself more powerful than nature.

The Trudeau experiment in the Adirondacks spanned the transition phase between "primitive" medicine and the enormous leaps in scientific discovery that followed Pasteur's proof in the 1860s of the existence and importance of bacteria. Gonorrhea, typhoid, diphtheria, infection from wounds, puerperal fever, and dozens of other once-fatal afflictions were curable by 1900. When Trudeau first went to the Adirondacks, he could not have cured one of these illnesses although he had had what was considered to be excellent medical training.

The shift made a great difference to the village of Saranac Lake. Like so many other Adirondack towns, it had begun as a poor, pioneering

The earliest known photograph of Saranac Lake was taken in 1877 from the Saranac River. *Photo courtesy of the Saranac Lake Free Library, Adirondack Collection*

settlement in the 1830s, inhabited by a few families working hard to carve a meager living from the land. Logging transformed the place in the 1860s. After the publication of William Murray's book in 1869, the hotel—built in 1849 about five miles south of the village—became so crowded that the proprietors had to pitch tents in the yard to accommodate guests. Even before Trudeau came, Saranac was a favorite spot for consumptives; in fact, this encouraged Trudeau to move there. By 1880 the village had about 100 buildings, a rather bleak accumulation of frame and log structures with barely a single tree or shrub to ease the starkness. Though people swarmed to the Adirondacks to take advantage of nature, the village of Saranac Lake seemed almost bereft of its influence, at least in the way of greenery, in the early days.

In the 1880s, Trudeau and perhaps 100 fellow consumptives had taken up residence all year-round in the village. Many townspeople were able to earn a living tending the sick in boarding houses or, before it was recognized that tuberculosis was contagious, in the hotels.

Arriving invalids couldn't help noticing the increasing number of healthy summertime visitors leaving after the "season" or arriving at its beginning. Saranac Lake had gained a reputation for being an excellent stopping-off place for one of the most popular camping and sporting areas in the Adirondacks. "Our woods still abound with game and our streams and lakes are alive with fish," boasted a writer for *Forest and Stream* magazine in 1881.

Tourists and invalids converged. Even when Saranac Lake came to be regarded as alive with germs as well as fish, and stories flew around about tourists speeding through town, whipping their horses and holding handkerchiefs over their noses, it remained a tourist center of some repute, thanks largely to its good, central location.

Many residents felt deeply ambivalent about the thriving health industry. At once grateful for decent year-round jobs in the sanatoriums but resentful that the town's prosperity depended so heavily on invalids instead of on robust, free-spending sportsmen, some people lamented that at least half the town's year-round income was based on health services.

In 1954, the dilemma vanished. The incidence of tuberculosis as a cause of death had been slashed by more than two-thirds as early as the 1930s. As a result of such great strides in medicine, spurred by Trudeau's own work, new, highly effective drugs had taken the place of rest, and the Trudeau Sanatorium closed, a victim of its own success. Stoneywold and Gabriels sanatoriums, two other well-known clinics in Saranac Lake, closed soon after.

Many people were relieved, others were heartbroken. Few realized that the town of Saranac Lake, the entire Adirondacks for that matter, had long been administering to new illnesses, things like ulcers, heart problems, depression, high blood pressure, tension, all deriving not from germs, but from social and urban conditions. As it happened, many of the methods Trudeau used for treating the tubercular were even more effective in the treatment of the "bacillus urbanum," or the rat-race syndrome.

By the time the Trudeau Sanatorium closed, infectious disease was no longer the leading cause of death in the United States. Nor were physical conditions alone, cancer and heart disease notwithstanding, any longer the primary threats to health in America. Fully one-half of all those in hospitals were suffering from mental illness, a trend that continues to grow.

The Adirondacks came to be seen not as a cure for the body so much as a balm for the mind. In the 1880s, Saranac Lake was known as the town of the second chance. Within twenty years many millions of people had come to think of the whole Adirondack region as the place of the second chance, not entirely for renewed physical well-being, but for the benefit of the human psyche.

13

Roughing It

IN THE SUMMER OF 1900, two hundred and fifty thousand visitors went to the Adirondacks. Some stayed at one of the several enormous, posh hotels and rubbed elbows with the rich and famous of the world. Some stayed in smaller, perhaps more typical, hotels, inns, or boarding houses. Some were invited to private "camps," elegant or crudely rustic.

Nearly everyone hunted or fished. Some went to the Adirondacks just to do so and spent their vacations camping out. Others only took afternoon excursions led by hotel guides. They lolled on lawns and porches or spent lazy hours in special Adirondack boats, part rowboat, part canoe. They rejoiced in comparing views, either from the tops of mountains or from hotel windows.

William Murray's book, *Adventures in the Wilderness*, was still in print as late as the 1890s, and the fame of Adirondack air, scenery, and rustic comfort never stopped growing during the years after its initial publication. General and unprecedented prosperity enabled the widespread, if still novel, belief that a "great intimacy with nature and mother earth could have . . . nothing but a helpful and inspiring influence upon us," as an article in the July 1892 *Ladies Home Journal* put it, to reach millions.

Some historians call the years between 1870 and 1914, when the Adirondacks were among the most fashionable and popular resort regions in the nation, the Gilded Age of the mountains' history.

Who were these people, who fifty years earlier had probably never heard of the Adirondacks? There were Vanderbilts and Astors and other super-rich scions of American society, but there were also a great many people who can be characterized as "comfortable" economically, as

Arthur Fitzwilliam Tait's paintings were reproduced by the millions in Currier and Ives prints. Here, in *A Good Time Coming* (1862),Tait captures a timeless Adirondack scene, genuine "roughing it." *Photo courtesy of The Adirondack Museum, Blue Mountain Lake, New York.*

the well-respected travel book, *Baedeker's Guide to the United States*, published in 1893, reported. Certainly it is true that the beneficiaries of prosperity and philosophy alike who transformed the Adirondacks into such a popular resort area were, for the most part, members of the middle and upper-middle classes.

In spite of a few well-appointed private camps and estates where the very well-to-do recreated — Camp Pine Knot, for instance, a Swiss chalet-inspired compound built by the railroad-rich Durant family, another similar Durant camp bought eventually by J. P. Morgan (who rarely went there), and the summer places of Vanderbilts and their ilk—by far the most typical Adirondack lodging was a modest, wooden frame hotel, housing from 10 to 300 moderately affluent guests.

The Adirondack hotel, whether it was in a town, on a railroad line, or buried deep in the woods and accessible only by stagecoach, was almost always built of wood. Most were frame, though some were of unhewn logs resembling pioneer homes or Swiss mountain cottages. Almost all had porches of some kind, whether they were verandas or simply platforms big enough for a rocking chair or two. And all of them, whether they advertised French chefs and *haute cuisine* or plain country cooking, served the two North Country staples—trout and venison.

Some Adirondack hotels were very comfortable by the standards of the day. The Beede House in Keene Valley, for example, had two buildings, each with verandas on two levels, and total space for 300 guests in 1899, hot and cold running water on every floor, gas lights, "richly finished public rooms and parlors," as well as "the best of spring beds and hair mattresses."

The most luxurious hotel of Adirondack history was Prospect House on Blue Mountain Lake. Though it had a short life, built in 1879–80 and closed in 1903, it was known as the "uncanny wonder of the wilderness." It stood on a point of land jutting into the lake; wide, well-tended lawns ran right down to the water's edge. Double, peaked-roof towers at either end and in the center of the structure, verandas on three levels, space for 500 guests, opulent parlors, and meeting rooms with enormous oriental rugs would have made Prospect House attractive even in New York City. But since it was built in the middle of nowhere, from wood taken from the virgin forest and turned into lumber on the spot, it seemed a miracle. Its own generator provided power for electric lights in each room, and the hotel was said to be the first to install these luxuries, although the Hotel Vendome in Boston made a similar claim. There was an elevator between the six stories, a first-class dining room serving French food (or at least food with French names), regular mail delivery (a feat, since the hotel was thirty miles from the nearest railroad station), bowling alleys, tennis and croquet courts (both new sports in American life near the turn of the century), orchestra performances in the afternoons, steam heat, and a really standout outhouse of two stories with causeways connected to the main building, the last word in convenience.

The Astors, whose fortune derived from old John Jacob, the German immigrant and one-time beaver hunter whose earliest forays for black gold took him not far from the Prospect House site in what was then

The Grandview House in 1912 overlooking Mirror Lake and the village of Lake Placid. S. R. Stoddard's guidebook described the hotel as "nicely furnished,"

the entirely uninhabited, un-named wilderness, sipped tea on Prospect House porches along with Whitneys, Harrimans, Roosevelts, and assorted foreign royalty.

Prospect House was perhaps too fancy. Its management never made profits, and while it was, as historian Harold Hochschild wrote, "probably the most fashionable highland resort in the northern states" between 1882 and 1890, its standards turned out to be too expensive to maintain for the short, two-month summer season.

It was the "good all around" houses, as a guidebook called them, that survived longer and were the backbone of the tourist trade. Places like the Leland House on Schroon Lake, where adequate plumbing, fireplace heat, good, simple food, and reasonable beds were available, or Holland's Blue Mountain Lake Hotel, a respected, pleasant, and far more enduring rival to Prospect House, or several hundred other attractive but not luxurious hostelries were what most Adirondack visitors knew and loved.

Yet a stay at one of these neither very fancy nor very humble places added up to a rather expensive vacation. "Somewhat high," was the judgment of the researchers for the Baedeker guide. To pay for room and board plus the services of a guide to take you on an outing into the woods could easily run more than $9.00 a day in the 1890s. The very best Saratoga Springs hotels, the Grand Union or the United States, both elegant, vast, Victorian structures with ballrooms, crystal chandeliers, breezy piazzas, and wealthy clientele, charged an average $5.00 a day.

Also it was much easier and cheaper to get to Saratoga than to

with "beds of the very best make." Rates were $3–4 a day. *H. M. Beach, Remsen, New York. Photo courtesy of The Adirondack Museum, Blue Mountain Lake, New York*

most of the well-known Adirondack watering spots. Trains ran regularly from New York City to Saratoga in 1893, and the one-way fare was $4.20. Yet it cost a minimum of $8.00 one-way to get from New York City to Plattsburgh, one of the chief gateways to the popular Paul Smith's Hotel on Lower St. Regis Lake, or to the villages of Saranac Lake or Lake Placid. Since the train from New York to Plattsburgh took fourteen hours, most travelers paid an extra $2.00 for a sleeping car. Therefore, it was twice as expensive to get only two-thirds of the way to the Adirondacks as it was to get to Saratoga Springs.

Once you arrived at one of the Adirondack gateways, Utica or Plattsburgh or Saratoga, for instance, a great deal more traveling awaited. Journeys over a series of narrow-gauge railroad, steamboats, or even canoes, and usually stagecoaches and sometimes plain buckboards over rutted roads followed.

One Adirondack regular was a man by the name of Fred Hodges. He had been a society photographer in Boston but gave it all up to live in his native Upstate New York and spend every possible moment in the mountains he had loved as a child and continued to love as an adult. He became one of the most famous photographers of the region and was well known to natives and vacationers alike. His first trip to the Adirondacks took place in 1897, when he was nine years old. His memories of the journey from Rome, New York, to the Cohasset Hotel on Fourth Lake in the Fulton Chain provide a neat, overall view of what "going into the mountains" meant for thousands of people.

"At the old New York Central station in Rome," Hodges wrote,

The Glenmore Hotel, Big Moose, N.Y., near Old Forge. To reach this family hotel, travelers took a steamer from Old Forge to the head of Fourth Lake in the Fulton Chain, then a series of small boats and carries. Getting there was part of the fun.

"we got on the train for Utica. There we changed to the Mohawk and Malone division, destination Thendara, where we again changed cars, this time for Old Forge. From there we walked to the dock and boarded the Steamer 'Fulton,' for the last leg of the trip." (These and other memories are from Hodges' diary, edited and published by another Adirondack writer and photographer, Maitland Desormo.)

Visitors bound for Blue Mountain Lake had an even more varied trip. They had to cross two different lakes, on two steamers, riding a trolley between the two. The Adirondack Museum at Blue Mountain Lake, today one of the nation's best regional museums, portrays the journey in an enchanting diorama.

Many Adirondack vacationers in the Gilded Years remembered the special joys of getting there with nearly as much pleasure as the stay itself. "The mere fact of going on the little steamer [the "Toowahloondah" which plied the waters between Blue Mountain Lake and the Marion River carry] with the vast and reverberatory name is not all there is in this trip, although of itself is a pleasure," wrote the guidebook author S. R. Stoddard in 1889. Something about going deeper and deeper into the woods, slowly, as all boats and coaches went, getting gradually closer to the increasingly wild land, seemed to engulf people, relax their minds and open their hearts. Many lamented the encroachment of better, more

H. M. Beach, Remsen, New York. Photo courtesy of The Adirondack Museum, Blue Mountain Lake, New York

extensive roads and the ultimate convenience, the automobile. Modernity seemed to strip the journey of its romance. Speed of entry deprived people of the delightfully gradual adjustment to mountain ways and scenery, just as the air travel seemed to strip a European vacation of its glamour, much of which was the ocean-liner voyage.

The railroads, however, which crisscrossed the Adirondacks by the 1880s, did give easier access for more and more people of modest to comfortable means, like the Hodges.

Many such people were able to get detailed information about transportation, lodging, cost, activities, and other features of an Adirondack vacation from reading the many guidebooks published during the last quarter of the nineteenth century. "Adirondack" Murray's successors were perhaps more realistic but certainly no less effusive about the Adirondacks. Their works make amusing reading today. Seneca Ray Stoddard and Edwin Wallace, for example, both wrote Adirondack guidebooks full of much flavor and information.

For one thing, both these and other guidebooks warned readers over and over that genuine "roughing it" was only for the experienced woodsmen. Ironically, only the poor and the rich were likely to be skilled enough to undertake such cost-free (or at least inexpensive) jaunts, since the rich had the time and leisure to perfect their hunting and camp-making skills and the poor were often forced to do so. The middle class vacationer needed both guides and hotels, the expensive combination.

To go into the woods without a guide and without practiced woodsman's skills, wrote E. R. Wallace, was "fraught with perplexity, hardship and absolute discomfort. . . . Those who are so unwise as to adopt such a policy invariable do so to their great regret.

But for both devoted woodsmen and city-soft vacationers the Adirondacks had something other resorts lacked. In the Massachusetts Berkshires, for instance, where at Lenox a summer colony of celebrities like Fanny Kemble, the English actress, Henry Ward Beecher, the colorful, charismatic preacher, and writers and intellectuals like Herman Melville, Henry Wadsworth Longfellow, and Edith Wharton spent summers in large, country manors; or in Bar Harbor, Maine, where wealthy Americans developed a special brand of rustic, oceanside opulence; or Newport, Rhode Island, where snob appeal drew many, things other than natural beauty came to dominate the resorts' characters. In the Adirondacks the primary drawing card was always nature.

The scenery, the air, the rolling hills, the vistas, the forests, the wildlife, the birds, these were the compelling features to which hotels, guides, and visitors deferred and for which they came. There was the "air of newness and morning freshness, as if just awakened from a long and refreshing sleep," as guidebook writer E. R. Wallace promised. "The wondrous scenes [that] are revealed by the strong light," "the charmed circle of sublime, ennobling and refreshing influences," such were the phrases used to lure people to the Adirondacks, and such were the things visitors came to look at.

Above all else, perhaps, were the views. The panoramas from Mount Marcy or Tupper Lake or Lake Placid were described over and over with loving attention in every guidebook. Nearly every hotel succeeded or failed on the strength of its views, which guidebooks and advertisements took pains to report.

The artists and writers who helped make the Adirondacks famous came for the same reason, to see, paint, or write about nature. The print-makers, Currier and Ives, reproduced millions of the out-of-doors paintings of Edwin Fitzwilliam Tait, who made scenes of the Adirondacks his special field in the mid-1800s. People such as Mark Train, Somerset Maugham, James Fenimore Cooper, and Edmund Wilson, from their various countries, eras, and perspectives had in common their trips to the Adirondacks, and every one of them wrote about the natural beauty there.

Perhaps more than any resort in America, the Adirondacks represented, indeed embodied, raw nature and all that came to be associated with it—adventure, excitement akin to the pioneers' experience (which after 1850 was already being mythologized), relaxation, peace of mind, change of pace. People went north, traveled for days, paid high prices for the privilege of *seeing* forests, lakes, and mountains. Even those who could not afford the additional expense of hiring guides to take them into the woods, or who didn't want to rough it for real, could sit all day rocking on one of the wide or narrow porches, just looking at nature, drinking it in from a safe, comfortable distance.

Comfort in the wilds, in fact, became more and more available and well advertised. Visitors delighted in rustic but adequate substitutes for cutlery and bedding: pottery mugs and crude forks instead of porcelain or silver set on leaves instead of linen; balsam boughs instead of mattresses excited the imaginations of city-folk. "There is such a novel charm about the old forest, and such a fascination in being removed from ordinary daily life and of living a sort of romantic holiday," wrote Jessamy Harte in the *Ladies Home Journal* in 1892.

No one needed to worry about being uncivilized, Harte took time to explain. Camp clothes were chic, if simple. Dances, even "balls," were held as they were in the city, only they were outside. Meals prepared by the guides were delicious and different. By the end of the nineteenth century, people talked about "roughing it" with tongues in cheeks, for it came to mean being outside but not working very hard at it.

A trip to the wilderness in the Gilded Age was rarely billed as a test of one's survival skills or endurance. "You are presumably out for pleasure," Stoddard remarked. "Do not, therefore, make severe labor" of the trip. Unlike California's Sierra mountains or Wyoming's Tetons, where dedicated mountain climbers and well-trained, self-sufficient nature lovers alone could travel (as was once the case in the Adirondacks), the Adirondacks in their Gilded Age served those whose commitment to nature may have been sincere but whose approach was hardly primitive.

It was not unremitting roughness that made the mountains appealing but comfortable roughness. The camping trip Jessamy Harte described for the *Ladies Home Journal* took place on Long Lake. The spot seemed isolated and remote, with lean-to's, a rustic dining hall without walls, a gorgeous view, and the sense of wilderness. But it was only an hour or so by rowboat from the nearest hotel and near enough to other camps for the outdoor dancing parties, lit by Japanese lanterns hung from trees, to be arranged with ease. (The invitations were written on pieces of birch bark, a touch Harte particularly enjoyed.)

Nature at the end of the nineteenth century was plain fun; and Americans loved to play. It was, as James A. Garfield noted when he campaigned for the presidency in 1880, their "second fight for civilization — what shall we do with our leisure when we get it." In a sense as pleasure replaced religion, even health, as a reason to go to the Adirondacks, the mountains took their place alongside other new diversions sweeping the country: forty different circuses touring the nation in the last quarter of the century, Wild West shows, Sarah Bernhardt, vaudeville, ragtime, religious camp revivals, the Elks, the Moose, the Knights of Pythias, the American Order of Druids and the Concatenated Order of Hoo-Hoo, 5 of more than 500 secret societies whose total membership was more than 6 million people, about the same as the entire population of New York State.

Between 1872 and 1891, roughly the peak of the Adirondacks' Gilded Age, the Audubon Society, Yellowstone National Park, the Metropolitan Opera, the first American Golf Club (in Yonkers, New York), basketball, and the "safety" bicycle—the one with two wheels of equal size — were born, all to accommodate a yearning for entertainment, diversion, and often nature.

Old notions about nature were overturned. In fact, it was the city, once the safe harbor of civilization, the symbol of man's victory over nature, that came to represent the darkness, gloom, danger, and evil once associated with natural wilderness.

City life spawned what was proclaimed in the late 1800s to be the national disease, "neurasthenia," a general term for anxiety and tension, coined by New York City physician George M. Beard, who wrote a book entitled *American Nervousness* in 1881. The widespread use of coal (the fuel that transferred the iron industry from the eastern United States to the South and Midwest) made cities dirtier than the earlier pollution of horse manure and roaming pigs. People were increasingly anxious about their jobs, their bills, their cramped lodgings, and their lack of domestic help in a day before many household conveniences. Personal anxiety among the growing and prosperous middle class was often compounded by concern for the dismal conditions of the poor, whose plight inspired books with such titles as *The City Wilderness*. In New York City more than a million persons lived in thirty-two thousand tenement houses, many of them the notorious dumbbell buildings with central hallways, sunless, windowless rooms, and without heat or water. Social welfare emerged and was preached by a new professional breed, social workers. It was they who dreamed up the idea of summer camps, a concept quickly adopted by the middle class.

Nature was good copy, too, for magazine and newspaper editors. *Forest and Stream* was established in 1873; indeed, general magazines such as *Century, McClure's,* and the venerable *Atlantic Monthly* all published nature articles by the hundreds.

Many forces were at work in the process that transformed the love of nature from a rarefied, intellectual precept into a popular one. Four men stand out as leaders in the movement. Two of these were influenced, as were many other leading conservationists later on, by an association with the Adirondacks. All of them became national, even international figures as they helped reshape Americans' attitudes toward nature.

John Burroughs and John Muir are now revered authors of nature writing. Unlike their intellectual mentors, Emerson and Thoreau, both Muir and Burroughs achieved immense popularity during their lifetimes. Both published books and articles that spread the transcendental gospel, more or less literally, in vivid, real-life style but with a lot more sophistication than William H. H. Murray was ever up to.

John Muir was a Scotsman whose family emigrated to the Wisconsin wilderness in 1849, when young John was eleven years old. He grew up on the frontier farm, working long hours with his father. Instead of nurturing a desire to go to the city, as did many other farm boys of the era, Muir longed for more nature, the wilder the better. Eventually, although he was a talented inventor and mechanic, Muir dedicated his life to living in and writing about wilderness. His works publicized the American wilderness in ways that made people want to get out and hike. And Muir cajoled, enticed, and in some cases demanded that portions of America be set aside as parks.

John Burroughs was in every way a gentler man. He also grew up on a farm, in the Catskill Mountains of New York, and he, too, developed a great love of nature but was never so much the publicist as the acute observer. He once characterized himself as the "insects' Sherlock Holmes." Muir, on the other hand, was more the insects' press agent.

Both actually lived the ideas outlined by Emerson and Thoreau. Muir was outspoken, even shrill in his advocacy of nature as the "conductor of divinity." In the 1890s, he led many battles through the thickets of state and federal bureaucracies to preserve certain of America's remaining wilderness areas. He also did Thoreau one better by living not on the banks of a tame pond but in the Sierra Nevada of California, truly wild, primitive, rocky precipices where only mountain sheep survived easily. He was a vigorous tourist, too, and sought out the wilds of Alaska and other remote spots. His most famous adventure, perhaps, was his thousand-mile walk from Indiana to the Gulf of Mexico in 1867.

Muir carried on a lively correspondence with the aging Emerson.

When Emerson was nearly seventy years old, in 1871, Muir invited him to share "a month's worship with Nature in the high temples of the great Sierra Crown." Emerson stayed in a hotel instead, disappointing Muir enormously.

Burroughs' admiration of Emerson was so profound that his first published articles seemed almost to be direct copies of Emerson's work. The *Atlantic Monthly* editors, in fact, combed through Emerson's work to make sure the younger man had not plagiarized them. And Burroughs, like Emerson, remained more closely in touch with the civilized world. As a young man, he lived in Washington, D.C., where for ten years (1863–73), he worked in a most urban, un-natural job, as a clerk in the currency department of the United States Treasury. Later, he returned to his native Catskills, where he lived and wrote quietly, resumed farming, and sold celery and other crops.

Burroughs always thought of himself, and was considered to be, a man of letters with interests in dozens of fields, including nature. His twenty-six books and his essays that fill twenty-four volumes explore not only nature but also literary criticism, theology, and philosophy. It was he who brought the attention of the public and the literary world to the genius of his close friend Walt Whitman.

For all their differences, Muir and Burroughs did for nature what Murray did for the Adirondacks. Muir spewed out books and transmitted a sense of extreme urgency. "There's a far-away look in his face and eyes," Burroughs wrote of Muir, "as if he saw the heights and peaks beckoning to him." Burroughs was the sensitive person, both to nature and to other men. He was thoughtful, measured in his pace and judgment. He weighed things, pondered them, and shared his thoughts in lovely, graceful language admired today as much for its literary value as for its content. Muir was a polemecist; he was out to make the world change radically and quickly. Muir wanted to shape other people's ideas to make them fit his own. Burroughs wanted to perfect his eye so that he could train his readers' eyes to see nature for themselves. Between the two nearly everyone in search of a better understanding of nature could be satisfied.

One of Burroughs' earliest nature essays, the first in a series to be published by the *Atlantic*, was about the Adirondacks called "With the Birds." Later renamed "The Return of the Birds," this became the first chapter of Burroughs' first book, *Wake-Robin*. Burroughs had discovered the work of John James Audubon, whose drawings and writings about birds rekindled the fascination with ornithology Burroughs had enjoyed since childhood.

In 1863, the summer before he went to Washington and just after his romance with Audubon's work, he took a trip to the Adirondacks. He was "curious," he wrote, "above all else, to know what birds I should find in these solitudes." He was somewhat disappointed to find that relatively few species lived there. The dense forests, the absence of settlements, and the climate discouraged large populations of birds.

But the Adirondacks had other delights for Burroughs. The water and the forests thrilled him. On the shores of a lake he "was conscious of a slight thrill of expectation, as if some secret of Nature might here be revealed." He felt a profound but instructive loneliness, "a dumb kind of companionship; one is little more than a walking tree himself," he imagined. "The woods were Nature's own. It was a luxury to ramble through them—rank and shaggy and venerable, but with an aspect singularly ripe and mellow."

This essay appeared in 1866, three years before Murray's book. Its effect was not so immediate as Murray's but turned out to be far more enduring. People still read *Wake-Robin*, in which "The Adirondacks," another essay about the mountains, is the third chapter. And they still delight in what Burroughs found to be "the wordless intercourse with rude Nature. . . . It is something to press the pulse of our old mother by mountain lakes and streams, and know what health and vigor are in her veins, and how regardless of observation she deports herself."

Burroughs returned often to the Adirondacks after that first trip, his eye ever more acute, his senses ever more attuned to the mountains and their ways. As he grew older, he seems to have appreciated the opportunity to have clean, dry, comfortable hotels where he could sleep in a bed, wash, and find decent food after tramping through the forest. While Burroughs was one of the most devoted of all American nature lovers, he shared with many thousands of other Adirondack visitors a need for both wild nature and civilized comfort. If both could be had at once, as was possible by the late nineteenth century in the Adirondacks, all the better.

Burroughs and Muir gave their contemporary conservationists a great deal of ammunition and data which continue to fuel the efforts to preserve wilderness areas.

There were others in the ammunition factory, too. In 1864, just a year after Burroughs' first trip to the Adirondacks, a man by the name of George Perkins Marsh, a diplomat, scholar, and amateur naturalist from Vermont, finally persuaded his publisher to bring out a book he had been writing for more than seventeen years. The title Marsh wanted to use was "Man the Disturber of Nature's Harmony." The publishers were wary.

Marsh had been known as a linguist and man of letters. He had had three major works published in the early 1800s, and these established for him a fine reputation as a humanist. He counted among his friends many of the most famous people of the day and had in recent years been an ambassador in Turkey and Italy. But his book on natural history, with such a shocking title, was out of his professional line.

Nevertheless, the publishers took a chance with Marsh's work but changed the title to *Man and Nature*. The thesis was that nature is an active, harmonious entity, whereas, the things on which man sets most store—agriculture, industry, architecture—are far from being signs of his superiority. Instead, these are the tools by which he is destroying nature. Man, in Marsh's view, is "to be regarded as essentially a destructive power." Nature, however, is benign.

Man and Nature describes and analyzes the ways man rapes the earth. Marsh combed all history and traveled extensively in his search for evidence. One-third of the book studies forests, how they were stripped from hillsides and flatlands, in China, Greece, and America, and how virtual deserts replaced them. Marsh was one of the first Americans to document the theory that a natural mountain forest was a collector and distributor of water. Without such forests, he believed, either drought or flood resulted, both of which were alien to the natural process. By cutting trees, man destroyed the means by which vegetable mold accumulates on forest floors and acts to absorb water from rain, snow, and springs, and also acts to disperse water gradually via streams and rivers. A dense forest, he thought, also modifies extreme temperatures, helps prevent widespread forest fire, and serves as a buffer for high wind. Even small clearings in a forest can make the whole vulnerable to fire and destruction from wind because clearings can create wind tunnels which fan fires and reduce the effectiveness of forests as buffers.

"The face of the earth is no longer a sponge," Marsh wrote of deforested land, "but a dust heap, and the floods which the waters of the sky pour over it hurry swiftly along its slopes." If the sky withholds its "floods," Marsh added, the result is drought since without a forest, there is no reserve water.

Thus does man destroy the earth, and himself. Nature, however, if left alone or tended carefully, does not, of its own accord, allow such destruction. Marsh shrugged when he considered things like hurricanes or earthquakes or "natural" forest fires. He believed these to be part of the natural process and noted that nature, the great healer, immediately begins the reclamation process. The only permanent, irreversible damage is caused by man.

Because man is the only creature on earth capable of altering his environment so dramatically, he must be separate from nature. Man must be *above* nature, Marsh concluded, because he was able to manipulate the land, but at the same time man was *beneath* nature, morally, because of his ignorance of the virtues of natural order. Balance, judiciousness, care, all incorporated beautifully in nature, had to be learned by man, the only being who seemed not to be born with such intuitive knowledge.

Marsh's purpose was to warn man of his imminent danger, to point out that he was responsible for it, and to teach him how to take better care of the earth and himself. His book was a best-seller of its kind. Around one thousand copies were sold within a few months of publication, an excellent record for a long, sometimes tedious text. The rather turgid prose, footnotes that took up more space than the text, and lengthy references to obscure authors and historical events could never have allowed the book to be popular. But Marsh did cause something of a stir in the academic community. The reviewers praised and agreed with him. Today *Man and Nature* is known as "the fountainhead of the conservation movement."

Marsh knew the Adirondacks and was among the first to insist, in *Man and Nature*, that they be protected by the state. He was also one of the first to point out the importance of the Adirondack forest as "a reservoir to supply with perennial waters the thousand rivers and rills that are fed by the rains and snows of the Adirondacks," which, in turn, fed the mighty Hudson River and the Erie Canal. These vital transportation routes on which so much of the East's economic prosperity depended had, at all costs, to be retained. To do so meant that the forests of the Adirondacks had to be recognized as the primary water suppliers.

The Adirondack forest, Marsh wrote in 1864, before logging had reached its peak, "still covers far the largest proportion of the surface. It is evidently a matter of the utmost importance that the public, and especially land owners, be roused to a sense of the dangers to which the indiscriminate clearing of the woods may expose not only future generations, but the very soil itself."

Little Adirondack land was suited to farming, anyway, he thought, so if "the forest [were declared] the inalienable property of the commonwealth," minimal economic loss would be felt. Much, in fact, would be gained. The rivers and canals would be safe, the rich farmlands in central New York would be assured of water, and of equal importance, a gorgeous natural environment would remain pure.

If retained, the Adirondack forests would be "at once a museum for the instruction of the student, a garden for the recreation of the lover of nature, and an asylum where indigenous tree, and humble plant that loves the shade, and fish and fowl and four-footed beast, may dwell and perpetuate their kind, in the enjoyment of such imperfect protection as the laws of a people jealous of restraint can afford them."

George Perkins Marsh, then, was one of the first to present the argument in favor of preserving the Adirondacks. And he was the first to say that preservation was not just desirable for esthetic reasons but absolutely crucial for economic reasons.

Marsh's conviction that man was *not* a part of nature separated him from other nature lovers. John Burroughs, for example, wrote, "Hedge or qualify as we will, man is a part of Nature. . . . Can there be anything in the universe that is not of the Universe?" "No," Marsh said in response to a query from his publisher. "Nothing is further from my belief, that man is a 'part of nature' or that his action is controlled by laws of nature . . .; man, so far from being . . . a soul-less, will-less automation, is a free moral agent working independently of nature."

The debate, even among the most influential advocates of nature's worth and beauty, stayed lively. That Marsh and Burroughs reached similar conclusions from two such opposing positions indicates how complex the question of man's relationship to nature can be.

The last of the four men who helped so much to reshape Americans' ideas about nature in the nineteenth century was neither scientist, conservationist, *belletrist*, nor philosopher. Yet more people read his books, perhaps, than all those who read either Marsh or Muir or Burroughs.

The book most people read in the last half of the nineteenth century was *McGuffey's Reader*, or one of the six in the series written between 1836 and 1857 and revised five times until 1901. McGuffey's books were for children. More than 70 million copies were published, bought, and used in American homes and schools. It is not too much to say that a generation of Americans, at least one half of all American school children in the era, received the precepts of generosity, obedience, kindness, piety, propriety, and patriotism from *McGuffey's Readers*.

The bulk of the stories in *McGuffey's*, memorized, recited, and remembered by millions, were about nature. Birds, kittens, puppies, and sunlit mornings were the "characters" in the stories. They were usually very good: dogs were kind to each other, birds sang sweet songs and shared their food. Mornings were always bright and sunny, even if previous afternoons may have been temporarily stormy. Children were supposed to copy the behavior of these animals and plants and weather patterns. Children, in fact, were meant to model their speech, actions, and thoughts after a nature which was generous, well intentioned, and *good*.

William Holmes McGuffey was a real person, with a background similar to John Muir's. His parents were Scottish and immigrated first to Pennsylvania, then to Ohio in the early 1800s. McGuffey's experience on frontier farms, however, did not inspire him to get closer to nature, as had Muir's and Burroughs'. He left the farm and became a college professor of languages and natural and moral philosophy as well as a minister. His attitude towards nature seems to have derived more from the moralistic ideas he preached than from his direct experience with nature. Many a nineteenth-century school child was tempted to challenge McGuffey's statements that birds were always pleasant or that mornings were always bright, knowing from experience that such was not the case.

By writing so many poems and pointed stories based on a carica-ture of nature, McGuffey probably did not intend to distort truth. Yet millions of Americans grew up with the idea that nature was a kind of exemplary schoolroom. Such principles, drilled into young minds, may well have helped shape the late nineteenth-century attitude that nature was not a threat but a noble friend.

It may not be too far-fetched to surmise that among the thousands of people who visited the Adirondacks in the Gilded Age, most had grown up and learned to read with *McGuffey's*. The intellectuals among them would have gone on to read Marsh; the literary would have known Burroughs' work; budding conservationists would have read Muir. And most, as they sat on wide porches, admired the views, set out to "rough it" for real or in fun, would have learned to read at all from McGuffey's tales of a benign, gentle, exemplary nature.

Those who knew Burroughs might have shared with him the wonder and joy of the bird songs, "rising pure and serene as if a spirit from some remote heights were slowly chanting a divine accompani-ment. . . . It is very simple, but I can hardly tell the secret of its charm. 'O spheral! spheral!' he seems to say; 'O holy, holy! O clear away, clear away!'" Others, equally open to the wonders of nature, may have had McGuffey to thank for their appreciative ears. Somewhere deep in their memories was a song many had memorized: "There's a merry brown thrush sitting up in the tree,/He's singing to me! He's singing to me!"

People no longer listened in fear for the "howl, howl, howl" of the wilderness. Instead, they went by the thousands to the Adirondacks in search of nature's clearest voice which was no longer threatening, but was as lovely as mist on the lake, as serene as daybreak.

One of those Adirondack visitors was able to combine a poetic love of nature akin to Burroughs' with a hardnosed practicality akin to Marsh's in a way that made more than a personal difference in his life. It made all the difference to the future of the Adirondacks.

14

A Public Pleasure Ground

Iₙ THE EARLY 1900s, citizens going about their business on the streets of
Albany, New York, clucked their tongues and shook their heads when
they passed the familiar figure of Verplanck Colvin, shabbily dressed,
muttering to himself. Quite dotty, they said. Some may have remembered
who the old man was, that he had come from a wealthy, distinguished
Albany family. Some may have known that Verplanck's father was a
well-respected lawyer and that the son, when young, had also been
trained in the law. Then, he had been tall, handsome, and vigorous, with
an enviable future.

Some, sympathetic perhaps, may have remembered that Verplanck Colvin had done more than any other single person to insure that
the Adirondack Mountains remained a natural sanctuary. If they remembered that, they could see him in what a later Adirondack chronicler,
William Chapman White, called a "pleasanter" way than his appearance
at the age of sixty evoked.

Many have loved the Adirondacks, but Verplanck Colvin, in his
youth and middle age, literally devoted his life to his adoration of the
mountains. His romance with the Adirondacks began in the 1860s, when
he was eighteen years old and went on a wilderness vacation there. His
hobby was map making, and the still relatively empty Adirondacks were
a wonderful place to practice his surveying and measuring skills.

In 1868, when he was twenty-one years old and already an expert
on the terrain of the Adirondacks, Colvin presented his passion to the
public for the first time. For the next thirty-five years he made it his
full-time business, having abandoned the law, to publicize the beauty of
the Adirondacks and to hammer into the minds and hearts of the people
that they must do something to preserve that beauty.

It may have been that a few Albany citizens in 1900 remembered that summer afternoon in 1868, when the youthful Verplanck Colvin drew a fairly large crowd at the tiny post office in the village of Lake Pleasant, New York, an Adirondack community on the southern edge of the mountains, about midway between Utica and Saratoga Springs. Just what prompted Colvin to make a speech at that time is not known, but speak he did, in the spontaneous, colorful manner that became his style. He may have been encouraged by the kind of people who formed his audience. They were largely hunters and fishermen in the pre-Murray days of Adirondack vacations. Lake Pleasant, being relatively accessible to Albany and other New York towns and cities, had become a convenient stopping-off place for sportsmen. What Colvin had to say was bound to be of interest to them because his subject dealt directly with what they had come to find — privacy, good hunting and fishing, and wilderness.

Colvin did not quibble. He believed the region to be especially suited to sport and said so. And he did not mince words when he came to the part about what people should do to keep it that way.

A state park, he said, should be created. The people had a precious heritage in their back yard. The Adirondacks were no less magnificent than the Rockies or the Grand Canyon, where he had recently been camping. Furthermore, he knew the Adirondacks as well or better than anyone else, he said, and was prepared to spend his time and money impressing upon the citizens of the state the vital necessity of preserving the Adirondacks.

Colvin's first public speech that afternoon in 1868 contained the outline of what became a crusade for preserving the Adirondacks. Articles, speeches, even demands followed. He spent every moment possible in the mountains, but Colvin's idea of fun was not to loaf or even to hunt or fish. It was to comb every inch of the more than 6 million acres of mountains, forests, and lakes, following the old maps, testing their accuracy. He tramped the same woods Emmons had explored. He was that rare person, financially secure enough to spend his life doing what he most loved, without having to earn a living from it.

Colvin, like Murray, was at the right place at the right time. The idea of creating a forest preserve of some kind in the Adirondacks had been proposed before but without much success. In 1864, for example, the *New York Times* had run an editorial suggesting the creation of a park in the Adirondacks. Colvin's urgent appeals and his conviction, however, made people listen and think and act. Some even began writing letters to legislators, and the first trickle of public support for a park or preserve began in the late 1860s.

Verplanck Colvin. *New York State Assembly, New York State Survey 7th Annual Report*

In 1870, Colvin, armed with his surveys and his energetic spirit, did an unusual thing. He submitted a report of his observations and ideas to an organization to which he did not belong and which had not solicited his advice. He had just finished a second expedition up Mount Seward, a peak in the northern central section of the Adirondacks where lumbermen had not yet penetrated. What he saw for miles around was unbroken wilderness. It was "wilderness everywhere," he wrote, "lake on lake, river on river, mountain on mountain, numberless." Joy and fear welled up in his heart: joy that such a scene existed and fear that it would eventually be destroyed.

So he sent a report to the Board of Regents of the State of New York, an official group of men who prepared, among other things, the annual report of the New York State Museum, the institution Emmons' and James Hall's collections had spawned. Hall, meanwhile, had become one of the most famous paleontologists of the day. Colvin figured that if any man would be interested and powerful enough to command attention in the legislature, it was James Hall.

With that in mind, Colvin's report contained details about his surveys as well as a plan by which the entire Adirondack region might be surveyed with more accuracy than ever before. The rationale behind the survey was not idle map making. It was the skeleton on which the fight for a public park could be built. Colvin had already thought out the major points of his argument and presented them clearly.

There were, he wrote, enormous economic advantages to be gained from preserving the Adirondack wilderness. The sheer beauty of the region, of course, was important; but the key fact was that the Adirondacks were the source of the most important water supply for the entire eastern United States.

The Adirondacks, he wrote, were the "secret origin" of the mighty rivers of the state. The wilderness "contains the springs which are the sources of our principal rivers and feeders of the canals. Each summer the water supply for these rivers and canals is lessened, and commerce has suffered."

The reason? Logging, mainly. Loggers were wantonly destroying the forests, the cradles of the water. Lumber camps invited fires and what was not felled by the ax was likely to burn. Without the forest, the waters were drying up; without the waters, New York State was in trouble.

The only thing to do was to wrap up the Adirondacks in legislative protection which could enforce restraint in logging and other human activities. Legislative action alone could protect the forests for the economic benefit of everyone while it also protected the interests of sportsmen.

The argument was so lucid and convincing that the Board of Regents read it and sent it to Governor John T. Hoffman. He was impressed enough to mention it in his annual message to the legislature.

Colvin didn't stop there. He kept up pressure, continued to make speeches to anyone who would listen, wrote articles, and button-holed friends, acquaintances and legislators.

The legislature, in turn, having received many letters from those sympathetic to Colvin, began to worry about the fate of the Adirondacks. In 1872, it authorized two measures designed to accommodate the increasing pressure to do something about the Adirondacks.

First, legislators granted to Verplanck Colvin $1,000 to complete his survey of the mountains. Then they created a Commission of State Parks and named a group of men to investigate the possibility of making a park within the counties whose boundaries fell within the Adirondack region. Colvin was named to sit on this commission.

Within a year of his twin appointment as surveyor and commissioner, Colvin turned in two reports. The first was a vivid account of his state-authorized survey. Colvin was a skilled craftsman in the art of writing readable government reports. He wrote rather more in the style of Murray's adventure stories than in the typical officialese of most such reports. This one, the first of many, detailed his exploration along the Sacandaga River and contained acute observations of the weather and the terrain, and descriptions of the places he camped, the food he ate, the trials and tribulations and joys he experienced.

On July 31, he said, he completed his measurement of Speculator Mountain. The next day he pressed ahead to Lake Pleasant, the scene of his first talk three years earlier, and plotted his course east toward Lake Champlain. He was a hard driver. He wore out everyone else, survived on very little food, often only trout broiled over a fire without seasoning or oil.

Sometimes he and his assistants ate only bread, and stale stuff it must have been since they had been carrying it for days. Colvin cared nothing for comfort and even looked upon the worn-out shoes and torn clothing of his companions without sympathy. Such trivialities meant nothing to him, and like many surveyors before him, he had endless trouble with his staff. They complained and sometimes quit, but Colvin went on, at times relieved to be alone, grateful for not having to cope with other souls.

Colvin's report to the legislature was so well written, so exciting, so filled with adventure and vivid details that people actually bought copies of it. Other, later reports—there were eight in all—were equally popular.

The second document Colvin prepared in 1872 was a summation of the work done by the Commission on State Parks. His points reiterated his earlier conclusion about the waters of the state. In a detailed analysis of the effect of deforestation upon the state's water supply, the report echoed the theories in George Perkins Marsh's *Man and Nature*, published eight years earlier.

One of Colvin's fellow commissioners was a man by the name of Franklin B. Hough, the son of a country doctor in Lewis County, New York, just beyond the far western slopes of the Adirondacks. Young Hough had been trained as a physician too, but by 1872 he was already better known as a friend of forests. Traveling around the country, he had been impressed by the way Americans abused their forests, thinking, apparently, they were endless and inexhaustible. Hough had launched a crusade of his own and became the father of American forestry and an early conservationist of great influence. It was probably through Hough that Colvin came to know Marsh's work and theories, for while Colvin may have arrived independently at the same idea, his conclusions were remarkably similar to Marsh's.

The Park Commission was temporary. After it had conducted its study, it was dissolved. Another twelve years passed before its work led to tangible results. But the groundwork it laid proved invaluable.

Meanwhile, Colvin continued his survey. For the next six years he covered nearly every acre of the Adirondacks. He reached Lake Champlain in August 1872, and began to work west again, toward Mt. Marcy.

In September 1872, only a few months after he began his official survey, Colvin made the discovery for which he became most famous.

It was a cold, foggy, rainy day when he and his reluctant crew reached the base of the mighty mountain. He insisted, however, that they climb it anyway. It was, after all, the tallest peak in New York and its precise measurement was vitally important.

They could barely see. Everyone shivered and complained. They complained even more bitterly when they finally reached the top and had immediately to come down again. It was too dark and misty to see anything at all. But the next day, up they went again, this time in clear, sunny weather.

Colvin's eyes were always darting around him, scanning the distant horizon with as much pleasure and interest as he investigated the tiniest fern. It was with such feverish curiosity that he noticed a tiny stream near the top of the mountain. Tracing the water's flow, he found the source of the stream in a small pond, nearly triangular in shape. There was no pond higher with an outlet for southerly flowing water.

The waters from this minute trough dribbled out on the west side

Colvin's map of the Hudson River's "most elevated lakelet," Lake Tear-of-the-Clouds. *New York State Assembly, New York State Survey 7th Annual Report*

of the pond and fell through a tiny stream bed. Gaining momentum as it trickled down the steep, rock-strewn mountain, and picking up other spring and rain-fed brooks, the stream swelled into Feldspar Brook, a madly rushing but still narrow brook whose course was about one thousand feet, downhill all the way. At an altitude of about three thousand feet, Feldspar met the Opalescent River, a stream whose waters splashed over the gleaming mineral labradorite which sparkles like opals in the sun.

A thousand feet further down, the Opalescent jagged sharply westward, then south again; only after its southern turn was it called the Hudson River. Due north of where the Opalescent dog-legged, another lake fed the Hudson, Lake Henderson, named for the mining executive David Henderson. Lake Henderson was a mile long and for many years had been thought to be the main source of the Hudson.

Colvin found out the truth. He realized that while many streams fed the Hudson on its 300-mile journey to the Atlantic, its true origin was not Lake Henderson, but there in that tiny tear-shaped pond near the top of Mt. Marcy. The mightiest river in the East began on New York's highest mountain.

Colvin was astonished, thrilled. He was the first to discover the true source of the greatest river in the East, some said the loveliest river in the United States. He wrote: "It was the lake, and [it] flowed, not to the Ausable and the St. Lawrence, but to the Hudson, the loftiest lake spring of our haughty river! . . . First seen as we then saw it . . . dripping with the moisture of the heavens, it seemed, in its minuteness and its prettiness, a veritable Tear-of-the-Clouds, the summit water as I named it."

Finding the source of the Hudson was no less a triumph for Colvin than discovering the source of the Nile River in Africa had been six years earlier for the British team that had spent many years looking for it. The origin of both great rivers, one so vital to the establishment of ancient civilization in the Western world, the other so crucial to the growth of New York and to the emergence of the United States as a world leader, were found within a decade of one another by men whose determination made a place for them in history.

No other achievement gave Colvin's crusade to preserve the Adirondacks so much force. The basis of his argument for a park was the existence of the Adirondack watershed. To have found the source of the mightiest river of them all, the kingpin of the East's water system, was his triumph. So eloquent was his description of the tiny tear of the clouds that the name was adopted by the state legislature and today is one of the most lyrical of all lake names in America.

Discovering the precious fountain on that September day in 1872 must have made measuring the mountain an anti-climax. But Colvin did not dwell on past achievements and pressed ahead. He corrected the measurement of Mt. Marcy and came within ten feet of its actual height, 5,344 feet.

By 1880, Colvin had completed the most thorough topographical survey ever conducted in the Adirondacks. But an enormous chore was still to be done. The privately owned and publicly owned land had to be sorted out. Ever since the Totten and Crossfield Purchase of the eighteenth century, when surveying was an imprecise science at best and was least accurate in rugged regions like the Adirondacks, boundary lines had been disputed. As lumbering operations delved deeper into the forests in the 1870s, many men simply cut trees wherever they found them without bothering to determine who owned the land, if, in fact, ownership could be established at all. Even the state did not know how much it owned. Much acreage had reverted to New York when landowners had clear-cut it, then abandoned responsibility—and the obligation to pay taxes — for it. Colvin, with his usual zeal, set out to put the record in order.

Based on his work, a growing mass of precise literature developed about the Adirondacks. But more and more people did not need to read government reports or study surveys to recognize what Colvin did. The last years of his survey were less lonely. In the 1890s, he wrote about the "ubiquitous tourist, determined to see all that has been recorded as worth seeing." Realizing how much of the record he himself had documented, Colvin had mixed feelings about the tourists. He knew they shared with him a love of the land, and he rejoiced in their appreciation. After all, it was for them that the park should be created. But, he wrote, "The air resounds with laughter, fun and jollity," sounds which tended to obscure the hush of the forest he loved so well. Such was the "genius of change," Colvin admitted; new problems always grow wherever the old ones seem to be healed.

Then, after thirty-five years of steadfast, perhaps frenzied work to understand the Adirondacks, Colvin gave up. It seems to have happened suddenly. He quit his job as surveyor and began to behave strangely. He refused to turn over his maps and other documents to the state and stopped talking about the Adirondacks or the park or the dangers of deforestation. He even tried to manage the building of a railroad through the mountains. It was then that he began roaming the streets of Albany, talking only to himself. Some said he was insane, some said he had brain fever. He died finally, friendless, in a hospital for the mentally ill in 1920.

While he never put all his information together in one place, he did leave the most detailed maps and the most accurate topographical information ever collected about the Adirondacks. And he left his eloquent, substantial arguments in favor of a park. He had been a practical activist and at the same time a poet. He straddled the world of the romantics, who believed nature was *ipso facto* good, deserving to be saved for that reason alone, and the world of the pragmatists, who believed usefulness alone warranted action.

Colvin gave both muscle and musical prose to those who were garnering increased support for preservation. He gave the world one of its most beautiful place names, Lake Tear-of-the-Clouds. He was a man of contrasts and contradictions, as was his legacy, the Adirondack Park and the Adirondack Forest Preserve, entities that in large part owe their existence to him.

Verplanck Colvin also straddled the transition in the history of the Adirondacks. He knew the region in the 1860s, when neither loggers nor tourists had had much effect upon the environment. And he lived to see the day when man exerted his control over the wilderness in such a way as to assure its continuation as wilderness. Between the two periods he saw the effects of logging and mining and what happened when man fought nature and won.

The sequence whereby ideas and attitudes toward nature were reshaped in the American mind by philosophers and artists, spread in popular form by men like Murray, refined and analyzed in terms of the latest scientific discoveries by people like Marsh and Hough, and polished into poetry by writers like Burroughs, took place in the course of Colvin's lifetime. He was forced to be an integrator. With purpose and political sophistication he did something about Marsh's ideas, yet he framed his hard-nosed arguments in lyrical prose that made people listen to him.

While Colvin lived, the definition of wilderness in the Adirondacks changed. When he was born, the wilderness meant the virtual absence of man; when he died, wilderness meant a conscious presence of man in the Adirondacks not as exploiter but as watchdog in charge of keeping nature natural. After Colvin, the terms on which man and nature forged alliances and fought battles could never be the same.

THE CONTEMPORARY WILDERNESS
(1885–Present)

15

Wilderness Economics

O N MAY 15, 1885, NEW YORK GOVERNOR DAVID B. HILL, a bachelor from Elmira, a former lieutenant governor, a man whose hobby was literature and whose ambition was to be president, signed into law a bill he had urged the legislature to pass. Chapter 283 stated that nearly seven hundred thousand state-owned acres in the Adirondack Mountains would be kept forever wild as forest lands. What trees there were on those acres could not be removed, nor could the land designated as Forest Preserve ever be sold or exchanged by the state. The Adirondacks (or the state-owned portions of them) were to be saved from the hostile hand of man forever.

Governor Hill had had his problems with that bill. He had been in office only two months when he signed what has since been called the "forever wild" law. His predecessor, Grover Cleveland, had left the New York capital to begin his term as United States president. Dave Hill, taking over in midterm, had inherited a government with a good reputation for efficiency in a state known for its sharp businessmen and astonishing commercial success in the private sector.

Recently, however, the clamor for reform of all kinds had been growing: people wanted full employment; labor unions were getting more powerful; the eight-hour day was a big issue. Politicians who could boast a concern for humanity, honesty, and who could prove their integrity were doing well with voters. (Grover Cleveland had even defied what most people thought was political suicide by frankly admitting that he had sired an illegitimate child. His forthrightness about the matter seemed to moderate the scandal.)

Dave Hill, then, had to garner support both from reform groups of all kinds and from the wealthy business interests who could help finance his bid for the presidency if he was to get to the White House, or even be re-elected governor.

What to do about the Adirondacks nicely demonstrated his problems. People like Verplanck Colvin had organized an effective campaign in favor of saving the Adirondacks, a movement lumped generally with other reform efforts. Business interests, however, ridiculed such efforts, calling conservation types "denudatics" and scorning their efforts to lock up perfectly good commercial land.

A battle over Niagara Falls had previewed the problem Dave Hill faced over the Adirondacks. Beginning as early as 1830, groups of people had been upset about "the abominable fungus" of souvenir vendors who were polluting the natural wonder in western New York. By 1883, such famous, influential figures as novelist Henry James and Frederick Church, a leader of the Hudson River School of painters, were writing letters and working hard to "Save Niagara Falls," as the campaign was called.

Saving one of America's most popular tourist attractions from cheap commercial exploitation, however, smacked of "denudaticism," in the view of many who had another form of exploitation in mind: electric power. By the late 1880s, electricity was quickly becoming the primary source of power in the United States. San Francisco and Cleveland were using electricity for street lights by 1879. A year later New York City installed electric lights on Broadway making the avenue famous as the "Great White Way." The future was electricity, many believed, and it had long been recognized that Niagara Falls was potentially the great electric power plant in the East. Business interests were not about to tolerate any measure that might threaten that potential.

The struggle over Niagara Falls, foretelling what was in store for the Adirondacks, was, in fact, thought by some merely to be a preparatory gesture for an even more hard-fought battle to make an Adirondack Park.

Grover Cleveland partially solved the Niagara Falls crisis in 1883 by signing a measure creating the Niagara Falls Reservation, which was the first state park in the nation. Commerce was not allowed, but no ban was placed on the actual water. Power companies were soon harnessing the falls for electricity, but nature lovers were at least spared souvenir hawkers as they contemplated the view.

Governor Cleveland had at first been reluctant to support conservation, but as president he became an outspoken advocate of the new attitude toward nature. His support for the Niagara Falls Reservation

helped Governor Hill make some decisions about the Adirondacks, and
the state legislature made things even easier for the president when in
early 1885 it authorized funds with which to buy more land around
Niagara Falls for the "reservation." Hill now had two important prece-
dents. Cleveland had established the right of the state to ban business
from state land, and the legislature had shown its willingness to give
financial support to parks.

Meanwhile, the federal government, too, got into the conservation act. President Ulysses S. Grant signed into law an act to create
Yellowstone National Park in 1872. (Grant, incidentally, spent the last
years of his life in the Adirondacks.) A portion of the Yosemite Valley in
California had been set aside as a "resort and recreation" area in 1864,
although the "Niagara Falls problem" had cropped up there. "A flourish-
ing tourist-catering business soon altered its wild character," according to
a historian of the conservationist movement in the United States,
Roderick Nash.

In New York, Governor Hill could also look back to 1876 when the
legislature, responding to pressure from people like Colvin, had banned
further sale of state-owned land around Lake George. Theoretically, the
ban meant that publicly held land was to be preserved, since the state
itself did not conduct logging or other commercial endeavors on its own
land. In 1883, when the furor over Niagara Falls was at its peak, the
legislature took another step toward preserving the Adirondacks. All sale
or exchange of state land in the Adirondack counties of Clinton, Essex,
Franklin, Fulton, Hamilton, Herkimer, Lewis, Saratoga, St. Lawrence,
and Warren was forever banned.

Some people think that this 1883 provision was really the most
important in the history of the Adirondack Park. The underlying principle
of the law, though it was not explicitly stated, was that state land in the
Adirondacks was to stay as it was; man was not to touch it. To make sure it
wasn't touched the State Fishery Commission, a body which had been in
existence for fifteen years, was assigned the additional duty of watching
over the Adirondacks.

By 1885, then, Governor David Hill could tell business interests
with an eye on the Adirondacks that the expressed will of the people, as
represented in the legislature, was that portions of the Adirondacks be
protected from commercial exploitation. There were, however, many
who were not likely to be impressed by such an explanation. Hill, therefore, needed a genuine, pressing *economic* reason to preserve nature in the
Adirondacks to persuade businessmen of the wisdom of the act.

Of course, the economic reason was already there. George Perkins Marsh, Franklin Hough, and Verplanck Colvin had worked it out, and Governor Hill used it.

New York, David Hill believed, faced a terrifying threat. The Erie Canal and the Hudson River, kingpins in the economic health of the state, depended upon the watershed in the Adirondacks for their water. The delicate balance of mosses, humus, trees, springs, and rivers there allowed the rivers and canals of the state to flow regularly, dependably, and without alternating floods and droughts. Destruction of the forest at the hands of loggers and miners was serious enough, but the fires resulting from their activities were as dangerous. The towns and villages that had grown up as loggers and miners encroached upon the wilderness added to the diminution of water sources in the mountains.

The threat was not somewhere in the future but was imminent. At least two-thirds of the Adirondack forest had already been razed, it was claimed. Lumbermen showed no signs of restraint; they were taking trees wherever they found them, on state land, private land, no-man's land.

Preservationists argued that the 1883 law banning sale of state land was far too loose, nor was the Fishery Commission powerful nor large enough to protect state land from loggers. Abuses were rife.

These potent arguments, combined with the one in favor of preserving the Adirondacks for recreational purposes, gave Governor Hill the means to please both nature lovers and commercial interests.*

Colvin's work helped, too. His extensive surveys and maps enabled New York to know exactly what it owned and where. About one-fourth of all the Adirondack land in the counties mentioned above belonged to New York and was thus public. But the public land was not in one piece. Tracts had fallen to New York when owners defaulted on their taxes. Other tracts had been state possessions since the Revolutionary War. Still others were presumed to be public since incorrect surveys, the tangle of deeds and patents left over from land speculation days, and the simple immensity of the region had left them unclaimed. State-owned land, then, was scattered all over the mountains, a thousand acres here, fifty acres there, ten thousand acres elsewhere. Loggers can be forgiven occasionally for taking timber from any land they came across simply

---

*Hill was adept at creating strange-bedfellow alliances. For example, he gained support from labor reform groups when he instituted a State Labor Day, later adopted nationally, and when he took a stand against child labor. Meanwhile, he refused to support another hot reform issue, prohibition of alcohol. In a day when Prohibition was almost always linked with labor and other reform issues, Hill's dual support from liquor interests (obviously not in favor of Prohibition) *and* from reform groups was quite a coup.

Harper's Weekly, December 6, 1884, published these drawings of cut-over, burned-over Adirondack forest

because they couldn't figure out what belonged to them and what belonged to the people any more easily than anyone else.

As a result, the creation of an Adirondack Park, modeled after Yellowstone and Yosemite, was impossible. The only way to do that was for New York to buy *all* the Adirondack land it didn't already own. Even for the wealthiest state in the Union, such a purchase was prohibitively expensive. In terms of acreage it would have been like buying all Connecticut plus half of Vermont.

There was, in 1885, no question at all about the inalienability of private property. Watershed or no watershed, the state could never presume to restrict logging or anything else on land owned by a private company or individual. It had taken decades to persuade the New York Legislature to ban business from *state* land around Niagara Falls. Few even considered the possibility of mentioning such a ban on any property other than the state's.

Therefore, when Governor Hill agreed to enact "forever wild" and create a Forest Preserve in the Adirondacks, state protection extended only to state land, scattered though it was throughout the mountains and abutting private land at every turn.

The fact that Forest Preserve land remained scattered among private land in the Adirondacks had enormously important consequences in the twentieth century. There was some talk in the 1890s about buying all the Adirondacks for the state. It never happened. As a result, some contemporary problems were made inevitable as far back as 1885. Today, New York owns under half the Adirondacks and pays taxes on its property just as private owners do. But the state land is no more unified now than it ever was, and the term "Forest Preserve" still applies only to state land. The term "Adirondack Park," as it is now used, means something entirely different from what it meant in 1885. Then it was sometimes used interchangeably with "Forest Preserve." Today it applies to the whole Adirondack region and represents state control of a sort no one could have imagined 100 years ago.

Modern problems, however, were invisible to Governor Hill and preservationists in 1885. The creation of the Forest Preserve, which was to remain forever as wild land, was a great victory for people like Verplanck Colvin. It was one of the "milestones in the early history of American wilderness preservation," Roderick Nash wrote.

The 1885 law was much more explicit than its predecessor of 1883. State land could never be "sold, nor leased nor taken by any person, corporation, public or private." Additionally, fire wardens and marshals, inspectors and monitors were named, giving teeth to paper provisions.

Three men were named forest commissioners. They had a small staff and the responsibility for filing regular reports about the status of the forests. Furthermore, they were expected to initiate reforestation projects, conduct wildlife surveys, and institute fire prevention measures.

The deed was done. Some people even today question the motives of those who worked hardest to save the Adirondacks. Some accuse wealthy landowners in the Adirondacks of wanting the state simply to protect their own private sanctuaries. There is evidence suggesting that those who persuaded Hill to sign the "forever wild" law were indeed great landowners themselves, less interested in the public welfare than in their own wilderness experience and property. Others still dislike the economic justification used to support "forever wild," claiming that purity of preservation for nature's sake was sullied. If an economic rationale was used then to save the Adirondacks, they fear, such reasons could again be used to exploit the Adirondacks if precious ores or other resources were found later.

Nevertheless, "forever wild" became a part of New York State law. Somewhere between the ideology of wilderness appreciation, the profit motive, and political maneuvering — somewhere between greed and altruism, the same combination that provoked the first systematic survey of the Adirondacks in 1836 — a large portion of the Adirondacks was saved from man's exploitation. If nature was to be respected and tended for man's enlightenment, as Emerson had urged, or if nature was to be protected for man's financial security, as Cicero might have argued, it was still saved.

Dave Hill did not become president, nor was the Adirondack Forest Preserve really his idea. He was, however, the governor who created it, and he is remembered more for that accomplishment than for any other.

16

The Mellowing

THE DRAMA OF "FOREVER WILD" SUBSIDED. During the forty or so years after 1885, a kind of mellowing took place in the Adirondacks. It was almost as if the confrontation between man and nature, having passed through a tumultuous childhood and adolescence, settled down into a quieter, perhaps more harmonious middle age.

Historian William Verner, former curator at the Adirondack Museum at Blue Mountain Lake, has divided Adirondack history into several phases. He believes the pre-Murray era, when only a few dedicated, responsible woodsmen and nature lovers knew the Adirondacks, to be a kind of Golden Age. He calls the big-hotel, roughing-it era the Gilded Age. Extending his divisions a bit, the early "forever wild" years are here called the "mellowing" because many people with different interests seemed to be relatively happy with what was possible in the mountains. The Adirondacks, in short, seemed for a time to serve campers, loggers, nature lovers, and conservationists—often enemies—with nearly equal success.

There were problems to be sure. But the very difficult dilemmas of the 1960s, when the Forest Preserve's scattered quality and proximity to private land seemed to threaten seriously the sanctity of "forever wild," had not yet emerged—nor had the problem of overuse of recreational resources.

Logging in 1885 was still nearly twenty-five years away from its peak year. Hotels stayed busy, and year-round residents could find jobs in lumber camps and in resorts. While life in the mountains has never been easy, severe poverty at the turn of the century was not widespread either.

If the Erie Canal represented a kind of equilibrium between man and nature in New York in the mid-1820s, the years between 1885 and 1920 in the Adirondacks marked a kind of similar balance. The old adversaries and new friends, man and nature, appeared to be doggedly working out the newly defined terms of their relationship on three major fronts: "forever wild," forest maintenance, and fire.

"Forever wild" was a victory for Verplanck Colvin and his supporters, but it also meant only a step toward permanent preservation in the Adirondacks. The concept had to be refined, and the laws had to be enforced and, in the minds of many, strengthened. In the beginning, the definition of a park and a forest preserve had been virtually identical, but in 1892 the two were differentiated.

In that year the Forest Commission, in charge of things in the Forest Preserve, outlined a new plan for the Adirondacks. Its annual report to the governor included a map of the entire region on which the commissioners had drawn in blue pencil a rough circle which took in portions of ten counties and nearly all the Adirondacks. This entity, the report said, should be called the Adirondack Park. Within it were the patches of Forest Preserve, of course, as well as the remaining private land. The commission wanted to call all of it a park, since it recommended that New York plan to buy up all the private land and turn the whole region into a unified Forest Preserve—or Adirondack Park.

The so-called Blue Line thus at first designated a proposed park, one that encompassed the whole Adirondack region but did not really exist since the state only owned a little more than a quarter of it.

The legislature liked the idea and in 1892 passed Chapter 707, creating the Adirondack State Park. This was really only a promissory park, however, even though some state money was set aside as a guarantee that more land in the Adirondacks could be bought and added to the Forest Preserve. The legislature also amended the "forever wild" law of 1885 to allow land outside the Blue Line, even if it fell within the Adirondacks, or Forest Preserve, to be sold in order to procure more funds for buying land inside the Blue Line.

Soon after the creation of the Park, however, there were signs that the five-man Forest Commission and the state were backing down on their commitment to purchase all the land inside the Blue Line. In fact, there were indications that the Forest Commission was not living up to its mandate to prevent the sale or exchange of Forest Preserve land even inside their own Blue Line.

Lumber interests were finding loopholes in "forever wild." Some state land was, in fact, sold to those who planned to log it. In 1894, the

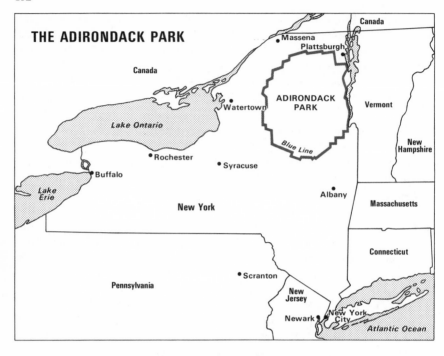

Forest Commission even approved the application of a railroad company to build more track through Forest Preserve acres. Such was fuel for scandal, and the *New York Times* that year exposed a shocking plot, it said, to erode "forever wild." It seems the Forest Commission had taken a straw vote and discovered that three of the five men would vote yes to the new track. The prorailroad commissioners scheduled the date of the official vote near Christmas, when the two antirailroad commissioners were likely to be out of town. For one man who was in favor of the tract, however, questionable arrangements were made when he was also out of town. He made it to Albany for the vote on a special, private train.

Some believed the balance between man and nature was quickly slipping over to the side of man, and a new effort to correct the balance had to be organized.

It happened that in 1894, the year of the railroad scandal, 175 men from each district in New York met in Albany to revamp the state constitution. Among these men were several Downstate representatives who had read the *Times* and shared its outrage over abuses to "forever wild." To them the Adirondacks were a gorgeous natural sanctuary where they could escape the "trials and tribulations and annoyances of business and everyday life," as one put it. Some owned land in the Adirondacks, too, and didn't like the idea that nearby acres might be ruined.

The man who spoke so eloquently for the beauty of the Adirondack wilderness was David McClure, a colonel in the army and a delegate to the constitutional convention from New York City. Conservation groups had asked him to represent their interests. The chairman of the convention was himself a devoted conservationist. Joseph Choate was a founder of the American Museum of Natural History, in fact, and McClure rightly guessed that Choate would support his pleas to strengthen "forever wild" by making it a part of the new constitution.

The only article during the convention that was passed without a single dissenting vote was Article 7, Section 7, which read in part: "The lands of the State, now owned or hereafter to be acquired, constituting the forest preserve... shall be forever kept as wild forest lands. They shall not be leased, sold or exchanged, or taken by any corporation, public or private, nor shall the timber thereon be sold, removed or destroyed."

The people of New York passed the new constitution by a wide margin. As a result, "forever wild" became sacrosanct. It was no longer in the hands of a fickle legislature or subject to the changing mood of governors. Only the people, by approving constitutional amendments in referendums, could change it.

Article 7, Section 7 introduced little that was substantially new; however, it did show determination on the part of New Yorkers to preserve their wilderness. Within five years, a Fisheries, Game and Forest Commission, the body that eventually became the present Department of Environmental Conservation, was at work protecting six hundred ninety-six thousand acres of Forest Preserve, still scattered, but more secure than ever. There was still the Adirondack Park to consider, too. The state continued to buy more Adirondack land for the Forest Preserve so the park's size increased, but the early goal to create a kind of Yellowstone out of the Adirondacks was a long way off.

However clearly the terms of the constitution seemed to state the will of the people, there was conflict over just how the Forest Preserve should be treated. Some people, for example, called Article 7, Section 7 the "Gibraltar of Forestry," in the hope that the science by which trees may be treated as crops could flourish in the state's most heavily wooded area. These people argued that if the forests were managed, they would remain as wild and beautiful as ever, yet would also provide income to the state through the sale of timber. That money would make the new Forest

Commission nearly self-supporting or at least capable of buying all the Adirondacks and fulfilling the dream of a total park.

Others believed forest management to be anathema to the principle of preservation. To cut even old, mature trees, they thought, was inimical to the whole idea behind "forever wild." The constitution stipulated, after all, that no Forest Preserve trees could be removed. Period.

The argument had been hot for years. John Muir, for example, felt that *any* cutting, in any protected forest, anywhere, was wrong. Franklin Hough, however, who had done so much to get the Adirondack Forest Preserve started, contended that selective, scientific, scrupulously careful cutting was actually beneficial to a forest. Woods which yielded their mature trees for timber looked as wild and beautiful as any "wilderness" but were actually healthier.

The contention between managers and hands-off believers grew into a schism, splitting nature lovers into two groups all over the country. The *con*servationists, who thought forest management was desirable, and the *pre*servationists, who felt it was not, barely spoke to each other. Many a friendship, once strong and energetically fighting to set aside natural parks all over the United States, ended. And so did the once effective unity among many wilderness groups.

Forestry in the Adirondacks was bound to cause trouble, and it did. Today the debate rages on, but scientific forestry became a dead issue in the Adirondack Forest Preserve when the one and only experiment with it succeeded—but succeeded just the way the operation did in an old medical joke. The patient, in this case a school of forestry, died anyway.

In 1898, Governor Frank Black told the legislature that he believed forestry, or the scientific management of trees, would enable New York to "reap a large revenue for itself and still retain the woods." The Adirondacks, of course, offered the best location in the state for the study and practice of forestry, and Black insisted that a plot of land there should be devoted to both. He suggested that the commission in charge of the Forest Preserve use some of its money, earmarked for future purchases of "forever wild" land, to buy an experimental tract.

The commission was not happy about the idea but felt it had no choice. It revealed its pique, however, by choosing thirty thousand acres around Tupper Lake, the worst possible tract of land the commission could find and the cheapest. A lumber company had clear-cut it several years earlier and was happy to be rid of it.

Meanwhile, the legislature searched for someone to head the experiment. With typical flair, they chose one of the most famous foresters in the nation, Bernhard Eduard Fernow, a German who had studied at the prestigious Hanover-Munden Forest Academy in Prussia. Forestry was an established academic discipline and practice in Europe, where extensive forests had not existed for centuries. If France or England or Germany wanted wood products and forests, managed cutting was vital.

Fernow had been shocked to discover that forestry was almost unheard of in the United States. He set himself the task of educating the public when he arrived in the country in 1876, twenty-five years old but already in possession of the respected German title "Forstkandidat." He wrote articles and worked for private industry and eventually became chief of the Division of Forestry in the United States Department of Agriculture.

Governor Black hired Fernow in 1898 to create a school of forestry out of that thirty thousand acres in the Adirondacks. Fernow's first task was less the management of existing trees than the creation of a forest he could, at some later date, manage. But he was determined, and with energy, an efficient if brusque style, and Governor Black's backing, he set out to make and manage his forest and to create his school.

Some of the methods Fernow and his talented student, Clifford R. Pettis, developed to raise thousands of seedlings and transplant them successfully are still being used. Pettis went on to become a much-loved woodsman and forester, and today a memorial forest to him stands near Saranac Lake.

No such memorial to Fernow exists, however. He was an unquestioned professional, and after five years his project promised to be a notable success. But he was irritating; he hadn't the inclination or the skills to cajole or compromise, and he tended to demand things. He was no Dave Hill, somewhat less than wholeheartedly in favor of preservation perhaps, but able to get some things done.

The legislature, in effect, fired Fernow in 1903. They refused to grant any more money to the school. Fernow left New York, wrote two major books on forestry, and established a school of forestry in Toronto, where he died.

It was several years before a new State College of Forestry in New York was established in Syracuse. Today, as part of the State University of New York, it is the second largest school of its kind in the world, and one of the best.

If forestry was dead in the Adirondacks, reforestation was very much alive. In the early 1900s, more than five hundred thousand new trees—larch, Scotch pine, Norway spruce, and the former forest denizen, the white pine — were planted in one year. In the 1920s, the state authorized the planting of more than three million more seedlings on Forest

Preserve land. Many of the methods Clifford Pettis and his teacher, Fernow, worked out today make the Adirondacks seem as dense with mature trees as they were when Samuel de Champlain fought Indians on the shores of Lake Champlain in 1609.

It seemed perfectly clear that New Yorkers wanted their forests in the Adirondacks to stay inviolable from all use—except people's enjoyment. While hardly a legislative session went by between 1885 and 1914 when some amendment to "forever wild" was not introduced, only one was brought before the people in a referendum and passed. That was in 1913, and New Yorkers allowed 3 percent of the Forest Preserve to be used for water storage or reservoirs.

Nevertheless, things were changing in the Adirondacks. Many of the most famous hotels and their keepers died. Paul Smith died in 1912. The proprietors of the Beede House, where thousands of tourists had enjoyed their colorful hosts, aged and died. Successors to John Cheney and other guides were often as knowledgeable about woodcraft, but somehow they seemed less original.

After 1900 other resorts became popular. Seaside hotels, especially, attracted many of the people who had once found such novelty in the Adirondacks. Atlantic City, Cape May, and Cape Cod, for instance, offered stiff competition to Saranac Lake, even Saratoga.

The Adirondacks, while still popular, became less fashionable. The automobile was partly the cause. The wealthy and chic liked to motor to their favorite resorts in the early ninteenth century, and roads in the Adirondacks were, for the most part, far too crude for such travel. Snob appeal, for a brief time an Adirondack magnet, declined.

If, however, in the summer of 1909 a visitor went to the Adirondacks, he was likely to find something new and rather nice, a new trail leading up Whiteface Mountain. It was well kept and easily accessible, just the thing for a leisurely hike. But it was not meant for visitors' use. It was a fire trail, one of several new ones recently built to help fight and prevent the great Adirondack scourge, fire.

Fires were getting worse: in 1903, nearly five hundred thousand acres of forest burned before June; in 1908, another spate of serious fires, as many as 500, destroyed another 350 thousand acres. Logging camps, trains, careless campers, and lightning all contributed to such disasters, as did a nearly total lack of fire fighting equipment.

In 1909, three fire stations, somewhat rickety wooden towers with platforms, enabled fire wardens to watch for fires. Soon, six fire towers, strategically placed around preserve territory, allowed the Forest Commission to begin to solve the problem. New trails by which fire fighters could reach all parts of the forest more easily also helped.

By 1925 the automobile had changed things in the Adirondacks, but when this picture of Saranac Lake was taken, the horse-drawn sleigh had not disappeared entirely. *Photo by W. F. Kollecker, courtesy of the Saranac Lake Free Library, Adirondack Collection*

In 1912, the annual report of the Conservation Commission, the latest incarnation of the body in charge of the Preserve, noted that the general public was using the fire trails for pleasure. The Forest Preserve had been administered so strictly that even campsites on state land were not allowed, and the commission pointed out that perhaps such measures were too strict. The fire trails were so popular as to indicate a need for better public facilities.

The same year the state constructed simple, but permanent, campsites on Forest Preserve land. These were really only platforms for tents which the camper had to provide for himself. They were supposedly built only for fire wardens, in compliance with "forever wild" laws, but nowhere did official literature say campers could not use them.

These simple trails and camps previewed the modern system of shelters and other conveniences for tourists. But in a way, it was the tourists who simply took them over from fire wardens without asking.

While the Adirondacks were adjusting to "forever wild" and the tourists were discovering new ways to enjoy their public wilderness, the world was changing in ways that did not allow the Adirondacks a very long mellowing. In 1914, another Blue Line, in the pine-covered hills of the Vosges Mountains of Alsace, the long and bitterly disputed province between a chauvinistic Germany and a defensive France, replaced the Adirondack Blue Line as a point of contention and controversy. Legislators in New York bickered over the precise meaning of "forever wild" while the world was preparing for the most devastating war yet fought.

What Samuel Eliot Morison called the "Great Change" was under way. World War I seemed to speed things up, but the elements of the change were apparent before it began.

Before 1908 the automobile was a luxury. After the war it affected the Adirondacks more dramatically even than the Reverend Murray's book did in 1869. Henry Ford, who made it possible for better than one out of two families in the Northeast to own a car by 1925, even designed a special touring auto—possibly the first recreational vehicle—complete with stoves, bedding, and ice chest for an Adirondack camping trip with his good friend John Burroughs.

Conservation had not been alone among reform movements in the United States at the turn of the century. Governor Hill in supporting "forever wild" did so at least in part to fend off other reform measures that seemed more threatening to the established order of things. He couldn't stop the tide, though. By 1920 universal suffrage, Prohibition, and conservation were all familiar and well-supported movements, as was the fight for shorter work hours, higher wages, the right to a vacation every year, and access to nature.

The Adirondacks played a part in helping Americans articulate their changing attitude toward nature. The consequences of the change altered the balance between man and nature permanently. "Forever wild" soon faced new challenges that made Governor Hill's dilemma seem tame. And a period of relatively peaceful accommodation between man and nature in the Adirondacks came to an end.

17

Love Unto Death

In the fall of 1881, people living on the West Side of New York City, then one of the wealthy residential neighborhoods in the city, received a leaflet. It was election time, and the citizens were accustomed to a barrage of circulars and posters and campaign speeches. But the well-to-do who received this particular pamphlet were surprised to read that Theodore Roosevelt, of the New York Roosevelts, was running for the state assembly.

It was not the sort of career one expected from a young man fresh out of Harvard (*magna cum laude*, class of 1880), with respected ancestors, secure social position, presumed moral integrity, tendencies towards foppishness, an inclination toward literature (many heard he was writing a book on naval history), and a childhood history of chronic ailments.

Roosevelt was elected, however, to three terms in the assembly, where he built a political base from which he ascended, almost without setback, from one important post to the next. He was Civil Service commissioner in Washington, assistant secretary of the U.S. Navy, police commissioner in New York City, governor of the State of New York, vice-president of the United States, and finally president (1901–1909) for one partial term as successor to the assassinated McKinley and one full term as the choice of the people. Throughout his public life Roosevelt enjoyed immense popularity, and if anything, history has accorded him higher accolades for sense and sensibility than those awarded him during his lifetime.

Among his many achievements, Teddy — a name he hated — valued perhaps above the others his keen love of nature and his role in convincing the public and the government to take care of it. "The

Roosevelt Era" has been universally lauded as one of the most important in the history of conservation.

During Roosevelt's presidency, nearly 200 million acres of land were set aside as wilderness preserves, national forests, and tracts for conservation experiments. When Roosevelt left office the amount of land owned and administered by the federal government for the purpose of preservation and/or conservation had increased more than six times.

Yet if there was ever an unlikely candidate for such a record, it was Teddy Roosevelt as a child. He had been skinny, nearsighted, and subject to severe bouts of asthma and other ailménts. He never attended a school but was given his elementary and secondary education by private tutors, partly as a concession to his frailty.

His physical weaknesses, however, were more than compensated for by strength of character. He attacked his frail body as if it were an enemy, following a self-imposed regimen of exercise and outdoor activity. By the time he was twenty-five, he was nearly six feet tall with a barrel chest and a passion for horseback riding, hunting, and strenuous exercise of all kinds. Only thick eyeglasses hinted at his childhood puniness.

Young Roosevelt, like the tubercular Edward Livingston Trudeau, embraced nature as a cure for, rather than a cause of, disease. Also like Trudeau, Roosevelt spent time at Paul Smith's hotel on St. Regis Lake in the Adirondacks. In the 1870s, he spent three happy, memorable summers there, and it is not too farfetched to say that the Adirondacks shaped Teddy's personal passion for nature.

Roosevelt, like John Burroughs, was fascinated by birds. While the Adirondacks harbored relatively few rare species, the birds there were close, easy to observe. So Teddy began to make a list of the ones he saw. He counted ninety-seven species in all, and his catalog, assembled when he was still a teenager, was the first ever compiled for Adirondack ornithology.

As an adult, Roosevelt traveled all over the world and visited many wilderness sites, Africa, South America, and the American West. But he often returned to the Adirondacks, and it was while he was vacationing at the Tahawas Club, one of the largest private forest preserves in the mountains, that Roosevelt, then vice-president, learned that President McKinley had been shot in Buffalo.

Roosevelt was climbing Mt. Marcy on the afternoon of September 13, 1901, when a messenger, having scrambled as fast as possible up the mountain, declared that McKinley, unexpectedly, was dying.

By the time Roosevelt got to Buffalo, after a legendary midnight relay ride via horse-drawn buggies over notorious Adirondack roads to

the train station at North Creek, McKinley was dead. Roosevelt technically became president sometime after midnight, on a foggy, pitch-black
trail somewhere between the Tahawas Club and North Creek.

Roosevelt was the twenty-sixth president of the United States. At
the time he was the youngest man ever to assume the office. He had
grown up as the cult of wilderness appreciation was gaining momentum.
Exploiting his personal love of nature, his energy and popularity, he was
able to translate a growing national love of nature into public policy.

Yet even for Roosevelt, who knew John Burroughs and John Muir
well and agreed with their commitment to nature, there remained a
certain ambivalence. Roosevelt, the complete outdoorsman, outspoken
advocate of vigorous confrontations with raw nature, personification of
physical and moral integrity, was also known for his sophistication, wit,
even elegance. The style he set in the White House was sometimes
criticized for being too pompous. He hired coachmen and dressed them in
glittering livery, making them look a bit like decadent European royalty.
He lavishly entertained the most urbane of America's citizens as well as
many of the most eminently "civilized" European aristocracy. He was no
frontiersman, as Andrew Jackson was, but a well-bred, highly educated,
even bookish gentleman. He represented the best American civilization
had to offer; he was, in effect, a product of the pioneering battle to
conquer the American wilderness and wrestle it into submission.

For Roosevelt, however, this conflict between his breeding and
background and his love of the out-of-doors was not a serious problem.
He proved that a person could combine genuine love of nature with a
civilized life. He set an example that enabled millions of people to admire,
even emulate, the rugged experiences of the American pioneers (whom
Teddy adored and wrote about) but on a part-time, sporting basis. In
short, Roosevelt helped resolve an old American dilemma. He said that
people could enjoy and love nature and at the same time harness parts of
it for profit and in the interests of civilization.

Such, too, was his approach to the growing conflict between
conservationists and preservationists. For the most part, he was able to
satisfy both groups. More than 10 percent of the land Roosevelt managed
to have set aside was quite explicitly marked as resource preserve—not
necessarily for recreation or wilderness value, but for future sources of oil,
coal, or water power. Roosevelt often used the economic argument
perfected by Adirondack "forever wilders," and he used it well. In this
sense, the history of "forever wild" was a good working model for many
national battles.

Meanwhile, the taste for what Roosevelt called "delight in the hardy life of the open," spread quickly. The love of nature was even organized and institutionalized.

The Sierra Club, formed by twenty-seven men in 1892, grew apace after the turn of the century, as did the Appalachian Club, formed in 1876. The American Scenic and Historic Preservation Society (1895), the American Park and the Outdoor Art Societies (both formed in the 1890s), the Isaak Walton League of America and the Wilderness Society (formed by Robert Marshall, who like many leading preservationists developed his love of nature as a boy at his family's camp in the Adirondacks) enjoyed great success in the early years of the twentieth century.

A tamer version of the trend appeared in the growth of the Garden Club movement, which spread across the country and instructed millions of urban women in the principles of natural history. The Boy Scouts began in 1910, and their *Handbook* became the best-selling book in United States history, after the Bible. The summer camp phenomenon exploded; by 1915, more than 300 private camps for affluent children existed.

"Anything can happen now . . .," wrote F. Scott Fitzgerald in his novel, *The Great Gatsby*, which epitomized the 1920s, "anything at all."

The sentence applies to the booming love of nature as well as to the other phenomena of the 1920s. A sense of the excessive was evident everywhere. There was a "more of everything" tenor to the Twenties, as Samuel Eliot Morison wrote, more "money, leisure, cars, sexy movies, dance halls, jazz," short skirts, bobbed hair, wild parties—and longing for nature. The longing was perhaps less pure than the brand Roosevelt and his friends John Muir and John Burroughs developed and practiced, but it was explosive.

Until the 1930s curtailed, for a time, some of the footlooseness of the 1920s, the Adirondacks felt their share of the exuberance. In 1923, the Conservation Commission, then filling the role of administrator and annual reporter on how things were going in the mountains, noted that during the summer months that year, one hundred thousand people had used the four large campsites which had been built on Forest Preserve land in the previous ten years. In one village near the Sacandaga River in Hamilton County, a staggering crowd of fifteen hundred people turned up one day in July.

The Conservation Commission, under the leadership of an energetic advocate of preservation, George DuPont Pratt, had worked hard to make the Adirondacks attractive for hikers and campers by building lean-to's, carving trails, and making other recreational improvements. Proud of its work, the commission had in 1921 printed and distributed one hundred thousand pamphlets describing the camping facilities, shelters, fireplaces, trails, and other recreational facilities in the Forest Preserve. Apparently the pamphlets had done their job, for within two years, one tourist for each pamphlet turned out to follow its advice.

In addition to state recreational resources, several private clubs had formed among nature lovers who banded together to buy large chunks of land. The Adirondack Mountain Club, for instance, was founded in 1922, and members bought a large tract of land in the High Peaks region. Theirs was a kind of private nature preserve, maintained as wilderness, featuring only a few campsites and hiking trails built voluntarily in strict accordance with "forever wild" mandates. The Adirondack Mountain Club was careful, for example, to clear only pre-existing trails so as not to have to cut trees, and their club buildings were appropriately rustic and woodsy. Club membership increased steadily. Branches were established in dozens of cities, and requirements for admission included a proved commitment to "forever wild."

One of the most famous private clubs in the Adirondacks, however, was one of the least typical. The Lake Placid Club in the village of Lake Placid, on Mirror Lake, was the brainchild of Melville Dewey, the New York librarian and inventor of the Dewey Decimal System. He had first gone to the Adirondacks in the 1890s for relief from hay fever, where Paul Smith advised him to buy land and build a hotel. Dewey did, but his resort was not just any hotel; it was an exclusive club where only Dewey's approval would do for admission.

He had some peculiar ideas: he refused all invalids (ironic, since he himself had been one before his arrival in the Adirondacks), all Jews, and all those who did not show evidence of adding to the club's atmosphere of upright enjoyment of nature. "Stranjers," he advised in his simplified phonetic system of spelling—a pet project that prevailed at the Lake Placid Club, but unlike Dewey's Decimal System, did not catch on elsewhere—"should refer to prominent citizens" for application.

The club was popular, however. Within twenty-eight years of its organization in 1891, membership had grown from eighty to more than one hundred thousand. A handsome, sprawling clubhouse, now a public hotel, housed guests. Dairies, gardens, golf courses, and, of course, stretches of wilderness added to their comfort and pleasure.

These private clubs to a degree replaced the vast hotels of the 1880s and 90s. For ordinary people lakeside cabins, overnight lodges, and the like replaced the boarding houses. And state camping facilities met the needs of thousands who no longer went to the Adirondacks in order to sit on porches and pass the time rocking back and forth or play at roughing it. They went mainly to experience the vigorous life in the open, to confront nature as their ancestors had done and as their beloved Teddy Roosevelt had urged.

By 1923, too, the Adirondack forest was beginning to look primeval again. More than 20 million new trees, some planted by the state, others by private groups, were growing to maturity. Signs of logging were beginning to disappear. The new forest looked a bit different, of course. More hardwood trees grew; new species, the Scotch pine and the Norway spruce, for example, were doing well, too. Experiments to replace everyone's favorite tree, the white pine, had not been very successful. Seedlings imported from Europe had Blister Rust, a fungus to which American trees had no resistance. Blister Rust acts like a blood clot in the human body. It cuts off the vital moisture-bearing passages between a tree's roots and its branches and causes certain death if allowed to spread. And it spread before anyone realized what was happening. Those white pines that survived the fungus then proved susceptible to a particularly nasty weevil known as the white pine weevil. Only about a quarter inch long, reddish with white splotches, the weevil attacks, eats, and destroys the juicy terminal sprouts on young trees, forcing the young trees to grow sideways instead of straight up.

Wildlife also changed. Like the white pine, the white-tailed deer has always been thought to be *the* Adirondack mammal. Ironically, there were probably more of them in the 1920s than there had been in Champlain's day. The full-grown male that needs six pounds of good browse a day was much happier in a deciduous forest than it had been in a conifer one.

Even in an environment so suited to deer, hunters began to outnumber them. In 1883, the year state land in the Adirondacks was withdrawn from public sale, certain restrictions were imposed upon the number of deer a hunter was allowed to kill; one hunter could take three. A hunting season of sorts had existed in New York since 1788, when people were allowed to hunt deer only between August and December, but the law was impossible to enforce. With the creation of the Forest Preserve and the mandate of its administrators such laws were made to work. And they became stricter. In 1895, the hunting season was shortened from August 16 to October 16, and only two deer per person were allowed. By 1897 it was thought that killing deer that were in water was unsportsmanlike and the practice was banned. One of "Adirondack" Murray's favorite sports, jack-hunting, or attracting deer at night by strong light, was disallowed in 1904.

By 1920 deer hunting season in the Adirondacks lasted only one month, from October 15 to November 15 and in 1926 hunters had to buy licenses. Still, hunters took between seven and twelve thousand deer each year in the 1920s.

Man-imposed restrictions and the new Adirondack forests allowed deer herds to thrive again. And thrive they did, so dramatically that after about twenty years they literally outgrew the environment. Too many deer and too little food meant that more and more were dying not from hunters' bullets but from starvation. Herds of famished deer threatened the tender young forests men and women had worked so hard to raise and plant.

Conservationists began to see that allowing hunters to kill more deer was a way of thinning out herds, for their own benefit and for the benefit of the forest. Hunting, therefore, was encouraged, and by the 1960s about twenty thousand Adirondack deer were shot by hunters annually. In 1970, a total of forty-seven thousand deer were legally killed.

Managing the deer population was not the only example of wildlife management to take place in the Adirondacks. A group of conservationists decided in 1904 that the beaver, the creature that had enticed white men into the Adirondacks in the first place, should be returned to the mountains. Beavers had not been wiped out entirely, but by the turn of the century were so rare as to be exceptional. Having collected them from the northwest, conservationists released six adult beavers into the Adirondack woods near Old Forge. Two years later, fourteen more western beavers were released and with trapping made illegal, everyone hoped for the best.

Within ten years the beaver population had more than doubled. Within another decade beavers were so numerous and so busy building dams, flooding forest lands, even disrupting village water supplies, that trapping restrictions were rescinded.

Programs to hatch trout and restock streams were also started in the 1880s. Under the direction of the Commission of Fisheries and with $5,000 from the state, a hatchery for "trout and other fish natural to that locality" was built in 1888 at Mill Creek, near Round Lake in Hamilton County. The hatchery operated for fifteen years but proved only marginally successful. Later, more scientific attempts were adopted so that today trout restocking in Adirondack lakes and streams enables the region to boast the best trout fishing in the state.

Some restocking experiments were less than beneficial. One near disaster was the introduction of bass into the Adirondacks. Unfortunately, the bass had a great liking for baby trout, foiling many an effort to restock the favorite Adirondack fish. Another disastrous "success" was the introduction of yellow perch, which turned out to be even more voracious than the bass, and ate both trout and bass. "This most nondiscriminating appetite with fins will turn out eight thousand eggs at a clip, sometimes twice a year," William Chapman White remarked ruefully of the perch. As a result, by the 1950s there were more than four times as many yellow perch as trout in Adirondack waters. Experiments to remove all fish from certain ponds in order to reintroduce only desirable species have been controversial in the Adirondacks, but in some cases they have been successful.

Such was the lot of the anxious conservationists trying to return the Adirondacks to a condition similar to that of the 1850s. The successes confirmed in the minds of many that the proper role man should take was bold management. But the failures suggested to others that in a genuine wilderness preserve, man had no business whatever and should let nature take whatever course it chose. The dilemma over man's role in nature was not solved.

Yet more and more men and women were seeking nature, and in spite of certain objections, the managers of the Adirondack Forest Preserve, which by the 1930s had grown to include nearly twice as much land as it originally encompassed, were making nature more accessible.

The people of New York voted an amendment to "forever wild" in 1927, only the second time they had agreed to any change since 1894. The change was to be a highway—a memorial to World War I veterans— eight miles long leading from the little town of Wilmington, a hamlet in the northern part of Essex County, to the summit of Whiteface Mountain, the fifth highest peak in the Adirondacks. The amendment was extremely controversial, requiring as it did the destruction of trees on Forest Preserve land. But the desire to see the world by automobile was becoming as compelling as the desire to respect the letter of "forever wild" law, and the road was finished in 1928.

Tourists, by this time, not only saw the Adirondacks in automobiles, but also on foot, on skis, on skates, and on sleds. Winter sports sprang up, at first at the Lake Placid Club where toboggan runs, outdoor skating rinks, cross-country ski trails, and even a ski jump appeared at the request of members in the 1920s. "By 1924," reports Adirondack observer Paula Metzler, "special trains were being run from New York to Placid with banners reading 'We are bound for Lake Placid and the Ski Jump!'" Thirty-five hundred people went to Lake Placid in 1925 to see one of the first ski jump competitions in the United States.

In fact, Lake Placid was bidding to become the most famous winter sports resort in the United States by the 1930s. The man who has

The 1932 Olympic Games in Lake Placid brought thousands of people to the Adirondacks, but the crowds then seem unimpressive next to the expected thirty thousand visitors a day for the 1980 Games. *Photo courtesy of the Saranac Lake Free Library, Adirondack Collection*

been called "the father of winter sports in America," was largely responsible for such fame. He was Godfrey Dewey, son of Melville, and it was his leadership that won for Lake Placid the bid to host the third Winter Olympic Games in 1932. In the midst of the Great Depression, over a million dollars were raised for the Olympic facilities, many of which are in use today. There was a new stadium, an indoor ice-skating rink, where the figure skater Sonja Henie became a star during the games, and perhaps most spectacular of all, a bobsled run, the first in America and the finest in the world. It was 200 meters long, 44 meters longer than any in Europe and was designed for ultimate speed: a thrilling 65 miles an hour.

The bobsled run alone cost $200,000, a financial fact that was less shocking to many than the original plan to build the run on Forest Preserve land. A group of conservationists, including David McClure who had argued so eloquently for the forever wild constitutional amendment, had in 1902 formed the Association for the Protection of the Adirondacks. This group challenged the bobsled run in court, arguing that the state would have to destroy thousands of trees on Forest Preserve land for what could only be considered frivolous reasons. The state court of appeals upheld the argument, and the bobsled run was built on the side of Mt. Van Hoevenberg owned privately by the Lake Placid Club.

If "forever wild" was legally powerful enough to prevent the bobsled run, however, advocates of recreational facilities on Forest Preserve land proved equally determined in 1941. That year, New Yorkers voted a new amendment to the "forever wild" article by approving the construction of new ski trails, with ski lifts and other improvements, on Forest Preserve land on Whiteface Mountain. Meanwhile, the Conservation Department oversaw construction of new hiking trails, walking trails, nature trails, bridle paths, campsites, lean-to's, and increasingly sophisticated fire-protection systems.

By 1940 the Adirondacks were indeed the people's park. Not only could tourists camp, but they could ski, rent canoes, and, of course, climb mountains. There was also the first theme park in America, Santa's Workshop, in the town of North Pole at the foot of Whiteface Mountain, to visit. A Jay native by the name of Arto Monaco built the park after World War II and prospered; in fact, ten thousand people showed up one day soon after it opened.

Only during World War II, when many campsites were closed and even the Lake Placid Club turned into an army training center, did a lull in the onslaught of tourists occur. The rest of the time, the increase in tourism never stopped.

"It's too bad a man has to kill every step he takes," says a fictional character in one of the few novels written about the Adirondacks by a North Country native. Irving Bacheller, author of *Eben Holden*, put those words in the mouth of a lover and great respecter of nature. Many men and women share his insight. Even Verplanck Colvin, with his small team of surveyors, disturbed the environment, simply by being there, simply by trying to preserve it.

Increasingly, it became not the loggers or miners who threatened the sanctity of the woods and mountains and waters. Those who loved the Adirondacks for their natural beauty were becoming the primary threats to the environment — as they tramped the woods, fished the streams, drove the highways, scaled the mountains, built cabins, breathed the air, and admired the views.

After World War II it was no longer man the exploiter but man the appreciator who had to be watched, regulated, and warned. "The woods

Overhiked trail at Avalanche Pass, 1975. *Collection of the New York State Museum*

locked up against the few meant the woods opened up for the many,"
William Chapman White wrote optimistically in 1954. By 1964 it looked to
some as if the woods would have to be locked up against the many as well.

Teddy Roosevelt's joyful insistence that Americans "develop

hardihood, resolution and scorn of discomfort" by getting out into the wilderness had led to a revolution in American habits. Many who loved the Adirondacks were delighted. The revolution meant jobs and prosperity. Others were terrified. Whatever else a wilderness was, it was not, they believed, crowded with people who were threatening to love the Adirondack wilderness to death.

18

For Beauty's Sake

IN THE AUTUMN OF 1968, another New York State governor took his place among many predecessors who had been worried since the 1880s over what to do about the Adirondacks. How should they be preserved? How much could they or their visitors and inhabitants be regulated? What, in fact, was wilderness, a term whose meaning seemed to change with succeeding generations? Was the Adirondack Mountain region genuinely wilderness by *any* definition?

Such were a few of the problems Governor Nelson Aldrich Rockefeller faced in the 1960s. Mounting complaints about the condition of the Adirondack wilderness, increasing demand from visitors for pleasure in the wilds, and growing national concerns over environmental problems all put pressure on the governor to take a fresh look at New York's vast North Country.

After World War II the number of visitors to the Adirondacks exceeded all predictions or expectations. In 1952, for example, nearly seven hundred thousand people went to the Adirondacks to camp or hike, fish or picnic, ski or climb mountains. Two years later, nearly one hundred thousand people had to be turned away from public campsites, and in 1955, one hundred and fifty thousand were sent packing when they showed up at state recreational sites with their knapsacks, collapsible stoves, tents, and sleeping bags. There was simply no more room on the more than three thousand public campsites.

Demand for camping facilities was so enormous by 1965 that authorities estimated that the state would have to build camps, boat launching sites, trails, picnic areas, and other facilities for an expected crowd of 4 million visitors a year by 1980.

Many believe the sheer beauty of the Adirondack land is reason enough to
preserve it. *Photo by W. F. Kollecker, courtesy of the Saranac Lake Free Library, Adirondack Collection*

Such high estimates were still below the mark, however. In 1968,
the State Department of Commerce reported that 8 million people visited
the Adirondacks that year. In the 1970s more than 9 million people visited
the region annually.

The Adirondacks, only a few hours' drive from most of the East's
major cities, were accessible to more than one-third of the United States
population and two-thirds of the Canadian population. Near the geographical center of the highly industrialized, polluted, highway-ridden
Northeast, the Adirondacks, still wild and relatively pristine, were won-
derfully inviting. Their inexpensive campsites, their restaurants and
hotels, forest, and lakes lured millions.

And as surely as the effects of industrialization were giving
people the money, time, and inclination to go to the Adirondacks, so too
were the accoutrements of industrialization becoming a part of nearly all
vacations. Most people drove to the Adirondacks in automobiles after the

1940s, or people flew to the airport at Lake Clear, seventeen miles from Lake Placid. The railroads had practically ceased to operate.

Gradually, even the automobile came to seem rare as campers, trailers, and buses grew in number and comfort. Like turtles, Americans seemed to feel safer with their movable houses on their backs.

Driving to the Adirondacks became easier with the building of Interstate 87. Since the new highway had to knife through 300 acres of Forest Preserve land in order to connect Montreal and Albany, New Yorkers had to pass an amendment to "forever wild" before construction could begin. They did, amidst great controversy in 1959. The Northway, as Route 87 is called, was completed in 1967, and while people still argue about it, millions more Canadians and New Yorkers can get in their cars, drive swiftly through lovely scenery and be in the heart of the wilderness within a few hours.

People weren't just driving to the Adirondacks for a week's stay, however. Another phenomenon of the 1950s and 1960s was the boom in vacation homes. In the 1960s, approximately one-third of America's 50 million families had within their economic power the ability to buy second homes, if not campers or boats or trailers as well. Such houses could not, of course, be built on Forest Preserve land, but in 1968, 61 percent of the land within the Blue Line, or the park boundaries, was still privately owned. The age of real estate development meant hundreds of new second homes on small lots and the provision of more plumbing, power, water, and garbage collection and disposal. More people also tended to mean billboards, flashing signs, and traffic jams on winding mountain roads. Urban blight in the wilderness threatened people of the twentieth century just as the "howl, howl, howl" of wilderness wolves had frightened the pioneering Sheldons of the eighteenth century.

Since private land abuts public "forever wild" land at every turn, and since legal boundaries cannot contain noise, air pollution, and other side effects of civilization, a growing number of people became alarmed about the future of the Forest Preserve. The threat was twofold: too many people using the Forest Preserve put its wilderness quality in jeopardy; and too much hasty development on private land was likely to abuse the purity of the Preserve.

There were other matters about the Adirondacks to worry Governor Rockefeller. The jumble of official governing bodies charged with looking after the Forest Preserve was by 1968 as confusing as the patchwork pattern of state and private land. There were at least ten agencies whose authority extended to the region. The Department of Conservation was the primary agency in charge, but within its structure dozens of different offices oversaw the various aspects of Park and Preserve administration. Fire prevention and control, analysis of mineral resources, wildlife management, hunting laws and licenses, water purity, trapping regulations, camp maintenance, highway building, surveying, and reforestation were only a few of the things that had to be taken care of. Even the federal government was involved, since such national historic sites as the farm where the abolitionist John Brown was buried were inside Park boundaries.

So many controls upon a supposedly natural environment seemed ridiculous to many. To others inevitable conflicts of interest between agencies and departments seemed destined to preclude proper management of natural resources.

One solution to these problems caused almost as much controversy as the problems themselves. In 1967, Governor Rockefeller's brother, Laurance, a conservation advocate, Adirondack land owner and chairman of the New York State Council of Parks, proposed that the central Adirondacks be converted into a national park of nearly two million acres. The federal government alone, he argued, could afford to buy the huge tracts of private land that stood in the way of the unified wilderness he and others believed to be desirable. As Fred Sullivan wrote in an article for *Empire State Report* in 1975, "The Rockefellers seldom make public moves that do not precipitate big waves."

The national park proposal produced a wave of opposition. Land owners didn't want to give up their holdings to the federal government. Conservationists didn't trust the National Park Service which, they feared, was likely to set up tacky tourist centers. Lumber companies weren't about to sell tracts of good timber. Native Adirondackers and tourists alike objected because hunting in national parks is forbidden. Even today, when most people consider the national park idea to be safely dead, mere mention of it is *"the* most unpopular thing to say," according to the publisher of the *Adirondack Daily Enterprise*, William Doolittle.

Opposition to Laurance Rockefeller's proposal, however, brought the issue of land use planning in the Adirondacks out in the open. The Rockefellers claimed that was the purpose of the proposal anyway, and the governor appointed a Temporary Study Commission on the Future of the Adirondacks to analyze problems and suggest new solutions. So in 1968, a group of scientists, historians, nature lovers, lawyers, and others took its place alongside so many other, similar commissions over the years charged with recommending action to protect the Adirondack wilderness.

One of the earliest such commissions had met in 1872 to "inquire into the expediency of providing for vesting in the state the title to the timbered regions lying within" seven Adirondack counties. For those men, the watershed was the outstanding reason for preserving the forests. They recommended the creation of a park in the Adirondacks as the best means of protecting New York's major water supply. Only secondarily was recreation listed as a reason for preservation.

Over the years recreation acquired a new prominence in the minds of New Yorkers, so that by 1938, when the original "forever wild" constitutional amendment, Article 7, Section 7, was changed in a constitutional convention to Article 14, recreation as a rationale for preservation had become, if not paramount, at least as important as the watershed factor.

Even if the provision of recreational facilities meant the destruction or removal of trees from the Forest Preserve—technically forbidden under any circumstances—New Yorkers seemed willing to bend the spirit of the law if their public pleasures were at stake. Building of campsites and boat launching sites seemed immoral and unconstitutional to some strict interpreters of "forever wild," but to most the Forest Preserve existed primarily for recreation.

By 1968 both recreation and the watershed factor were so widely accepted they barely needed defense. Scientific investigation had upheld the principles behind the watershed, and the hordes of backpackers, campers, boating enthusiasts, outdoorsmen, skiers, and weekend pioneers testified to the new inclusion of recreation as a virtual right.

But something fundamental about preservation policy and philosophy had changed, too. The overriding concern of the Temporary Study Commission on the Future of the Adirondacks was neither watershed nor recreation. It was beauty, sheer beauty: its preservation, its maintenance, its sanctity. This was new.

The commission studied the Adirondacks for two years, and in 1970, the members submitted their report, a ninety-six page book filled with full-color photographs of trees and mountains and rivers and lakes. Obviously, the commissioners loved the Adirondacks with the passion of Verplanck Colvin, with the scientific awe of Ebenezer Emmons, and with the delight in nature of the Reverend Murray. The difference was that the 1968 commission did not need to wrap its arguments in terms of economics or religion or health, or even in recreational needs. They argued for preservation in terms of esthetics. What the commission urged, without cavil or qualification, was that the Adirondacks be saved for beauty's sake.

Not everyone accepted the argument, of course. Some felt the idea was little more than romantic balderdash among tasteful urbanites who didn't like tract houses and neon signs. Many who took this view believed the rights of the Adirondack inhabitants, who often depended upon building and the expansion of tourism and recreational facilities for a living, were the most important considerations in any new look at the Adirondacks. They feared that stringent governmental intervention in the interests of preserving the beauty of public land was bound to cause undue hardship for those trying to develop private land.

Nevertheless, the value of wilderness beauty and the need to protect it was an idea gaining acceptance all over the country. Many state and federal courts had sanctioned the right of government to intervene even in private actions if certain natural conditions seemed threatened. In 1954, for example, the U.S. Supreme Court upheld the right of a public agency to stop the activities of a private landowner whose building projects jeopardized the general public's right to beauty. "It is within the power of the legislature," the Court wrote in *Berman* v. *Parker*, "to determine that the community should be beautiful as well as healthy, spacious as well as clean, well-balanced as well as carefully patrolled."

In 1964, the Congress of the United States even defined wilderness, and in passing the Wilderness Act "accorded wild country unprecedented national recognition," Roderick Nash wrote. Henceforward, the Congress said, wilderness was "hereby recognized as an area where the earth and its community of life are untrammeled by man—where man himself is a visitor who does not remain"—a condition which once had made Americans eager to tame and transform the land into a useful, profitable, high-yielding farm or factory or lumber camp.

The commission studying the Adirondacks had plenty of support for its conviction that the mountains, forests, and lakes had to be protected for their beauty. Its report accepted the federal definition of wilderness as a guiding principle behind its recommendations. It was clear that a genuine wilderness could include man only as a transient, and a passive transient at that. The report to the governor quoted William Chapman White, who believed that the Adirondacks as a natural environment should remain a vehicle by which man could "stand on a rock . . . and be in a past he could not have known, in a future he will not see. He can be part of time that was and time yet to come."

As things stood in the 1970s, the man standing on the rock was likely to see all too many signs, not of eternity, but of the polluted present. "The private owner of a lovely Adirondack shoreline property may now, if he likes, build on its shores a movie theater or an amusement center or a trailer park," the commission report stated. Whatever else a movie theater or a housing development might mean, it was not in accordance with wilderness beauty. And however elitist, interventionary, or romantic state control of private owners' ventures might seem, the public wilderness, in the commissioners' opinion, had to come first. The state, as the protector of the general public's good, was therefore obligated to take "massive" action. "Man's survival is at the core of this concern," the commissioners believed. "Forever wild" was at stake.

It would be impossible to get further from "forever wild" than the pioneer ideology whose precepts guided the builders of the United States. To them, survival depended absolutely on subduing wilderness. People cultivated in their children a fear of the woods. The protagonist in the Adirondack novel *Eben Holden* expressed such a need when he said of the North Country wilderness in the eighteenth century, "I got the impression that it was a country of unexampled wickedness and ferocity in men and animals." Above all, a person needed "the fear of the woods or [he] would have strayed to [his] death in them."

Descendants of the pioneers believed precisely the opposite. Only by refining his love of the forests, and making sacrifices in order to preserve them, could man survive, the commission argued.

Yet just as the general pioneer ideology revealed, on closer inspection, a glimmer of appreciation for the beauty of wilderness, so too was the apparently extreme position in favor of natural beauty complicated in 1970 by a remnant of practicality. However much members of the Temporary Study Commission may have wanted to make the Adirondacks a true wilderness, "untrammeled by man," they did not, after all, recommend that the Adirondacks be withdrawn from public use altogether. Although such withdrawal was the only way to achieve the ideal situation, it was hardly possible.

Instead the commissioners compromised, concocting a system in which the whole park might be saved from the worst aspects of civilization while some parts would be made pristine wilderness. Transition areas could be adapted for the conveniences of man, for his recreation and pleasure; some areas could even be used for light industry.

While the commission's recommendations, later adopted as laws by the legislature, may have represented an ideological compromise, their application also meant the curtailment of certain individual rights. The extension of governmental control over private property was bound to cause trouble, and it did.

Nevertheless, the politics of beauty prevailed. If the needs of nature did not entirely dominate the needs of man, man's interests were made to seem so dependent upon the interests of nature as to put trees

Natural beauty and recreation are interdependent in today's Adirondack Park.
Collection of the New York State Museum

and water and mountains before the immediate needs of many men and women.

   "It is now settled," decided the New York Court of Appeals in 1972, "that aesthetics is a valid subject of legislative concern." For proponents of natural beauty for natural beauty's sake the issue was settled, too. But a settlement implies a victory, in this case a victory of nature over man. For many, the tentative truce between man and nature in the Adirondacks was at an end. Victory for one side only meant festering discontent for the other and the preparation for a renewed war.

The temporary commission tried to tie up all the strands of Adirondack history, human and natural, into a neat package designed to benefit everyone. With the best of intentions, they had not included every strand. The old problem of man and nature was not completely solved.

THE NEW PROBLEM OF
MAN AND NATURE

19

Saving For or From?

THERE WERE 181 WAYS TO SAVE the Adirondacks, reported Governor Rockefeller's Commission on the Future of the Adirondacks in December 1970. The foremost was naming a single agency with responsibility for the Park and only the Park. Then all the land in the Park, both state Forest Preserve and private property, could be analyzed carefully to determine how much use it could withstand. After such a survey and analysis, the agency in charge might decide and monitor just what could and could not be done in the interest of the total environment.

The overarching theme of the commission's plan was that the Adirondacks needed to be seen as a whole, and the whole should be made to seem as wilderness. No longer could a concern for separate units — rivers, forests, villages, lakes — administered by separate agencies or municipalities or landowners, hope to preserve the sense of open space or natural wilderness.

There were problems enough on the Forest Preserve. Recreational overuse threatened the delicate ecological balance in such beautiful but fragile spots as the High Peaks region where too many hikers had worn away the thin soil on the very popular trail to the top of Mt. Marcy, for example. Furthermore, trash and litter along the Mt. Marcy trail was so bad the Conservation Department was having to dispatch helicopters, sometimes on a weekly basis, to gather up the cans and paper and other debris. Increasing numbers of snowmobiles generated noise pollution and, more seriously, endangered new growth on young trees as the machines raced through woodlands.

One particularly insidious problem affecting the whole Adirondack region was so-called acid rain. Increased levels of inorganic acids, emitted mainly as a result of heavy industrial use of fossil fuels in the Midwest and Northeast, mix with the atmosphere and, in effect, pollute rainfall. Thin Adirondack soil is unusually susceptible to the sulfuric and nitric acids in the polluted rain because the less soil there is, the lower its capacity to assimilate acid. At elevations above twenty-five hundred feet, where rainfall is heavy and soils very shallow, whole lakes can become so drenched with acids that no fish can exist. Furthermore, as Carl L. Schofield of the New York Department of Natural Resources writes in *New York's Food and Life Sciences*, "if an acid episode coincides with a species' spawning period or the presence of sensitive eggs and larvae, a complete loss of a year class could result." Acid rain is a problem no one yet knows how to solve, but since it threatens all the Adirondacks, public and private, it points up a need to study the region as a whole unit.

For the Study Commission, other problems on privately owned land seemed nearly as intractable as acid rain. Even though almost 80 percent of the private land in the Adirondacks appeared to be cared for with as much concern about natural beauty as on the Forest Preserve—in many places in the region, the commissioners noted, it was impossible to tell the difference between private and public land—"unguided development on the 3,500,000 acres of private land will destroy the character of the entire park if immediate action is not taken."

Indeed, more than half the Adirondack Park was owned by individuals or companies. Most of the private land was in the hands of large companies and single large tract owners, but 28 percent of the 3.5 million private acres was owned by the so-called "little guys," those with only a few acres apiece.

While big companies were accustomed to government regulations of all kinds, individuals were not. What the commission most feared was "unguided development," mainly in the form of residential subdivision and its inevitable attendant, "urban blight." "Throughout this country," the commissioners pleaded, "unplanned development of both private and public land is despoiling resources once considered limitless. . . . Smog-ridden cities, suburban sprawl, billboard jungles, polluted lakes and rivers, and a disrupted ecosystem have contributed to a reconsideration of the relationship between man and his environment."

In the Adirondacks such disruptions could only occur on private land. Therefore, there was little choice, in the commissioners' opinion, but to impose strict regulations upon everyone in the Adirondacks.

The state had long since given up the idea of buying all the land in the mountains, thus enabling it to assume undisputed control as the federal government had in the creation of the national parks. New York could only regulate its private citizens' activities and hope they would accept the regulations gracefully, recognizing how important they were to the retention of the "sanctuary" the Adirondacks had so long provided from urban ills.

In short, the commission recommended, and in 1971 the state legislature accepted, what turned out to be the most comprehensive zoning program ever enacted in the United States up to that time. The Adirondack Park Agency (APA) was created as the authority given responsibility for the total park. This agency was to implement recommendations of Rockefeller's commission by which the Adirondacks could be saved. Agency headquarters were set up in the tiny village of Ray Brook, about midway between Lake Placid and Saranac Lake, at the foot of a wilderness trail leading to Mt. McKenzie. From there, scientists, lawyers, and nature-minded administrators began their job of making sure the Adirondacks remained a sanctuary from the "unrelenting pressures of an increasingly urbanized society."

The commissioners expected, indeed planned ahead toward the day when the 104 towns and villages of the Adirondack region would eventually take over land use control of their own territories. Meanwhile, however, the park agency set up as interim measures specifications by which expansion or improvements had to be planned and approved.

Land developers were to be restricted, as were summer residents wanting to add a room to their lakeside cottages, and motel owners wanting to build new wings, and large-lot owners wanting to sell. There was, the commission and its successor the Park Agency insisted, plenty of room for expansion and growth, even development, but there was no room for unplanned expansion or ugly accretions.

The Adirondack Park Agency was thus handed the job of saving the Adirondacks *for* New Yorkers and mankind, and at the same time *from* man's abuse. There was a very fine line between the two. No backpacker, no motel owner, no lumber company, no school child or government official could escape the irony inherent in the new policy.

One of the great American nature lovers, Henry David Thoreau, who learned so much from Emerson, has been a guiding figure to environmentalists throughout the years. But Thoreau's spirit of independence, self-sufficiency, and his distaste for regulation of any kind could have made him a hero to many of those who were indignant about the Park Agency and its powers. "As if nature could support but one order of understandings," Thoreau had written in the mid-1800s, ridiculing those who tried to pin down nature with restrictive definitions. In the 1970s, many would ask how the Adirondacks, where one-eighth of a million people lived year-round, trying to earn a living, raise children, carve out a decent existence from a recalcitrant land, could be expected to support only one order of understanding about nature in the Adirondacks, and a state-imposed order of understanding at that.

Some of these Adirondack residents began to suspect that it was they from whom the Adirondacks were to be saved. The governor's commission's warnings notwithstanding, it was hard for them to cite another "enemy." Most logging operations, once the biggest threat to the wilderness, were practicing good forest management in such a way that their property looked as wild, often, as the Forest Preserve. Some paper companies allowed hunting, fishing, camping, hiking, and other wilderness pastimes on their land, and visitors found their forests as beautiful as any in the Adirondacks.

The two major iron mines in operation in 1968, the largest garnet mine in the United States at Gore Mountain, the huge talc, titanium, and wollastonite mines as well as the stone and gravel quarries—traditional abusers of Adirondack scenery and forests in the past—were operating to the approval of the state's Science Service. Evaluating the mining activities with an eye to pollution and deforestation, the service found that noise, water, and air pollution were minimal.

Tourists were among the contributors to environmental problems, to be sure, but some state government voices seemed to be saying that it was largely for them that the Adirondacks should be saved.

Who then was left to ruin the mountains? Land developers, yes, but their activities were being strictly regulated by the new Park Agency. What, many asked, about those one hundred and twenty-five thousand residents whose existence depended upon some form of exploitation of the natural resources? It was nice to appreciate beauty, but what about the need to survive now?

Surviving in the Adirondacks on a full-time basis under any circumstances had never been easy. As early as the 1840s, Joel T. Headley, the frail minister who went to the Adirondacks for his health and wrote several books about them, noted that "not a man here supports himself from his farm." Few single occupations ever supported people. Generations of Adirondackers had combined skills, talents, and occupations— guiding in summer, logging in winter; farming and trapping; taking in boarders and hunting; and more recently, working Downstate during the week and commuting home for weekends; even rum-running during Prohibition. Such versatility and enterprise had helped spawn a reputation for courage, independence, self-reliance, and pride for which North Country natives have been admired for over 100 years.

Adirondack literature is full of stories about North Country families who lived decent, honorable lives, sparing of comfort but noble in spirit. They were praised for their "rugged strength, their simple ways, their undying youth," as novelist Irving Bacheller wrote in his story of the Adirondacks, *Eben Holden*.

But in the twentieth century, Adirondackers' will and strength had been tested in ever more challenging ways. Logging, once a steady, well-paying, part-time or full-time occupation, had declined after the early 1900s. After World War II, when it picked up again, its practice almost required a college degree in forestry. The lumber and wood-related industries were able to employ only about 19 percent of the population, even though the two remained among the biggest employers in the region.

Mining had always been a risky occupation. Lay-offs, mine closings, and erratic demand for Adirondack ores and minerals combined to add more miners to the welfare rolls than to the labor market.

Only about 10 percent of the land in the Adirondack region had ever been suited to farming, and by the 1960s a good deal less than that was being plowed and tilled. The number of working farms decreased by more than three-quarters between 1930 and 1970. Abandoned farmhouses became as characteristic of some landscapes as the mountains themselves.

The big hotels of the Gilded Age, where so many had found summer jobs, were no more. Big private estates or camps, once in need of large staffs, were beyond the financial means of even many wealthy people by the 1970s. Many stood for sale but were unbought; others had been turned over to the state.

Motels and lakeside cottages, having replaced the boarding houses and small hotels, seemed to suffer as often as thrive. A rainy summer or a snowless winter could put them out of business in a season.

Modern tourists seemed to go to the Adirondacks not to spend money at motels and villages, but to camp in the woods, to hide out from civilization rather than subsidize it. While tourism increased, it often seemed that tourist-generated income decreased.

"Oh we got troubles, all right," lamented a former town supervisor of Westport, as reported by Burton Bernstein in 1971 in his profile of Essex County, *The Sticks*. "There are the natural ones of the weather, the soil, the short growing season." And there were, and continue to be, the unnatural problems. "If we were a foreign nation," said a businessman from Lake Luzerne in 1977, "we could qualify for aid to underdeveloped countries."

Wilderness living has never been easy. *Photo by W. F. Kollecker, courtesy of the Saranac Lake Free Library, Adirondack Collection*

In 1961, Essex County was declared a depressed region by the federal government when its unemployment rate reached 12 percent; ten years later, things had become even worse. About one-third of the working population in the Adirondack counties was out of work in the 1970s. In Saranac Lake, 23 percent of the work force was unemployed in 1977.

The percentage of those on welfare throughout the region exceeded that in Harlem. Severe fuel shortages in a climate whose winter lasts eight months threatened the health of many, as well as the ability of many fuel suppliers to stay in business.

And perhaps more serious in a region noted for the fierce pride of its people, a disgruntlement verging on despair became evident. Population was declining, welfare dependency was going up, and alcoholism was more widespread in the Adirondacks than anywhere else in the state.

Governmental intervention in the form of welfare, economic development programs, and even the provision of the majority of jobs in the region by 1970 seemed not to lessen in many cases a growing resentment. What amazed many natives was that the traditional means by which Adirondackers had always managed to keep themselves going—the exploitation of natural resources—were being stripped away as new demands imposed by well-off, urban outsiders seemed to be increasing.

The Adirondack Park Agency, although an arm of the same state government that paid taxes on its own land at the same rate private land owners paid, and thus provided a large portion of what economic flow there was, became the perceived instrument of the trouble in the minds of many. The agency staff appeared to be composed of city-slick outsiders, romantic esthetes, and descendants of the "denudatics" who had so annoyed nineteenth century businessmen. The new Park Agency's rules and regulations as a means of coping with nature seemed opposed to the traditional Adirondack ways of endurance, practicality, hard work, and self-reliance.

Among the many ironies of the situation, one of the most poignant was the fact that it was often the grandfathers or uncles or cousins of many Adirondackers who had instilled an appreciation of the Adirondack wilderness into city-folk. The grandchildren, nephews, and cousins of those wilderness-struck city-folk of the nineteenth century were now in charge of maintaining the wilderness in the 1970s—often, it seemed, at the expense of those who first knew it and first loved it.

Increasingly, protests, even violence, characterized the uneasy relationship between "forever-wilders" and the native Adirondackers soon after the Park Agency's formation. Bumper stickers with antipreservation and anti–Park Agency slogans appeared on automobiles. One night in November 1975, a truckload of manure was dumped onto the lawn of APA headquarters in Ray Brook. Forums designed to allow people to air differences turned into shouting matches. Adirondack natives formed alliances and committees to fight what they believed to be untoward governmental intervention in their lives. Representatives of Adirondack voting districts brought their constituents' problems into the public arena by organizing lobbying efforts and counterproposals against the Park Agency. Some tried to make up in publicity what the Adirondack region lacked in voting clout.

While the Adirondack region as a whole occupies one-third of the state, and the parameters of the Park alone make up one-fifth of the geographical area of New York, less than 5 percent of the total state population of 18 million lives in the Adirondacks. Set against the vast majority of New Yorkers, 85 percent of whom live in urban areas, Adirondackers are a distinct minority. The sense that they were being given a kind of preservation poison was perhaps more virulent for being concentrated among so few. Adirondackers in the last ten years or so have felt neglected at best, abused at worst.

The question of minority rights was not new to preservation, but it had been raised before as an argument in favor of wilderness. The man who expressed this view most eloquently was Robert Marshall, who in the 1930s defended the right of a minority to the preservation of true, primitive wilderness.

Like so many other prominent defenders of the environment whose interest in nature was stimulated and/or reinforced by an association with the Adirondacks, Robert Marshall shared with Ralph Waldo Emerson, George Perkins Marsh, Theodore Roosevelt, Verplanck Colvin, and many others an intimacy with the North Country mountains. Marshall was "a twentieth-century Thoreau," wrote William Chapman White, and Marshall learned his love of nature while spending every summer of his boyhood at his family's camp on Lower Saranac Lake.

As a teenager in the early 1900s, Marshall accompanied his brother on so many mountain-climbing jaunts that the two of them became the first to climb all forty-six Adirondack peaks over four thousand feet. The achievement made them charter members of a kind of club going strong today, the "Forty-Sixers."

Marshall's devotion to nature and wilderness was so strong that he made it his profession after taking degrees in forestry and plant pathology. He became a nationally known figure through his writings, through his important posts in the United States government and through his founding of the Wilderness Society in 1935.

Marshall fought not only the familiar battles to prevent industrial development of natural resources, but also the battle to preserve certain wilderness areas even from tourists and their need for recreational facilities. He wanted to be able to "escape to the primitive," as he said, and his advocacy of the utterly primitive represented a new, radical branch of the conservation movement. He believed that some areas on earth should be exempt from *all* signs of man, and his work formed the basis of the later, federal definition of wilderness as distinct from nature. As Roderick Nash wrote, "few have exceeded his zeal and effectiveness in crusading for [wilderness] preservation," and his careful analysis of the need for wilderness is today considered seminal.

Marshall realized that perhaps only a minority of Americans would share his need for total primitiveness, but he spoke for this small minority's rights loudly and persuasively. Although not taking a lead directly from Marshall, many Adirondackers believed that their minority rights were vital, too. They echoed many of Marshall's arguments but applied them to utterly different goals.

Beyond their personal concerns, many natives feared the growing power of big government. "I am wary of the awarding of that kind of power to an agency, any agency," one Adirondacker said. He and others worried about the effects a powerful agency like the APA could have on individuals.

The rights and urgent needs of the Adirondack resident minority were clear enough to command attention from the state. Even members of the Commission to Study the Future of the Adirondacks realized in a few years that maybe they had not given enough thought to the economic consequences of their plan to save the Adirondacks from what, after all, was more a distant threat than a present reality. Some admitted that the original staff of the Park Agency may have been a bit too zealous in their initial actions and attempts to implement the commission's radical plans to preserve the Adirondacks for beauty's sake.

New York State officials, therefore, took a second look at the Park Agency and the state's role in regulating man's activity in the Adirondacks. This time they spotlighted the economic plight of the Adirondack people. In 1975, the governor appointed a special assistant as Consultant on the Adirondack Area Economy, Roger Tubby, a twenty-five year resident of Saranac Lake, former press secretary to President Harry Truman, diplomat, and for many years editor and publisher of the *Adirondack Daily Enterprise*. Tubby knows both the people and the land, and his job is to balance the needs of both by studying ways to boost the economic health of the Adirondacks without putting stress on the environment. Like many environmentalists, Tubby believes the Park must be seen as a whole unit, but as an economic as well as an environmental one.

Even the Park Agency, from 1977 to 1979 led by Robert Flacke, a businessman from Lake George who has had long experience in Adirondack tourism, seems less rigid, a hopeful sign to some if an alarming trend to others.

And Adirondack natives themselves responded to the situation by making a successful bid for Lake Placid to host the 1980 Winter Olympic Games.

Not surprisingly, the Olympics elicit opposing views. At a cost of around $90 million, with the federal government contributing more than half, the new facilities and the newly renovated ones are transforming the village of Lake Placid into a boom town. A new 400-meter, refrigerated speed-skating oval, two ski jumps, a 20-kilometer cross-country ski trail system, slalom and downhill trails at Whiteface Mountain dropping 3,200 feet, a field house with the biggest total ice surface in the world, and special snow-making equipment are among the winter sports facilities being built. Over fifty thousand people a day are expected to be in Lake Placid during the two weeks of the games in February 1980. Hundreds of millions of people all over the world will see the games on television. Some expect the television publicity alone to turn Lake Placid into an internationally famous sports resort.

Olympic planners, enthusiastically hopeful about the economic benefits the games should generate, have taken pains to make all the new facilities pay off for the future. Coaches, trainers, and teachers for aspiring Olympic team members, tourists who come to watch the students and use the facilities, tradesmen who will have year-round customers, and participants in World Cup and other competitions should, according to the positive scenario, keep Lake Placid bustling and prosperous all the time. The railroad line from Utica to Lake Placid was reopened as a result of the Olympics. New jobs will be created in Ray Brook when the Olympic Village, where all the visiting athletes will live during the games, becomes a federal minimum security prison after 1980.

Such are the hopes of many. The same data fuel the fears and angers of others. The new ski jumps, seventy and ninety meters high, are visual pollution of the most offensive sort to many. Anyone climbing the High Peaks will see them. They mar the view from the grave of John Brown, the pre–Civil War abolitionist whose farm in North Elba is now a national historic site. "The structures are a monumental intrusion on the open-space character of the Park," writes Richard Beamish, former public relations officer for the Adirondack Park Agency.

A group of New York State ministers banded together to protest the creation of the prison which will occupy the Olympic Village buildings. "The moral image of the United States, New York State and the Olympics themselves is almost certain to be tarnished as foreign lands learn that their young athletes will be housed in a U.S. prison," the Reverend Graham R. Hodges from Watertown, N.Y., wrote to the *New York Times* in 1978.

Those who believe overuse threatens the Adirondacks are not happy about increased publicity of the region. More people mean less genuine wilderness. The Sierra Club sued the state for repairing a ten-mile stretch of Route 73, the only road to Lake Placid from the east. Efforts to widen the two-lane, twisting road, over which most Olympic traffic must travel, jeopardized the beauty of Cascade Pass, the Sierra Club contended.

For all these protests on the one hand and jubilant optimism on the other, many see the Olympics as a possible means to better economic conditions, at least in Lake Placid. One such cautiously optimistic man is

The 1980 Olympic Winter Games' facilities are changing the Adirondack land-scape. *Collection of the New York State Museum*

Roger Tubby, recently given an extra assignment as the Governor's Special Host for the Olympics. He is well aware that the Olympics could invite a honky-tonk atmosphere in Lake Placid or else attract too little attention. (He notes that Squaw Valley never burst upon the international sports scene after the Winter Olympics were held there in the 1950s.) He's hoping for a middle way.

Whatever happens as a result of the Lake Placid Olympics will probably neither assure the fortune of the High Peaks region nor seriously endanger the open-space quality of the area. As the extremists on either side of the man/nature dilemma continue to voice their opinion, they may be laying the way for more moderate solutions to the old dilemma.

Perhaps, as representatives from each faction soften after the hue and cry associated with the Olympics passes, "hands across the mountains" will gain increased favor as an Adirondack motto.

Some say there are ghosts in the Adirondacks to this day. The Reverend Murray saw a few and described them vividly. On the dark, cold winter nights when Mrs. Adolphus Sheldon and her husband were living in their isolated cabin, listening to the wind and the wolves, they too, perhaps suspected unearthly creatures might be out there. In our day when a blizzard knocks out all the electric power for a time, even the most practical Adirondackers probably cannot help feeling an eerie sense in the isolation.

If there are ghosts in the mountains of New York's Great Wilderness, maybe one of them belongs to Ralph Waldo Emerson, the man who made it easier for many Americans to accept and to transcend their ambivalence toward nature by advocating harmony and balance between man and nature. If so, Emerson is no doubt still exploring, still rejoicing, still mulling over all aspects of man and nature. "All are needed by each one," he may be muttering still. "Nothing is fair or good alone. . . . I yielded myself to the perfect whole."

20

Taking Charge

IT WAS WARM FOR NOVEMBER in the Adirondacks on Saturday, November 25, 1950. It had been raining heavily for several days. In colder weather the precipitation would have been snow. But just before Thanksgiving that year, during the last days of the deer hunting season, sportsmen and residents suffered unusually unpleasant, unattractive Adirondack weather—bone-chilling dampness.

Towards midday on November 25, however, the air suddenly turned strangely warmer. Wind began to rustle in the trees and whistle in people's chimneys. As it picked up a bit, buffeting the rain, hunters realized the wind was coming from the south, unusual because Adirondack storms normally come from the west and north. In fact, wind from the southeast, where this November wind was coming from, is relatively rare all over New York State. Most wind comes from the southwest, west, and northwest. Adirondackers are accustomed to raging, arctic winter storms, but this southern wind was different, and a bit eerie.

It kept getting stronger, and by nightfall it had whipped itself up to a raging 100 miles an hour in some places while the rain poured ruinously down without any sign of letting up. On Whiteface Mountain, where thirty thousand tourists had enjoyed the view the previous summer, four inches of rain fell in one hour that night.

What was happening was not a hurricane exactly, nor a tornado, nor even a weird and especially powerful thunderstorm. Weather experts called it an extremely low pressure system, a kind of wave of air surging like an ocean wave between two air masses of widely differing temperatures. Low pressure almost always means bad weather; the lower the pressure and the faster its descent, the worse the rain and wind.

Aerial view after the Big Blow, 1950. *New York State Department of Environmental Conservation*

On November 25, 1950, the pressure between two air masses dropped so quickly and to such a low point that it caused the most damaging storm in recorded New York history. It was worse than the tornado of 1845, the later hurricane of 1954, or any of the powerful snowstorms of any year.

High winds swept from Long Island to Ithaca, from Lake George to Potsdam. In Ithaca underground cables fastening buildings to the earth were ripped out of the ground. In New York City's harbor one boat, carrying two mooring lines, was literally swept up from the water and

One of many tangled, impassable trails after the Blowdown. *Collection of the New York State Museum*

dropped onto dry land. In the city itself, nearly seven thousand trees were uprooted.

But the worst damage was in the Adirondacks. The Big Blow of 1950, or the "Blowdown" as it was called for lack of more precise meteorological terms, caused more damage "than anything previously recorded in the history" of the region, the Conservation Department reported. No logging operation, fire, mine, or act of man had ever been responsible for more destruction at a single throw than the natural Blowdown of 1950. Nature outdid them all.

The few remaining stands of virgin conifer forests, which had stood here and there on a total of perhaps four thousand acres, were wiped out overnight. Softwood trees, especially mature ones like the 80–100 foot pines and hemlocks, were especially vulnerable to the wind; their shallow roots could not prevent them from toppling over or snapping off or pulling their roots out of the ground as they fell.

Around Meacham Lake in Franklin County, for instance, where the once-famous Meacham Lake House had been "embowered by majestic pines," as a nineteenth-century guidebook put it, over forty thousand spruce trees alone were blown down within a few hours. Whatever pines were left went too. In the old days, the very best logger could cut around seventy trees a day, and that was with luck, skill, practice, and good weather.

The Blowdown seemed to inflict the most damage on state land—the Forest Preserve. The Conservation Department estimated that 60 percent of all the damage in the Adirondacks was on state land.

All the figures were grim, however. In all, it appeared that the equivalent of 125 million feet of hardwood timber had fallen within the Blue Line. In 1908, the year that the most hardwood timber in any one year was logged in the Adirondacks, only 100 million board feet had been taken. Softwood trees fared even worse. On state land alone the equivalent of nearly 2 billion board feet was blown down in 1950, nearly six times the total taken in the peak year for commercial softwood lumbering.

"The woods are one grand jumble," said a shocked forester when the storm finally subsided and planes and rescue teams could get in and take a look at the destruction. Trees lay everywhere like giant matchsticks on the ground. If one hunter, stranded deep in the woods, was careless with a campfire, if the weather shifted and blew up a thunder and lightning storm, the possibilities for forest fires were frightening. Along with the trees, 148 miles of telephone lines, dozens of public campsites and private dwellings, and many fire observation towers were knocked down. Most of the 100 miles of Adirondack truck trails, built to accommodate fire engines, were so clogged with huge, fallen trees and brush as to be impassable.

Had a fire broken out within a few days or even weeks of the Blowdown, the entire forest, or the portion of it that was left, could have been destroyed. Those trees lying directly on the ground might rot relatively quickly, turning gradually to humus. Those on top of the piles, however, would simply dry out from exposure to air. In short, they could become kindling and stay kindling for years, inviting fires for a generation.

Foresters knew, too, that fire was not the only danger. Masses of dead trees invite disease and destructive insects of all kinds. One-quarter of the Forest Preserve trees had fallen. Disease in that quarter could spread to other living and dead trees within months.

Immediate action to prevent fire and disease was crucial. Only by removing as many trees as possible, as soon as possible, could New Yorkers even hope to preserve their wilderness. Yet the "forever wild" amendment to the constitution specifically forbade the removal of a single tree, dead or alive, for any reason, from Forest Preserve land.

The clean-up operation had to cover at least one-half million acres of state land and was going to be expensive. The costs of simply calculating the damage were put at around $200,000. Ultimate costs were expected to run into the millions. The New York constitution also forbade the sale of timber from Forest Preserve land for any reason, under any circumstances.

Within three weeks of the Blowdown, the Conservation Department raised all these problems with the attorney general of the state. The irony, of course, was the fact that rules designed to preserve the Adirondack forests were likely to cause their destruction if strictly interpreted. "On the face of it," the commissioner of the Department of Conservation wrote to the attorney general, "this Constitutional mandate ["forever wild" Article 14] might be construed as rendering the state helpless to act in this emergency."

The most pressing need in November and December 1950, was, in effect, "a major logging operation." And an obvious way to procure the vast sums of money needed to hire loggers, transport the logs, arrange for emergency fire protection and road repair was to sell the lumber and pulp wood that was felled.

Two months after the Blowdown, acting on the advice of the attorney general, the legislature passed a law allowing the Conservation Department both to remove and to sell the wood that had been blown down. It took five years for the clean-up to be finished, during which time more than 40 million board feet of lumber and over two hundred thousand cords of pulpwood were removed from the Adirondacks. Although disease and insect damage began to take their predicted tolls soon after "Operation Blowdown," as the rescue project was called, got under way, rendering a good portion of the wood useless, more than a million dollars were realized from selling the felled trees. Some of this money, almost $100,000, was used to purchase more Forest Preserve land.

But the effects of the Blowdown lingered. Many trees that had not been tipped over were weakened and vulnerable to later, ordinary storms. Damage in the wildest sections of the Adirondacks could not be cleaned up since much of it was nearly inaccessible. Disease and pests spread. The ambrosia beetle, for instance, infected many thousands of the hardwood trees. Downed spruce were attacked as well.

The physical effects of the Blowdown may have been outweighed, however, by the stinging reminder that nature can take charge of things as easily as man, and that nature's acts of assertion, like man's, are not always benign. Many people in New York became aware that the problem of man and nature cannot be outlined entirely in extremes, of destructive man and beneficient nature. Man who relinquishes all control over nature accepts grave risks as does man who takes full, exploitative control.

Many observers of society and history have noted that the only durable, workable constitutions, or governing bodies of laws, are those that can accommodate many conflicting views, attitudes, and traditions. The same is true of an approach toward the age-old dilemma of man and nature. Extreme positions allow for little flexibility. Asserting the omnipotence of either man or nature subjects both to unpleasant hazards, as Adirondack history reveals.

At least once, in 1950, however, it turned out that precisely the activity of man that had once nearly destroyed the Adirondack forests— the major logging operations of the nineteenth and early twentieth centuries — had to be marshaled in order to save the forests. The laws governing the Forest Preserve proved to be malleable enough to be bent, flexible enough to be reinterpreted for a specific emergency.

Since the old problem of man and nature is forever revealing new facets, raising unforeseen dilemmas, challenging new generations of human beings, many New Yorkers have worked hard to make laws governing the Adirondacks both explicitly clear and flexible—a difficult and not always successful balance. Many believe, however, that such a bridge is possible. Man should be able to retain at least the sense of wide, wild open space on six million acres in the Adirondacks and at the same time allow residents to survive in the ancient, inescapable way, by using natural resources to their advantage.

Many argue that recreation is the best way to achieve both goals since the retention of wilderness is necessary to attract visitors who generate income. So New Yorkers have, in effect, used Romantic rules, which would seem to exalt nature, in the application of Ciceronian pretexts, which suggest that man be totally in charge.

In few places in the eastern United States are man and nature still so directly engaged as they are in the Adirondack Mountains. The old problem of man and nature, then, lives on in an almost anachronistic way. Yet the dilemma, though age-old, presents future challenges as difficult and exciting as space exploration or nuclear research. And the tools man now has at his disposal both alter the terms of the dilemma and promise new solutions.

When George Perkins Marsh studied the Adirondacks in the 1860s and gathered evidence to prove how vital the watershed there was, science as we know it was still new. Yet scientific research, including the development of new fields such as ecology and environmental studies, played crucial roles in the movement to save the Adirondack wilderness.

Today, dozens of scientific disciplines enable man to take a fresh look at nature and his place in it. Strangely, or perhaps inevitably, increasingly sophisticated scientific perspectives reinforced *both* extreme views of man and nature. On the one hand, man can control nature more successfully than ever before; on the other hand, increased understanding of the complexity, harmony, even beauty of the natural process inspires ever more profound awe in men and women. Mastery *and* mystery multiply as man evolves.

A growing tension between the two demands new and better means of integration all over the world. In the Adirondacks a study of man and nature reveals a marriage of exploitation and preservation. The mountains are not only a kind of museum where the old problem of man and nature can be studied, but they can be a laboratory where vital experimental research on every level—scientific, philosophical, poetic— may perhaps afford many of the new, imaginative terms on which man and nature can better cooperate, integrate, and adapt to the pressing demands of each upon the other.

BIBLIOGRAPHY

The books and articles listed here represent only a few of those I have read, quoted, and borrowed from. With apologies to all the writers I have left out, I have tried to cite here those sources that might be of special interest to readers of this book.

Bernstein, Burton. *The Sticks: A Profile of Essex County, New York*. New York: Dodd, Mead and Co., 1972.

Broughton, J. G.; Fisher, D. W.; Isachsen, Y. W.; and Rickard, L. V. *Geology of New York: A Short Account*. Adapted from Educational Leaflet No. 20. Albany, New York: New York State Museum and Science Service, 1973.

Davis, George D. *Man and the Adirondack Environment: A Primer*. Blue Mountain Lake, New York: Adirondack Museum of the Adirondack Historical Association, 1977.

Donaldson, Alfred L. *A History of the Adirondacks*. 2 vols. New York: The Century Co., 1921.

Ekirch, Arthur A., Jr. *Man and Nature in America*. Lincoln: University of Nebraska Press, 1973.

Ellis, David M.; Frost, James A.; Syrett, Harold C.; and Carman, Harry J. *A History of New York State*. Ithaca, New York: Cornell University Press, 1967.

Flick, Alexander C., ed. *History of the State of New York*. 10 vols. New York: Columbia University Press, 1933.

Furnas, J. C. *The Americans: A Social History of the United States, 1587–1914*. New York: G. P. Putnam's Sons, 1969.

233

Graham, Frank J. *The Adirondack Park*. New York: Alfred A. Knopf, 1978.

Hochschild, Harold. *Township 34: A History, with Digressions, of an Adirondack Township in Hamilton County in the State of New York*. Blue Mountain Lake, New York, 1952.

Hyde, Floy S. *Adirondack Forests, Fields and Mines*. Lakemont, N.Y.: North Country Books, 1974.

Marsh, George Perkins. *Man and Nature*. Cambridge, Mass.: The Belknap Press of Harvard University Press, 1967.

Masten, Arthur H. *The Story of Adirondac*. Syracuse: Syracuse University Press, 1968.

Nash, Roderick. *Wilderness and the American Mind*. New Haven and London: Yale University Press, 1967.

Platt, Rutherford. *The Great American Forest*. Englewood Cliffs, N.J.: Prentice-Hall, Inc., 1965.

Savage, Arthur V., and Sierchio, Joseph. "The Adirondack Park Agency Act: A Regional Land Use Plan Confronts 'The Taking Issue.'" *Albany Law Review* 40 (3):447–82.

Schlesinger, Arthur M. *The Rise of the City, 1878–1898*. Vol. X of *A History of American Life*. Edited by Arthur M. Schlesinger and Dixon Ryan Fox. 12 vols. New York: The Macmillan Company, 1933.

Sullivan, Mark. *Our Times*. 6 vols. New York: Charles Scribner's Sons, 1936.

Temporary Study Commission on the Future of the Adirondacks. *Wildlife: Technical Report 2*. 1970.

―――. *Forest, Minerals, Water and Air: Technical Report 3*. 1970.

―――. *The Future of the Adirondack Park*. 1970.

Thomas, William L., Jr., ed. *Man's Role in Changing the Face of the Earth*. Chicago and London: University of Chicago Press, 1956.

Van Valkenburgh, Norman J. *"The Adirondack Forest Preserve: A Chronology,"* 1968. (Mimeographed.) Available from the New York State Museum, Albany.

Watson, Winslow Cossoul. *Pioneer History of the Champlain Valley*. Albany N.Y.: J. Munsell, 1863.

White, William Chapman. *Adirondack Country*. New York: Alfred A. Knopf, 1967.

INDEX

Acid rain, 213–14
Adirondac, N.Y., 106, 107; ——, *The Story of*, 107
Adirondack Daily Enterprise, 204, 221, 223
Adirondack forest, 56–76; characteristics of, 62–69; climax stage of, 71; glacial effects on, 63; reforestation of, 185, 194; "tree line" in, 67; tree varieties in, 63–72; zones in, 65, 68, 70
Adirondack Forest Preserve, 170, 173–79; agencies charged with protecting, 203–204, 215; defined, 178; effects of "Blowdown" of 1950 on, 226–30; fires in, 186; private ownership of land in, 178, 203, 214; recreational facilities in, 187, 198; state-owned land in, 176, 178. *See also* "Forever wild"
Adirondack Mountain Club, 193
Adirondack Mountains: geologic history of, 44–46, 48–55; glacial activity in, 52–53, 58, 60, 61; named by Ebenezer Emmons, 114. *See also* High Peaks, and names of individual mountains
Adironack Museum, 148, 180
Adirondack Park, 170, 178, *182*; approved by state legislature, 181; defined, 178; proposed creation of, 164, 181; sale of state land banned in, 175
Adirondack Park Agency (APA), 221; creation of, 215; opposition to, 219
Adirondack region: boundaries of, 10–11; early explorers of, 16–17; early names for, 111; early settlers in, 8–10; early surveys of, 36–37; geography of, 11–12; maps of *14–15*, 19, *47*, *182*; military tracts in, 39; surveyed by Ebenezer

Emmons, 111–16; surveyed by Verplanck Colvin, 165, 166–69; topographical features of, 43–44
Adirondacks: or Life in the Woods, The (Headley), 118
Adirondack Steel Manufacturing Company, 106, 107
Adventures in the Wilderness (Murray), 126–27, 134, 143
Agassiz, Louis, 54, 118
Albany, N.Y., 91, 161; importance of, in fur trade, 19, 22; importance of lumber industry to, 96, 97
Algonquin Indians, 16, 32, 114
Algonquin Peak, *57*
Allen, Ethan, 31
American Museum of Natural History, 183
American Park Society, 192
American Scenic and Historic Preservation Society, 192
Anorthosite, 48, 49–50
Appalachian Club, 192
Arnold, Benedict, 31, 100
Association for the Protection of the Adirondacks, 197–98
Astor, John Jacob, 22
Atlantic Monthly, 153, 154
Audubon, John James, 154–55
Ausable Chasm, 27
Ausable River, *13*, 27, 91
Avalanche Pass, *7*, 44, *45*, *199*

Bacheller, Irving: *Eben Holden*, 198, 207, 217
Balmat, N.Y., 48

235

Beamish, Richard, 222
Beauty, value of defended, 205–206
Beaver River, 91
Beavers, 73–74, 195; fur trade in, 18–23
Beaver Wars, 21
Berman v. Parker, 206
Bernstein, Burton (*The Sticks*), 29, 217
"Big Boom" (logging corral), 91–93, 96
Birds, 74; rare species of, 61, 74
Bishop, Morris, 17
Black, Governor Frank, 184
Black River, 91
"Blowdown" of 1950, 225–30; effects on Adirondack forest, 226–30; photographs of, 226, 227
Blue Ledge, N.Y., 93
Blue Mountain Lake, 145, 148; Adirondack Museum at, 148, 180; Holland's Blue Mountain Lake Hotel, 146
Board of Regents of the State of New York, 164, 165
Bogs, 62; and soil formation, 61–62; unusual wildlife in, 61
Boon, Gerrit, 39
Boonville, 39, 41
Boreas River, 93
Bouquet River, 26, 27, 91
Boy Scouts, 192
Brown, John, 38, 204, 222;——'s Tract, 38
Burroughs, John, 153–55, 158, 159, 188, 191; *Wake-Robin*, 154, 155

Canadian Shield, 46, 47
Carey, Governor Hugh, 223
Carson, Russell: *Peaks and People of the Adirondacks*, 50
Cartier, Jacques, 17, 20–21
Cascade Pass, 223
Central Highlands: geologic characteristics of, 50
Champlain, Lake, 17, 24, 166
Champlain, Samuel de, 5, 6, 17
Cheney, John, 114–16, 117, 118
Choate, Joseph, 183
Church, Frederick, 174
Clear, Lake, 203
Cleveland, Grover, 173, 174–75
Clinton County: iron mining in, 107
Colden, Lake, 7
Colvin, Verplanck, 161–70; discovers Hudson River source, 166–69; proposes creation of Adirondack park, 162, 164;

surveys the Adirondacks, 162, 165, 166–69
Commerce, State Department of, 202
Conservation Commission, 187, 192
Conservation, Department of, 198, 203–204, 227
Conservation movement: conservation vs. preservation, 184; early contributors to, 153–60; resisted by business interests, 174; "Roosevelt era" of, 189–90
Cooper, James Fenimore, 150; *The Last of the Mohicans*, 11, 24
Cooper, William, 80, 81
Cooperstown, N.Y., 80
Cranberry Lake, 95
Crapsey, Adelaide, 137
Crown Point, N.Y., 100, 104

Davis, George D., 60, 68, 71–72; *Man and the Adirondack Environment: A Primer*, 58
Davis, James F., 49
Deer: hunting season for, 194–95; presence of in forest, 72–73, 194
Desormo, Maitland, 96, 148
Dewey, Godfrey, 197
Dewey, Melville, 193
Donaldson, Alfred, 130
Doolittle, William, 204
Doyle, Larry, 130

Eben Holden (Bacheller), 198, 207, 217
Ekirch, Arthur, xvii
Elizabethtown: settled by William Gilliland, 27, 29, 33
Emerson, Ralph Waldo, xv, xvi–xvii, 154; on man's relationship to nature, xv–xvii, 224; *Nature*, xv, 120; visits Adirondacks, 118, 120
Emmons, Ebenezer, 53, *113*; Adirondack region survey of, 112–16; names Adirondacks, 114; names Mt. Marcy, 114
Empire State Report, 204
Employment, 216–19
Environmental Conservation, Department of, 183
Erie Canal, 4, 176
Essex, N.Y., 32
Essex County: iron mining in, 47, 107; iron

ore in, 100; *The Sticks* (Bernstein), 29, 217; unemployment in, 217–18

Farming, 217
Feldspar Brook, 168
Fernow, Bernhard Eduard, 184–85, 186
Fish, 74; restocking experiments with, 195–96
Fisheries, Commission of, 195
Fisheries, Game and Forest Commission, 183, 184
Fishery Commission, State, 175, 176
Flacke, Robert, 221
Follensby Pond, 120
Forest Commission: proposal of to create Adirondack Park, 181; and railroad scandal (1894), 181–82
Forestry, State College of, 185
"Forever wild": amended in 1892, 181; amended in 1927, 196; amended in 1941, 198; amended in 1959, 203; and constitutional convention of 1938, 205; in law of 1885, 173, 178–79; "Operation Blowdown" and, 229; and referendum of 1913, 186; in state constitution of 1894, 182–84
Fort William Henry: battle of (1757), 24, 26
"Forty-Sixers," 220
Fossils, 51–52
Fourth Lake, 147
Fox, Dixon Ryan, 4, 112
Francis, John, 38
Fur trade, 18–23

Gabriels (tuberculosis sanatorium), 141
Garden Club movement, 192
Gates, General Horatio, 31
George, Lake: battles over, 24; sale of state land around banned, 175
Gifford, Sanford R., xvi, *119*
Gilded Age, 143–52
Gilliland, William, 25–33, 100, 111; charged with treason, 31; colonial ambitions of, 29; loss of holdings of, 32; portrait of, *30*; settles on Bouquet River, 26–28
Glacial activity, effects of, 52–53, 58, 60, 61, 63
Glens Falls, N.Y., 87, 91; importance of lumber industry to, 96

Golden Age of Homespun, The (Van Wagenen), 71, 82
Gore Mountain: garnet mine at, 48, 216
Gouverneur: marble quarries near, 48
Grant, Ulysses S., 175
Grasse River, 91
Great American Forest, The (Platt), 18
Gregory, Duncan, 106
Grenville Province, 46
Guide to the Empire State, 42

Hall, James, 164; and founding of New York State Museum, 53–54, 112
Hammond, S. J., xix
Hansen, Marcus Lee, 35
Harte, Jessamy, 151
Hayes, James Truman, 86
Haystack Mountain, 68
Headley, Joel T., 130, 216; *The Adirondacks: or Life in the Woods*, 118
Heart Lake, 57
Henderson, David, 107, 110, 111; 114; assists survey of Mt. Marcy, 116; invests in iron mine, 103–106; lake named for, 168
Herkimer Country, 40; "Herkimer Diamonds," 48
Herreshoff, Frederick, 39, 100, 103
High Peaks, 11, 43; first surveyed, 36; geologic history of, 49; lichens and mosses on, 60; threats of recreational overuse to, 213; tree varieties in, 65–68. *See also* Adirondack Mountains
Hill, Governor David B., 173–76, 178, 179, 188
Hochschild, Harold, 146; *Lumberjacks and Rivermen in the Central Adirondacks*, 88
Hodges, Fred, 147–48
Hodges, Rev. Graham R., 222
Hoffman, Charles Fenno: tours the Adirondacks, 117–18; *Wild Scenes in the Forest*, 118
Hoffman, Governor John T., 165
Holbrook, Stewart H.: *Yankee Loggers*, 82, 91
Hotels, 145–47; Beede House, 145, 186; Cohasset, 147; Glenmore, *148–49*; Grand Union, 146; Grandview House, *146–47*; Holland's Blue Mountain Lake, 146; Leland House, 146; Meacham Lake House, 228; Paul Smith's, 147; Prospect House, 145, 146; United States, 146

Hough, Franklin B., 166, 184
Hudson River, 91, 93, 176; source of discovered by Verplanck Colvin, 166–69
Hudson River School, xvi, 174
Huron Indians, 16–17

Ice Age. *See* Glacial activity
Ilmenite, 47, 100, *102*
Indians, 16; and fur trade, 18–21; land claimed by, 34. *See also* names of individual tribes
Indian River, 91
Iron industry, 108. *See also* Iron mining, Iron ore
Iron mining: impact of, 108–109, 216; in Lake Champlain area, 107; problems with, 100. *See also* Iron industry, Iron ore
Iron ore, 46–47, 48, 100. *See also* Iron industry, Iron mining
Iroquois Indians, 100, 114. *See also* names of individual tribes
Irving, Washington, 41
Isaak Walton League of America, 192
Isachsen, Y. W., 49

James, Henry, 174
Jay, N.Y., 33, 198
Jogues, Father Isaac, 17
Johnson, Sir William, 133

Keene Valley, N.Y., 145
Keeseville, N.Y., 118
Ketchledge, E. H. (*Trees of the Adirondack High Peak Region: A Hiker's Guide*), 76

LaBastille, Anne, 56
Labradorite, 49–50
Lake Placid, N.Y., 147, 193; ——Club, 193, 196, 198; site of 1980 Winter Olympics, 221–22, 223
Lake Pleasant, N.Y., 162, 165
Land Office, New York State, 37
Land speculation, 34–37; British role in, 34, 36; Macomb's Purchase, 36, 37; Totten and Crossfield Purchase, 36–37, 103, 169

Land use planning: Adirondack Park Agency charged with, 215; need for, 204, 206–207, 214
Last of The Mohicans, The, 11, 24
Lewis County: mineral deposits in, 50
Lichens: in soil formation, 60
Long Lake, 151
Lossing, Benson J., 53
Lost Brook, *66*
Lowell, James Russell, 118
Lower Raquette River, 83
Lower St. Regis Lake, 147
Lower Saranac Lake, 220
Lumber industry, 79–98; at its peak, 92–93, 94; dangers of, 89, 93; in decline, 97; early days of, 83–84; employment in, 88–89, 90, 217; environmental impact of, 97–98, 164, 176; logging procedures in, 85–88; New York State's position in, 82–83, 92, 97. *See also* Wood
Lumberjacks and Rivermen in the Central Adirondacks (Hochschild), 88

McClure, David, 183, 197
McGuffey, William Holmes, 159; —— 's *Reader*, 158–59
McIntyre, Archibald, 103–107, 109, 111; mountain named for, 114
McIntyre, Mount, 67
McIntyre (later Adirondac), N.Y., 105, 106, 112–114
McMartin, Duncan, 103–104, 105, 111; mountain named for, 114

Macomb, Alexander, 36, 37; —— 's Purchase, 36, 37
Magnetite, 47, 48, 100
Man and Nature (Marsh), 156, 157, 166
Man and the Adirondack Environment: A Primer (Davis), 58
Marcy, Mt., 43, 44, 190; lichens on, 60–61; measured by Verplanck Colvin, 169; mineral deposits on, 50, 51; named by Ebenezer Emmons, 114; threats of recreational overuse to, 213; "tree line" on, 67
Marion River, 148
Marsh, George Perkins, 155–58; advocate for Adirondack preservation, 157–58; *Man and Nature*, 156, 157, 166

Marshall, Robert, 192, 220
Martineau, Harriet, 4–5
Masten, Arthur H. *(The Story of Adirondac)*, 107
Mathewson, Christy, 130
Maugham, Somerset, 150
Meacham Lake, 228
Merriam, Clinton, 19
Metzler, Paula, 196
Mill Creek (fish hatchery), 195
Mineral deposits, 46–48
Mineville, N.Y., 100, 108
Mining industry, 47–48, 102; employment in, 217; environmental impact of, 216. *See also* Iron
Mirror Lake, 193, *146–47*
Mohawk Indians, 16–17, 133; land owned by, 34, 36
Monaco, Arto, 198
Moose, 72–73, 74
Moose River, 91, *94*
Morison, Samuel Eliot, 5, 121, 192
Morris, William, 130
Mosses: in soil formation, 60
Muir, John, 153–54, 184, 191
Murray, Rev. William Henry Harrison, 58, 123–26, 128, 194, 224; *Adventures in the Wilderness*, 126–27, 134, 135; enthusiasm for Adirondacks of, 124; ideas about nature and health of, 133

Nash, Roderick, 175, 178, 206, 220
Natural History of New York (1842), 112
Natural Resources, New York Department of, 214
New York: A Guide to the Empire State, 134
New York's Food and Life Sciences, 214
New York State Museum, 52, 16; started from first geologic survey, 53–54
Niagara Falls, 174, 175; —— Reservation created, 174
North Creek, N.Y., 48, 191
North Elba, N.Y., 100, 103, 222
Northway, The (Interstate Route 87), 203

Old Forge, N.Y., 148; established in 1817, 100
Olympics. *See* Winter Olympic Games
Oneida Indians, 16–17; cede territory to U.S., 42; land claimed by, 34

O'Neill, Eugene, 130
Opalescent River, 50, 168
Oswegatchie River, 91
Outdoor Art Society, 192

Parks, Commission of State, 165, 166
Parks, New York State Council of, 204
Peaks and People of the Adirondacks (Carson), 50
Pettis, Clifford R., 185, 186
"Philosophers Club," 120
Platt, Rutherford, 63, 67, 68, 79; on fur trappers, 18; *The Great American Forest*, 18
Plattsburgh, N.Y., 147
Port Henry, N.Y., 100
Potash, 81
Pratt, George DuPont, 192
Pulp industry: demand for lumber of, 83, 95–96
Putnam, Gideon, 133

Raquette River, 83, 88, 91
Ray Brook: Adirondack Park Agency headquarters at, 215, 219; Olympic Village at, 222
Recreation, 205; facilities for, in Forest Preserve, 187, 198; nature as, 152; postwar boom in, 201–203; threats posed by, 213
Rockefeller, Laurance: proposes creation of national park, 204
Rockefeller, Nelson Aldrich, 201
Rome, N.Y., 147
Roosevelt, Theodore, 189–91, 220

Sacandaga River, 165
St. Lawrence County: mineral deposits in, 46
St. Regis Lake, 134, 190
St. Regis River, 91
Sanford Lake, 103, 104
Saranac Laboratory for the Study of Tuberculosis, 139
Saranac Lake, 140, 147, 185, *187*; origins of village, 83–84; site of Trudeau Sanatorium, 136, 137; tuberculosis and the growth of, 139–41; unemployment in, 218

Saranac River, 91
Saratoga Springs, N.Y., 133, 146–47;
    hotels in, 146
Schofield, Carl L., 214
Schroon Lake, 146
Schroon River, 83, 87
Science Service, 216
Seneca Indians, 81
Seward, Mount, 164
Sheldon, Mrs. Adolphus, 8–10, 16
Sierra Club, 192, 222–23
Simmons, Louis J., 84
Skene, Philip, 32–33
Smith, Paul, 134, 186, 193;———'s Hotel, 147,
    190
Soil formation, 58–62
Speculator Mountain, 165
Star Lake, 100
Stevenson, Robert Louis, 130
Sticks, The (Bernstein), 29, 217
Stillman, William James: and "Philos-
    ophers Club," 118–120
Stoddard, Seneca Ray, 148, 149, 151
Stoneywold (tuberculosis sanator-
    ium), 141
Story of Adirondac, The (Masten), 107
Strong, George Templeton, 6
Sullivan, Fred, 204
Surveys. See Adirondack region
Sylvester, Nathaniel Bartlett, 8
Syracuse, N.Y., 185

Trees. See Adirondack forest, Adirondack
    Forest Preserve
Trees of the Adirondack High Peak Region: A
    Hiker's Guide (Ketchledge), 76
Troy, N.Y., 82, 93
Trudeau, Edward Livingston, 131, 138;
    opens sanatorium at Saranac Lake, 136,
    137; pioneer in treating tuberculosis,
    136, 137–39; as tuberculosis patient,
    134–37
Trudeau Sanatorium, 136, 137, 141
Truman, Harry S, 221, 223
Tubby, Roger, 221, 223
Tuberculosis, xvi, 131, 134–42; Adiron-
    dacks a cure for, 137; importance of, to
    growth of Saranac Lake, 139–41
Tupper Lake, N.Y.: origins of, 83–84;
    school of forestry at, 184–85
Twain, Mark, 150

Unemployment, 218
Utica, N.Y., 147, 148, 222

Van Hoevenberg, Mount, 59, 198
Van Wagenen, Jared; The Golden Age of
    Homespun, 71, 82
Verner, William K., xvi, 180

Tahawas, N.Y., 47, 102, 106, 107;———Club,
    190
Tait, Edwin Fitzwilliam, 144, 150
Tear-of-the-Clouds, Lake, 61; map of, 167;
    named by Verplanck Colvin, 168; as
    source of Hudson River, 166
Temporary Study Commission on the Fu-
    ture of the Adirondacks, 204, 207, 221;
    and privately-owned land, 214; rec-
    ommendations of, 215; report of (1970),
    205, 206–207, 213
Thendara, N.Y., 148
Thoreau, Henry David, xvi, 215
Thousand Islands: in geologic history, 46
Todd, Rev. John, xix
Totten and Crossfield Purchase, 36–37,
    103, 169
Tourism: role in Adirondack economy, 217
Trappers: among earliest explorers, 18;
    character of, 22

Wallace, Edwin, 149, 150
Warrensburg, N.Y., 93
Watershed, importance of, 164, 166, 176,
    205
Watson, Winslow, 25, 27, 29, 32
Westport, N.Y., 33, 216
White, William Chapman, 42, 44, 75, 76,
    196, 199, 206, 220
Whiteface Mountain, 186, 196, 198; how
    named, 50; Santa's Workshop at, 198
Wilderness Act (1964), 206
Wilderness Society, 192, 220
Wildlife, 61, 69, 72–74, 194–96; endan-
    gered species of, 74; management of,
    195–96. See also Beavers, Birds, Deer,
    Fish, Moose
Wild Scenes in the Forest (Hoffman), 118
Willsboro, N.Y., 48, 100; first settled, 29, 33
Wilmington, N.Y., 196
Wilson, Edmund, 55, 150

Winter Olympic Games (1932), 197–98
Winter Olympic Games (1980), 221–24
   economic effects of, 222, 223; environ-
   mental impact of, 222–23
Wisconsin glacier, 52
Wolf Pond, 10–11
Wollastonite, 47–48

Wood: demand for, 81–83, 95, 108–109;
   types of trees logged, 83, 94–95. *See
   also* Lumber industry

Yankee Loggers (Holbrook), 82, 91

ADIRONDACK WILDERNESS

was composed in 10-point VIP Palatino and leaded 2 points,
with display type in VIP Palatino by Utica Typesetting Company, Inc.;
printed on 60-pound Warren acid-free Old Style Wove paper stock,
Smyth-sewn, bound with 80-point binder's boards and covered in Columbia Bayside vellum,
by Maple-Vail Book Manufacturing Group, Inc.;
and published by

SYRACUSE UNIVERSITY PRESS
SYRACUSE, NEW YORK 13210